Contents

Acknowledgements

I am still enormously grateful to all those who helped me so much prepare and publish the first edition of this book. For getting it into a second edition I owe particular thanks to Robin and Julie at Intellect Books and to Jonquil for all her support.

Author's Note to the Second Edition

It was gratifying to look through the letters and comments I had on the first edition and realise that this turned out to be a book that - despite some topical references - didn't date.

The principles of developing ideas into stories and then into screenplays have not changed that much since Aristotle. It remains as difficult to write well now as it no doubt did then.

Julian Friedmann
London, January 2000

How to Make Money Scriptwriting

Julian Friedmann

intellect™
Bristol, UK
Portland, OR, USA

First Published in Paperback in 2000 by
intellect Books, PO Box 862, Bristol, BS99 1DE, UK

First Published in USA in 2000 by
intellect Books, ISBS, 920 NE 58th Ave. Suite 300, Portland, Oregon 97213-3786, USA

Reprinted in 2003.

Publisher: Robin Beecroft
Cover Design: Bettina Newman
Copy Editor: Julie Strudwick

A catalogue record for this book is available from the British Library

ISBN 1-84150-002-X

The right of Julian Friedmann to be identified as the Author of the Work has been asserted by him in accordance with the Copyright, Designs and Patents Act 1988.

Printed and bound in Great Britain by 4edge, UK.

Introduction

Do we really need another book about writing? Shouldn't writers be encouraged to write, or at least read scripts, rather than read about writing or going on writing courses? Can writing really be taught?

Many writers, whatever their personal motivation to write, seem more interested in writing and in 'being' a writer, than in the nuts and bolts of the business. But in my experience writers who see writing as a real profession, a serious way of earning money, rather than seeing it primarily as the need to say something personal, tend to be more successful because they are more businesslike about their careers. For them, saying something personal is not necessarily the most important thing: succeeding in communicating it well is.

This is not a book about how to write. There are many of those, some of them very good. It's a book about making money by writing, so it will deal with writing from that point of view. One of the old Hollywood studio bosses once said, 'I used to spend 80% of my time making films and 20% of my time making deals. Now I spend 20% of my time making films and 80% making deals.' Deals will be as much part of your profession as good stories well told. One of the aims of this book is to enable writers to gain greater control over their careers and therefore to achieve better deals.

I hope that I will succeed in encouraging writers to spend more time on their deals. Indeed I hope that as a result of this book there will be more deals to spend time on! Measuring success by money alone is a pleasant but dubious process. But greater monetary success does tend to result in increased opportunities to choose what to write.

I have worked with writers in various capacities for over thirty years: as editor, publisher, agent. Prior to that my experience was somewhat less professional – my late mother was a writer, as were some of her friends. To me, as a child, writers seemed ordinary, if sometimes fairly neurotic, grown-ups. As an adult I came to realize that they were, underneath it all, not that different from the non-writers of my acquaintance.

For the last eighteen years I have represented writers as an agent. It is chiefly the experiences of these years that I hope will be of some value to writers, and to those who work with them. And since I am in the business of protecting writers' interests, I will generally take the writer's point of view in considering their business dealings with producers, broadcasters and agents.

Writing involves art and craft, culture and commerce. I believe that one cannot sensibly talk about content without talking about form. For the purposes of this book I am making the assumption that anyone writing a script or novel or short story is doing so with the intention of seeing it on the screen or in print. And that a writer wants to be paid for his or her work. Anything written just for the fun of it, poetry not for public consumption, diaries, with no intention of production or publication, is outside the scope of this book.

It has been said that 'Time spent in reconnaissance is seldom wasted'. This is even more true of writing than it is of espionage or war. For every published novel or produced script there are literally tens of thousands that never see the light of day. Most of them were never given a chance to live because they were written prematurely. As Truman Capote said of a novel by Jack Kerouac, 'This is not writing; this is typing!' I hope this book will provide direction for those writers who wish to increase their income and the quality of what they write, and to help in the reconnaissance process.

Quality and commerce are not mutually exclusive. In fact they usually go together. I do not believe that popular culture, whether a soap on TV or a Mills & Boon-type romantic novel, is less worthy than a BBC-TV classic or a distinguished literary novel. I do enjoy the ubiquitous Australian teen soaps that frequent British television, as they are so often brilliantly planned and executed, satisfying a large audience and providing profits for their producers. In other words, they are probably what their creators set out to achieve. Ultimately, it is the audience for whom it is written, not the writer.

I want to steer away, therefore, from the value judgements that permeate the discussions about film and TV, books and plays. For writers the key to success usually lies in knowing your audience, and creating a script or manuscript to satisfy that audience. This doesn't mean writing down, just because the largest audiences are – in socio-economic terms – 'down-market'.

It does mean making what you write accessible to the audience for whom it is intended. Not enough writers pay attention to their audience, which results in there being too many projects which fail to reach the target.

One of the keys to solving this problem lies in writers being aware of their own motivation. This is usually a complex mix of things, from making money to working out personal and psychological problems, overcoming the fears and challenges of writing itself, as well as the ego-trip of being creative. Without some understanding of why you are writing, it is not likely that you will understand why you write the way you do. Or why you have chosen to write whatever it is you are writing.

That choice is critical to your chances of success. Not only do you need to write what you are going to be good at, but you also need to write to a market that will respond, so timing matters too.

How do you know if you are writing the right project for yourself and for the market? Who can you ask? A good editor or agent might help, simply because over the years they will have read hundreds of scripts or manuscripts, and examined thousands of bestseller lists, box-office charts and ratings charts. They develop an instinct about what will succeed, and they usually have a sense of what is capable of becoming hot, rather than only of what is hot now.

As development and production lead-times for films, TV programmes and books is long, jumping on a bandwagon that is already rolling is starting too late. You need to be there at the outset.

It is possible to create the bandwagon yourself. That is the holy grail that drives many writers – to be the first, to create the new trend. Not a week goes by without our agency receiving several submissions prefaced with the words '...this has never been done before...' Usually with good reason.

If you work in the agency business it is extraordinarily satisfying to get a first, speculatively-written script sold and produced, or a first novel published. But the hoped-for warm glow of success must not distract agents from being realistic about the probabilities.

'Why is it so difficult to get a deal?' is the most frequent question from new writers at seminars, lectures and workshops. Variations on the question include 'Why does it take so long to get a response?' and 'Why can't I be told what is wrong with the script or manuscript?'

The truth is simple. The vast majority of scripts and manuscripts read by agents, producers, broadcasters, editors and publishers are not good enough. If they were produced or published they would not make money for the company investing in them. In fact, they would lose money.

That is the bottom line. Lack of awareness of this among writers is one of the main reasons for failure. Lack of talent is the other. Knowledge of the business in which they have chosen to work is not that easy to come by, except by experience. The knowledge is needed most before the majority of writers are produced or published.

Attempts to find the formula, to copy whatever has recently been successful, usually fail. Poor imitations flood across the desks of those in the industry who read. Apart from their frequent similarity to other submissions, the majority of scripts and manuscripts rarely stand out in any way.

Most writers, at the start of their career, offer original, speculatively-written scripts. But, as I will explain, there is an argument for a relatively new writer to also write, as a calling-card script, an episode of an existing series. If well done, it proves the ability of the writer to discipline himself or herself, something that might impress a TV series editor or producer, or an agent. Together, the two calling-card scripts are a stronger pitch for that writer than either one on its own.

As most original, speculatively written scripts are unproducible, they offer little incentive to script editors, producers or agents. Many agencies receive over one hundred submissions a week from writers wishing to become clients. It takes time even to read the covering letters, never mind reply constructively to the scripts and manuscripts. As a result, many rejection letters are late and unhelpful. We do not get paid to read and analyze prospective clients' material. That is what we do for our existing clients.

We want to know that the writer can write 'to order', as well as be original, develop characters from scratch and put together a structure that does not rely on an existing model. It may seem a lot to ask, but the competition is stiff. If we find a script that makes us sit up, brings a tear to the eye, quickens the pulse, we will normally commit ourselves to the writer, as long as we have the time.

There are no absolute rules when it comes to the best way to develop a writing career. By emphasizing the 'politics' involved in being a writer, I hope to show that the interpersonal relationships in the business are very important. Writing should not simply be the process of putting words down on paper and handing them over. Writers must not be mechanical or passive in these relationships.

Writers should be activists, particularly in view of the isolation of writing, not only joining writers' groups, but also playing a pro-active role in each of the professional relationships that writers must foster with agents, editors, producers, publishers, sales and marketing people, publicity and support staff.

Creativity and talent may be qualities that one either has or does not have. But much competent writing can be done by people who apply themselves, and use what creativity they have. Understanding the stages of preparation of the written material, something about the 'real business' of film and television, how to identify audiences and to target markets, how to use agents, all helps you sell yourself and your ideas.

After looking at creativity and writing, at the psychology of audiences and at markets – the 'pre-deal' arena – the book moves to the deal itself. Once you have written something and pitched it or had it read, and a deal is imminent, it needs to be negotiated. Setting up the preconditions so that the deal comes more quickly, and on better terms, may have nothing to do with the creativity of the writer, but a great deal to do with that writer's earning capacity.

In addition to some general principles of negotiation (which also apply in everyday life), there are other preparations that will help, including gaining some knowledge of the law and of contracts. The protection of ideas and scripts is something that worries most writers, so there is a chapter specifically on that.

The book ends with some brief notes on research, because there is invaluable information out there, easily available if you know where to look. Knowing how to find out whom to submit material to, how to read the 'trades', the box-office figures and ratings, can make the difference between getting a sale or not.

There is always money out there looking for projects. There are production companies, banks, broadcasters, all with sizeable sums which they want to invest in films and in television programmes, but they cannot find enough projects of a high enough standard.

By ensuring that your work is noteworthy, and by getting it to the right people, you increase the chances of making a deal. And with increased knowledge of the business you can ensure that it is not just any deal. The better-informed all of us in the business are, the more productive we will be and the stronger the industry. Despite the apparent competition that exists between writers, we are all better off if the industry thrives. The real competition is from other countries, especially the United States. I believe that we must beat the Americans at their own game. If they can tell stories in such a way that audiences all over the world flock to see their movies and tune into their television series, we must understand how they do it. Respecting the audience is the beginning of that process.

Most cinema and television drama is watched for the explicit purpose of enjoyment. Unfortunately, most of the scripts and manuscripts that we see in our agency do not seem to recognize this. The purpose of this book is to provide some alternative routes to better writing and more successful business deals.

The chances of stumbling on luck are small. You can make your own luck. It starts by taking the initiative and having greater control over your chosen career.

1   The Politics of being a Writer

Much of this book is inevitably about the tensions – healthy and unhealthy – that exist between the art and the craft of writing. For any individual there are always choices to be made. The process of writing is essentially one of selection: one word after another, one character trait instead of another.

The decisions you make as a writer may be informed either by instinct or by experience and training. Is the former 'art' and the latter 'craft'? This is a discussion that goes on in gatherings of writers and producers all over Europe. It would probably mystify Americans. While debate about writing is generally valuable to those doing the writing, there is no absolutely right or wrong way. Writing clearly isn't art only or craft only.

What is important is for writers to be open to new ideas, new techniques and to criticism. It is also important for them to be aware of why they have chosen one story, one character, even one word, over another.

Early Decisions

You start making choices when you're faced with a particular idea or story you want to write about. For example, if it is based on fact, you can choose to tell it as a documentary or a 'docu-drama'. If the latter, do you rely on the reader's interest and involvement stemming from his or her awareness that the story is true?

There are also choices when it comes to deciding on the format. You can get away with more violence and sex in a feature film than you can on television, and you can get away with even more when it comes to a novel. Or you can choose a more subtle way and focus on the emotions of the characters. Either approach is viable. But this decision raises another choice: which character to use as the main vehicle through whose eyes the audience will experience the film or programme.

Many treatments and scripts provoke the question: 'Who is the central character?' because the answer is not always obvious. If the central character takes us into the ebb and flow of his or her emotions, then the reader or the audience is going to come away feeling that they had shared the experience. How you choose to stimulate the emotions of your audience will depend on choices you make.

Let me give you an example. A teenager commits suicide. The police establish for us (the audience) that he had left home months before and had very sporadic contact with his parents. We then see the boy's mother arriving with a police escort to identify the body. We are unlikely to experience the mother's emotions ourselves. Something is missing in the telling.

The most powerful emotional moment occurs when she is told about her son's death. We must be present at that moment. We should see her going about her normal life until that fateful moment, which changes the course of her life. (In script-editing jargon the phrase is 'the incident that disrupts her routine'.) We must share with her the very first time she hears the news. We must empathize with the policeman or policewoman who has to give her the news. And we must see how she reacts to it.

We can then cut to the moment that they lift the sheet off the body in front of her. We do not need to travel with her from home to her son's flat. In most British or European films we would, but the pace should be speeded up by the cutting or editing. Later on, we will look at this in the context of the differences between European and American films.

How the audience's emotions will be engaged, how much 'breathing space' you allow them between scenes (some variation is necessary to raise the tension even more) depends on the choices you make. Don't assume your first choice is the best. Find ways of questioning your choices, push yourself to examine the implications of alternative choices. Every choice could be a wrong turn.

There is also much to be said for working out your story backwards from the final scene. This is more likely to prove successful than starting at the beginning without knowing where you are going. The temptation is usually to start at the beginning. It should be mandatory, once you've decided on the story and you've worked out more or less who you want your characters to be, to go back even further.

In other words, once you know what you want the ending to be, work out in some detail what happens to your main characters before your story starts. This exercise tends to force you to be ruthlessly logical about their motivation. The way you set up your characters and their situation can be of enormous benefit to you later. Much bad writing – unnecessary scenes, ambiguous characterization, misleading situations and poorly presented motivation – stems from the fact that writers rarely do enough homework about their characters.

Once you have a rough draft, look back from the end. Does the build-up lead inexorably and with sufficient twists, reverses and surprises to a satisfying climax? Play devil's advocate with yourself. Question yourself about the story and the characters as though someone else had written the script. Make sure that at every turn the motivation of each character makes sense.

If you write about something that you witnessed, be careful that your selection of words is not limited to re-creating the images in your own mind. This could turn you into a reporter. You must remember that anyone reading the script (it's got to be read before it's made) won't have a memory of the incident or event and you need to create the whole world of the incident for them, not the partial one necessary for it to come to life in your mind.

Whatever choices you make will determine whether your script or novel succeeds. External factors play a part too, and the way you handle relationships with your readers can help you to get more out of those with whom you will be working.

Accessibility – Giving them what they want

What do agents, script editors, producers and directors want from you (and each other) and how can you get what you want from them?

'Good writing' is what people in the business want from you. But what is 'good writing'? Apart from the fact that we aspire to it (or aspire to find it if we work in the business but are not writers), it is difficult to pin down. There are some objective criteria (for example, correct grammar), but there are also subjective factors which are important.

I believe that you should be able to consider your writing in terms of its intended audience, and that the single most important quality of good writing is its accessibility.

You therefore need to have a coherent sense of who your audience is and how they will relate to what you are writing.

If you have little understanding of your own psychological make-up, you are unlikely to understand why you write the way you do, or even why you choose particular themes or genres to write about. If you are writing for yourself, you may have trouble making other people respond to your work.

Much unsuccessful writing by otherwise talented writers is caused by their failure to separate themselves from their audience. If you didn't get on with your parents and you are trying to work this out in your writing, it may be difficult for someone who got on with his or her parents to relate to what you are writing unless you set the situation up well.

For a story or character to be accessible, the audience must understand, identify with or be able to relate to it. Accessibility is about the audience having a satisfactory experience in the cinema, in front of the television screen, or while reading a book or poem or listening to a piece of music. In other words, their expectations have been met. To achieve this you need to appreciate the audience's expectations. How do they know what it is that they are going to see or read?

A look at the marketing profile of a film or programme produced by the production company will tell you what the audience is predisposed to expect. It may, of course, be misleading hype, the result of over-enthusiasm on the part of the producers or the people they hire to promote and market the product. Advertisements, trailers, word-of-mouth, press and magazine publicity and reviews all determine that profile. A disappointed audience gives bad word-of-mouth.

What are the marketing angles of your idea? Don't wait until it is a completed script before you think of marketing angles. And don't say, 'But I'm the writer; someone else can think about marketing angles!' Make up several short pitches for your script. It is not an easy exercise, but it will focus your mind sharply on what you are writing and it will be rapidly apparent if you have encapsulated your central theme in the one- or two-line pitch. The exercise may reveal the fact that you have not really identified your theme at all!

If you understand something about how films are marketed, you will increase your chances of being successful. If you remain fixed in the belief – a common one – that you do not need to understand the context in which your work will be marketed, then you are more likely to join the ranks of the many thousands of writers whose speculative scripts – or even commissioned scripts – are 'just typing, not writing'.

In the course of this book I hope to show why accessibility, audiences and self-awareness must be kept in mind as you write.

Time is a key factor

If one looks at why so few scripts are really exciting, and why so many bad and unsuccessful films or programmes are made, some of the answers become clear. Very few scripts actually take their writers even six months of concentrated, single-minded effort. Yet the agents and the producers who might work on them or buy them, expect them to be complex, powerful, intriguing, clear and compelling enough to touch millions of people.

For their part, the writers, agents, producers – and script-editors – know that the script (even if it has not been given enough time to grow) must first enthuse the director, the actors and actresses, the art director, the cameraman, the marketing chiefs, the distribution company, the ad agency, and probably a banker or two. But the follow-through, to a really good finished script, is often lacking.

The reality is that most scripts are not accessible enough because the writers, agents, script editors, development executives and producers are too complacent, too unambitious and in too much of a hurry. Where a good script-editor does produce major rewrite notes, they sometimes come up against objections from the producer who liked it pretty well the first time, and is reluctant to commit more time and money to fix something they don't believe is broken. There is often a set of 'power' relationships between writer, script editor and producer. How the politics of that relationship is played out, is the result of personalities, dependency and who takes the initiative.

For example, it is worth highlighting here the importance of writers taking the initiative to ensure that they have enough time to do the work thoroughly. To do this, insist that time for rewrites is built into the schedule and the agreement. Make this clear from the beginning; you dramatically increase the chances of being the writer who does that rewrite, not to mention getting the next commission.

Unless you can come up with a script which has been thought through and is accessible – apparent for all to see when they first read it – the chances are not high that you will be the sole writer if the script goes into production. The same problem occurs when you are commissioned to write a script, but the first document you must write is a treatment. So you write the treatment and get fired because they don't like it or don't find it accessible. You never get to write the script, which is what you are good at. I will examine treatment writing at greater length in a subsequent chapter.

Other important points to bear in mind

There are a number of important generalizations to keep in mind during the writing. It helps if the people with whom you are in immediate contact are of like mind. If they are not, problems ensue. It is not necessarily the writer's task to stage-manage these relationships. But passivity does not usually achieve much except to let someone else get their way.

It is obvious, for example, that the biggest audiences have a short attention span. So how long are the scenes in your script? Scenes in American feature films are approximately half the length of scenes in European scripts. Should the writer plan the length of each scene, or write untroubled by such considerations, while the script editor has to deliver the bad news that the script is too long, the scenes are too long and the lovingly crafted dialogue will have to be cut? And have you, the writer, thought as much about occupying the audience's eyes as you have thought about the dialogue?

1. The Politics of being a Writer

Writers control two levels of communication with their audience as they write: what the audience sees and what they hear. It is very unusual for a British or Continental script to be characterized as strongly visual. It is also uncommon for a European film to be successful in a wide range of international markets.

Why is it so important to write visually? The answer is simple, but extraordinarily important: people tend to believe what they see, rather than what they hear.

It is a truism that people who cannot speak a language will be better able to follow a film in that language if the story is visually told, than if the film is dialogue-based. But like many truisms, it seems more difficult to do than one might think, judging by the dialogue-based scripts that pour over the industry's desks in Europe.

Keep thinking about your audience. What does the audience want from the experience you are constructing for them? If it is a cinema film then it needs to be something that they won't get on television. That means big screen, big emotions and action. Cinema audiences also want to have emotions. They do not want to sit eating popcorn and watch other people experience emotions.

Once you start asking what audiences need to get from the viewing experience (or, with books, the reading experience), the importance of the need to manipulate, to plant and payoff, to build rising climaxes, and all the other techniques you learn from books on scriptwriting or in creative-writing classes, should become clear.

Audiences are not monolithic. Each spectator brings to the viewing of your film, or reading of your book, different intellectual, emotional, cultural and educational baggage. You should give each and every one of them the optimum opportunity to relate to the characters.

Criticism and Rewriting

Your attitude towards criticism and rewriting can have a significant influence on your success as a writer. Script-editing, criticism and rewriting are all inextricably linked. Rewriting should be so normal, so common and so necessary that most of the time it is taken for granted. Instead, it is often avoided and the result damages not only the writer's career, but also the producer's, although producers seldom get adequately criticised for going into production with a script that is not ready. Script editing and rewriting have a whole chapter devoted to them.[1] Very few writers are clear-sighted and emotionally strong enough to tell the producer that the completed script is not good enough or ready, especially when the producer has said that he or she loves the script and, what is more, the schedule is tight.

Writers should always start out by encouraging criticism. It is not easy to be open-minded about criticism. It helps to be fairly confident. I am not ignoring the pain and apprehension criticism holds for writers. It is very real and unpleasant, but it is the Achilles' heel of too many writers.

Writers can sometimes determine the nature as well as the extent of the criticism they get. Having invited criticism from the agent, script editor or producer, the ball is then in their court.

Another point of contention between writers and those they work with intimately has to do with assessing the size of the audience, and the problems of writing for a larger audience. Established and inexperienced writers alike sometimes resist writing for the largest audience, as though their art puts them above such populism.

Using the size of the audience to assess the success of a show can lead erroneously to the assumption that a mass audience is unintelligent, undemanding, and has a short attention span. It is easy to make this assumption; it is also elitist. People who work in advertising don't make this mistake: their concepts are finely honed to sell a particular 'product' to a targeted section of the market. Pretentious assumptions and needing to be seen as an 'artiste' don't come into it.

If it is difficult to be objective about what other people have written, it is almost impossible to be objective about what you write yourself. Do not expect a director, who has a strong personality and attitude, to leave your script alone. He or she might actually improve the script, although that may depend on whose point of view you take.

The politics of being a writer involve juggling conflicting pressures, both within yourself and from outside forces. Compromise is inevitable for much of the time. Those who start with the right approach will ensure that they get constructive criticism and advice for the right reasons, rather than negative criticism for the wrong reasons.

Each of the key people with whom you will have a relationship – agent, script editor, producer and director – has their own agenda. They also have their own career paths and goals. They may be under even greater pressures than you to come up with something that will turn their careers around. Or they may be complacent and unwilling to take risks or speculate too much of their time on your script.

Try to empathize, put yourself in their position (which does not necessarily mean agreeing with what they say). Understanding what the other person wants in a negotiation (and all these relationships mean negotiating some of the time) is the first step to getting your own way, assuming that this is possible and seems sensible to others.

There are writers who will not let themselves be marginalized. They empower themselves, through networks of writers, professional societies and sheer professionalism. The position of the all-powerful writer-producer in long-running series on the US television networks may be more than most writers in Europe will achieve, but it is what they should aspire to.

Notes

1   Script editing and rewriting have a chapter (9) devoted to them because they are so fundamental to the development process. A survey of development in Europe has been written by media journalist Angus Finney: *Development Feature Films in Europe: A Practical Guide* (published by Blueprint for the Media Business School, Autumn 1995).

2 Creativity – Understanding the Sources of Ideas

Creativity involves inducing your imagination to reveal itself to you in a way that you can order and select from. It is putting into specific words your dreams and fantasies. That is why writers are encouraged to visualize, to fantasize. Dreaming is, for a writer, part of the creative business.

You have to be able to play the roles of all your characters. Many writers don't achieve this satisfactorily. They can play some of the roles, but others are harder. Some men can't write female characters, and vice versa. You need to subjugate your ego and sense of self, feel and think yourself into the personae of your characters, and then tell it like it is. It is a confidence trick made possible by a fertile imagination.

A finished film is the result of a massive series of confidence tricks, which requires literally hundreds of people to pull off. For the audience it is a flowing, natural whole. But it starts with the script and that is where the writer earns his or her money.

Remember the important distinction between reality or truth on the one hand, and believability on the other. It is very common in first novels and first screenplays to find a thinly dramatized version of the real world, usually autobiographical. It seldom works.

If you want to write about the real world, as it appears to you, stick to documentaries and non-fiction. But if what you write is described as drama or a novel, the audience or readers will have certain expectations. Finding a truth about themselves and the world they live in will be part of that. Successful creativity can make the unreal seem believable.

Some ideas or themes are very much of their time and reflect changes taking place in society. Others may actually change the nature of the society. One of the motivations driving writers to face the blank page day after day, is the satisfaction of the challenge to change society, the challenge that comes from being creative, from being a writer.

But in taking this approach, the writer faces a major danger: writing for oneself. It is not easy to know how other people will react to what one writes. Gaining an understanding of your audience will bring an awareness to your creativity and will enable you to write better. I will discuss ways of achieving this later. Being creative is not artistic licence to be self-indulgently anarchic. As I have already said, accessibility is of paramount importance if you are going to succeed.

Not that some great writing hasn't emerged out of just that sort of individual 'auteurism'. In a culturally rich society artists should be encouraged to experiment, to break new ground, without starving. But I want to look at something more banal, more predictable. Can you influence your success by choosing one idea over another? How can you determine what will work and what won't? Projects frequently fail because the basic idea they have chosen is either not a good one, is wrong for that particular writer, or it is the wrong time for the idea.

Will a bad idea in the hands of a good writer have more chance of success than a great idea in the hands of a bad writer? It all depends on how good or bad the writer, and how good or bad the idea. Writers have to live with their choices of ideas or themes for a long time. Often they snatch at ideas that seem appealing and begin writing long before there is real evidence that they may have made the right decision.

Certain types of idea or theme seem to remain consistently acceptable to audiences and therefore to the industry. Let's look at two well-known and popular genres, the thriller and the horror movie. These both have a sense of 'threat' at their core. The journalist John Lyttle has pointed out that in the past the threat was external – it came from a distance (often another planet) and intruded on the protagonists. In recent years, perhaps influenced by very successful mass-market authors such as Stephen King, the threat has moved closer. It is right next door or even in your own home or family. And it almost always starts by looking innocuous.[1]

> It could be that one night stand (*Fatal Attraction*). It could be the lodger in *Pacific Heights*. What about the new nanny in *The Hand That Rocks the Cradle* or the ex-client, fresh from jail in *Cape Fear*? It might even be the nice, handsome cop in *Unlawful Entry*, or your friendly flatmate in *Sitting Pretty* or *Single White Female*. Or even the respectable lawyer in *The Client*.

Lyttle goes on to make the point that the victims tend to be white and middle class. They are 'nice' people at the mercy of the manipulative and cruel random acts of fate.

> ... it's not the American family which is failing, it is the American family which is being failed. Film after film, the legal system is found wanting. The police can't help Michael Douglas or Matthew Modine (who's menaced, shot and flung behind bars) or *Cape Fear*'s Nick Nolte (a lawyer hoisted on his own petard). All the one-time targets finally take the law into their own hands. And the films all climax in bloodshed as vigilante justice prevails.

Creatures from outer space, giant ants or killer bees all touched our deepest fears in the 1950s and 1960s movies. Domestic violence, as well as films like *Kramer vs Kramer*, never mind *Fatal Attraction*, may also be exploitative. But nobody forces people to go to see thriller or horror movies. They do it because they want to. They go, as Hitchcock knew so well, because they want to be terrorized in the safety of the darkened cinema. Successful writers touch on the fears, hopes and aspirations that most people can relate to. We all know what it's like to feel threatened. We all know what it's like to laugh or cry. If you write scripts that an audience can relate to you greatly enhance the likelihood of your script being turned into a film. Do not assume you are the archetypal audience. And remember that movies happen in the present. You have to try to create in the audience a feeling of experiencing it here and now.

In a novel or a short story there is often the sense that the narrator knows that the story has happened in the past. In a film (or a television drama) the story is going to happen, and what gets us interested in the main character is a feeling of empathy or sympathy and a sense of anticipation.

Pascal Lonhay, one of the best script analysts in Europe, defined anticipation:

Anticipation forces the viewer to guess, because the characters have been given freedom to act in an unpredictable way. Anticipation offers alternatives whereas predictability asks the viewer to believe, to accept without alternatives.

That's what EM Forster meant when he said, 'Surprise me with the believable'. That's what good writing does.

Later we will look in some detail at the audience, from demographic, psychological and physiological points of view. It is only by combining these perspectives that writers can increase the likelihood of getting the viewer to think and feel what the writer wants them to, at exactly the moment that they are supposed to.

The Creative Process

So, what is involved in the process of being creative, of selecting what to write about and how to write about it? The ability to get an audience's juices flowing – whatever the subject – depends to some extent on the writers' understanding of his or her audience. And one way of learning that understanding is to be aware of yourself as an audience.

William Goldman, the distinguished writer of screenplays for *All the President's Men* and *Marathon Man* amongst other films, as well as the book *Adventures in the Screen Trade* (certainly the most amusing if not the best written on the subject of writing for the cinema), encourages writers to watch a movie several times in one sitting.

During the first viewing you are an average punter, paying your money for the seat and the popcorn, to be transported into another world. At the end of the movie, when the curtain comes down, Goldman recommends that you remain in the cinema for the next screening. This time be aware of the audience's reactions to the film. Watch a third showing – now look only at the audience, not the screen. Do you see the whole range of human emotions cross the faces of those in the audience, some perhaps more than others? This emotional stimulation is what they have paid for.

As a writer in the audience you may not have expressed your emotions so openly, perhaps because you were trying to see how the movie was written. There is a form of elitism that comes to affect many people working in the industry. It is easy to feel superior to one's audience; it is also dangerous. That is one reason why so many scripts fail: the writers have lost touch with their audience.

Getting in touch involves some understanding of how human emotions function (see also the chapter on the psychology and physiology of emotion) and also of the creative process that writing entails. This also involves being in touch with yourself as a writer. If you cry at the emotionally high moments in a film, you learn to tell, intuitively, what is likely to work on audiences. Once you develop your instincts about characters and storylines, you will have a rich vein into which to tap. I believe that the starting point is the need to get an emotional response. If you can get an intellectual response too, so much the better, as audiences operate on several levels when watching film and television.

Planning

Be conscious of your relationship with your audience. How do you intend to appeal to each of the three levels within the audience: guts, heart and brain? (These are described by Jon Boorstin, in his seminal book *The Hollywood Eye*, as the visceral level, the emotional level and the intellectual level.) And once you have written the first draft, go back and check each scene for this, but take it further: check how you have chosen to write the scene:

i)   what have you done to interest the eyes?

ii) what have you done to interest the ears? If it's mainly ears, rewrite it more for the eyes.

Remember also that the music in the film may be more important than your dialogue. Music, it is said, goes directly to the stomach. It is not mediated through the intellect. Anthony Storr's book *Music and the Mind* establishes beyond reasonable doubt the importance of music as a form of communication. Yet where is it in the writer's creative palette? Where does it play a significant part in scriptwriting books or courses?

I am generally in favour of reading books and attending courses. Virtually every course in creative writing teaches certain fundamentals which stories must have. Michael Hauge identifies the basics as:

- A central character or hero.
- The audience must empathize and identify with that character (otherwise the writer fails to engage the audience's emotions).
- The central character must have something which can be seen on screen (ie it is not enough for the character to want to be a better person – it has to be manifest) and the character must be nearly thwarted. No conflict, no emotional duress.
- The central character must relate to other interesting characters. The villain must be not only dangerous but attractive.
- These characters must also inhabit subplots, which link in to the main story so that they are all resolved in the final act.

None of this is new to you, I'm sure. But you'd be amazed how often these most basic elements are not present in scripts, even those written by experienced writers.

Credibility

So writers must make themselves aware of all these factors. As well as working out the storyline, developing complex and interesting characters, giving them sparkling and surprising dialogue to say, writers should, in some way, attempt to be original. It's not easy. We have a cartoon on the wall in our office. A writer is saying to an editor, 'You say this is difficult to understand! You should try writing it!'[2]

Without natural talent, it is difficult making sure that the audience is provoked by the film or programme, that the emotions are accessible. Note the difference here between the story and how you tell it. After 'accessibility', 'believability' is one of the most important qualities to strive for. Whatever film, play or novel you are writing, producing or directing, you have to ensure that the audience or readers believe in the universe you depict. (It is less important whether you yourself believe in it. But making your audience believe it is the essential challenge to your creativity.) Aristotle, commenting on drama, said, 'A plausible impossibility is preferable to an implausible possibility'. He was talking not about truth but about credibility.

Genre vs originality

Discussions about creativity often touch on the fact that truly original films are relatively few and far between. Genre is often defined in terms of its derivativeness. So can one say that creativity is dependent on originality?

We are back to the question about whether film is art or craft, culture or commerce. A successful genre piece requires a combination of discipline, imagination and mimicry. It may not be original, but if it is successful it will probably be well-crafted.

Writing within a genre means paying attention to the conventions of that genre. And it means being aware that the fans of that genre – the paying public – might know the genre better than you, and might care about it more than you. So change it, but only if you know what you are doing and why you are doing it. TS Eliot said, 'It is not wise to violate the rules until you know how to observe them'. Trite but true enough.

Most television series drama is genre drama. It can be easier to write, simply because detailed guidelines are available. For example, the characters exist, so do the locations and the world of the story. But if you add nothing, your script will be flat and repeat commissions will be unlikely. So your involvement has got to create something extra. Furthermore, other people's egos are also involved in a series 'bible' (the detailed proposal document for a series or serial) and in the storylines you may be given. Don't make changes just for the sake of it. Only make suggestions if they improve the work. And check with your script editor all the way. The concept of genres contains within it the notion of derivation. We know that audiences want more of the same, and there is a tremendous momentum to follow a huge success with a similar product. Hence the permanent vogue for sequels in Hollywood. When you buy another can of coke, you don't want a lemonade. You want a repeat experience.

This is important, because if you know who your audience is, you know what they expect. And you will then know how to surprise them. In television series, audiences can be unforgiving if changes are made to much-loved sit-coms or soaps. When Murphy Brown in the eponymous US sitcom had a baby the show lost audience share. They liked Murphy to be bitchy, funny and tough, not really the attributes of motherhood.

Francis Ford Coppola described the need to repeat similar experiences: 'People are particular about films, they don't want to be put into an unusual situation. It's like the little kid who says, "Tell me the story of the three bears again."'

It is not easy to come up with something really good in an established genre. It is probably as difficult as coming up with something really original. It is certainly easier to judge genre work, to make the obvious comparisons. If you choose to write genre scripts, don't be patronizing about the series or the stories. Established writers who condescend to do a few soap episodes seldom do them well.

Which leads me back to the problem of elitism among writers. Don't think that because you are creating something, you are superior to your audience. The danger of the creative ego is ever-present. You need the ego to help you face the blank page, to get you through the bad and tough times, and to help you face rejections, or producers' and directors' egos.

Choosing your subject and handling the characters

So what role should the ego have in your choice of material or storyline? Should you only write about that which you know? There are obvious advantages, less research for a start. Authenticity will be easier to establish. But don't lose sight of the need to engage an audience who need to believe in your characters and story, even if they are not true or accurate. How often, before you decide to write about something particular, or while you are searching through your sources of inspiration, do you ask yourself these two questions: Why are you writing? Who are you writing for?

They are perhaps the most important questions a writer can ask. It is easier to know the answer than to live up to it. The late Frank Daniel, doyen of scriptwriting teachers, asked a class I attended a similar question: 'When an audience sits in a darkened cinema, looking up at the screen, what are they looking at?' The answer, so obvious once he said it, is that they are looking at themselves.

I sometimes find it useful when working on a problem in a script, to analyse it using a model of the 'eternal triangle':

The writer's primary relationship should, of course, be with the audience or reader. Using this model we find that much that does not work in the scripts and manuscripts we see stems from writers being too concerned with their own relationships with their characters. It is not enough for characters to make sense only to the writer. Characters are simply a means to reach the audience. To succeed, the script has to move the audience. In order to terrify your audience you may indeed have to terrify one or more of your characters. But that is not the ultimate goal. This may seem obvious, but it is probably the single most common cause of inadequate character motivation. It is also far more prevalent in inexperienced writers.

Your identity, your self-image, all play a part in determining the way you write, even perhaps what you write about. Without some awareness of your own strengths and weaknesses, your fears and phobias, how will you know whether you are working something out for yourself, rather than enabling your audience to share the experience? Writers need to be able to stand back from their creation.

Professional readers, including agents, should be able to read fairly objectively and give a 'representative' reaction, even if the story or script in question is nowhere near the reader's personal taste or interest. Having selected an idea, not knowing whether it will appeal widely, how do you develop it so that it will have enough depth and edge to exert power over the reader or audience? In constructing the broad strokes of your story, focus on the theme and the central characters and ask what sort of backstory[3] you are going to create for those characters. Once you have done that, how much of the backstory do you need to reveal, in order for your characters not only to make sense but to become interesting? Too little and the characters can seem thin; too much and the narrative

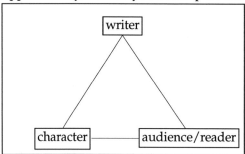

The Eternal Triangle

16

is impeded. But the richness of well-revealed characters can add greatly to the quality of the reading or the viewing if this can be done without slowing the pace.

Originality

Studying the classics or successful films and learning from their structure and the craft that went into making them is one way to identify (or eliminate) a theme or subject for a script. It can hinder your attempts to do something original if you are strongly influenced by a successful film. But knowledge of the industry means you are at least likely to know what has been done already. This means knowing when something you do is original, because it isn't enough for the material to be original only in your eyes.

Fatal Attraction, or its ending, was derivative, but to audiences all over the world (me included), no less satisfying for all that. When it comes to picking a topic or theme, there isn't much that hasn't been tried. You may not have come across a particular story or idea before, or a particular structure for a story, but the possibility is that someone else has. So don't rely too much on the buzz you get when you think that you have just invented the wheel.

The real problem here isn't only that you might put too much emphasis on the apparent originality to carry the writing, but that you will not put enough emphasis on how you are telling the story. The fact that it may not be original does not matter if you tell the story so well that it captures the imagination of millions.

The search for something that is different often leads to ignoring the basics of storytelling. Submissions prefaced by the words, 'I have come up with something that is different from anything that is around at the moment...' are often sloppy, resting on the laurel of being different – and rarely being that different anyway.

It is not likely, with hindsight, that many writers will be judged to have been truly original. This is not a bad reflection on those who are not original. There is little or no correlation between what writers who are original earn, and what the others earn, because a high proportion of successful films and books are not in any meaningful sense original. Look at the industry's relentless reliance on sequels, which are deemed safe by conservative decision-makers in the major studios. In fact, such is the premium on originality that the studio system not only recognizes the relative unattainability of originality, but has also created a new development industry reformatting films from other countries. This even happens outside the USA. David Puttnam produced a film in Ireland called *War of the Buttons*, which was based on a much earlier French film.

There is also money in reformatting television series. Britain has exported a number of series to the United States. *Till Death Us Do Part* became *All in the Family* (Alf Garnett turning into Archie Bunker). It also became a German programme called *One Heart and One Soul. Upstairs Downstairs* became *Beacon Hill*, set in Boston. The British classic *Steptoe and Son* became the American series *Sandford and Son*. More recently the Americans failed to successfully adapt the British hit sitcom *Men Behaving Badly*, and the American reformatting of *Cracker* was miscast and was not thought to be a success. Both these shows depend to some extent on an explicitness about sex and drugs that the American public (or is it the television executives?) don't want. It reminds me of the Monica

Lewinsky/President Clinton comment, made by an Australian: 'Thank God we got the convicts and they got the puritans!'

The British have also imported American formats. *Who's the Boss?* became *The Upper Hand* and *The Golden Girls* became the failed British sitcom *Brighton Belles*. ITV's adaptation of the American show *The Seventies Years* into *Days Like These* received such a poor reaction that it was taken off prime time before the end of the run. In general the shows that fail to 'translate' seem to do so because the remake does not come across as culturally authentic. Audiences are not easy to fool.

In countries like Holland and Germany reformatting has become big business. It is seen as safe and relatively inexpensive for broadcasters. Shows like *EastEnders* from Britain and *Good Times, Bad Times* from Australia are amongst those being translated into a European context. The Continental producers claim that one of the reasons they are reformatting shows is that they simply do not have enough experienced writers to create new shows. This means that hundreds of hours of drama on television can be taken up by programmes that could otherwise have been created by local writers. Some of them will get work on the reformatting – it might even prove a useful training ground for them. But it is not quite the same as the opportunity to write an original episode for an existing series or to create a new series.

In some cases, the reformatting producer will abandon the dozens of scripts purchased from abroad because the storylines and characters have taken off in a different direction. In effect, they end up commissioning original storylines.

Writers don't tend to earn a great deal of money when their scripts of an existing series are sold as part of a format deal. This is one of the reasons why a writer should attempt to retain the format rights if it is an original idea, or at least make sure that a respectable share of the format revenue is retained.

It is difficult to come up with accurate figures for what broadcasters pay. Everyone is secretive about figures like this, but a sum in the region of $5,000 per episode is probably quite common. It is possible to negotiate 'escalators' into format deals, so that if the new version is successful the purchaser will pay an increased figure for later episodes.

The small number of new series or serials which succeed, and last more than one season, makes it unlikely that inexperienced writers will be given the chance of creating original ideas for the longer-running formats.

Form and content

So what can a writer do to identify trends, to increase the chances of finding a topic or theme that will be of greater interest to a wider audience? To begin with, the fact should be borne in mind that form is as important as content. Then ask if your subject or background is topical.

What are some currently topical subjects? At the risk of dating myself, they could include the environment and ecology, the new man, political correctness, AIDS, the internet and virtual reality, to suggest a few obvious ones. Every time there are stories in newspapers or magazines about subjects like these, you should consider them as potential inspiration for story ideas. You and thousands of others, I'm afraid. But having chosen to explore your topic or theme, and who your central characters are, how are you going to use them in a way that will appeal to the audience?

If you cannot find a form to dramatize the theme, forget it. It is not enough to have an idea, even a very good one. Ideas have no value unless someone can execute them. When we get unsolicited submissions that consist of great ideas, but the writing is awful, we send them straight back. It is when we get lousy ideas with great writing that we get more interested. It is the talent to write that is rare, not the willingness to try. In other words, it is not really possible to judge how good a script will be when you are only told an idea. Writers are always asking what people think about this or that idea. 'I've got a great idea for a film' is a litany we hear so often.

In the case of a client whose work and abilities I know well, I may be able to guess. But even then it is not easy. Some ideas seem as if they should suit a particular writer but the finished product is disappointing. And an idea that seems quite wrong for another writer can turn out to be a wonderful script.

Arousing an emotional response

As I have already said, audiences pay for experiences outside their own immediate lives. Escapism is one reason, voyeurism another. Unless you understand your audience, your creative energy will probably be misdirected, rather than correctly focused.

Hitchcock was relentless in the pursuit of audience manipulation. In doing so, he was being very creative. He created the opportunities for millions of people to experience feelings – often fear – for which they were willing to pay.

Fear isn't the only experience you can have vicariously. Positive, uplifting, inspirational, life-enhancing qualities are all associated with successful movies, as are upbeat endings, commonly seen in American movies. They wear their emotions so openly because arousing strong emotion has been shown to make money. And that should not be thought of as pejorative.

The conventional wisdom is that Hollywood has proved that audiences want happy endings. Is this really true? Not always. Although three different endings were tested for the psycho-thriller *Fatal Attraction*, in the one finally used, the adulterous husband learned his lesson without paying the price. The cost: the single woman dies. Most audiences seemed to want that ending, although the producer, Sherry Lansing, apparently set out to make a film in which the man doesn't get away with it. It seems that there is a real divide. The network which made the television movie dramatizing the mass killings at David Koresh's compound in Waco, Texas, even wanted the film to have an upbeat ending. It could simply be that audiences seek to escape from the depressing recession and from violence in the streets. Happy endings do seem to be what they want most of the time.

The truth is probably more complicated. What audiences really want are emotional experiences, and the list of very successful films (and television shows – *Roseanne*, *Cheers*, *thirtysomething*, for example) in which the endings were not happy, is long. Films like *Sommersby* didn't go for the obvious upbeat ending, and if you look at the best films of the last thirty to forty years many of the classics don't either. *Gone With the Wind*, *Brief Encounter*, *Casablanca*, *Bonnie and Clyde*, *Butch Cassidy*, *Midnight Cowboy*, to name a few.

When we go the movies or watch television, part of the reason is to explore ourselves and our lives. 'What if?'/'How would I feel if?' The sense of anticipation is a vital ingredient in the make-up of the audience. Ian Katz, in an article in *The Guardian*[4] pointed out that American movies do have a certain predictability about them. 'You know exactly what you're going to get. Summer is also the time for 'feel-good' movies. In summer 1993 millions of people were hoping Meg Ryan and Tom Hanks would consummate their long-distance love affair in *Sleepless in Seattle*. (In summer 1994) they were rooting for Hanks again in *Forrest Gump*. The moral of these films is the same: to nice and good people of the world good things will happen, sooner or later.' In 1998 it was the ill-fated *Titanic* and *Shakespeare in Love*.

Katz concluded that the success of these films reflected 'a deep yearning for simple, uplifting parables in a complex, morally confusing world... Their appeal is...less complicated than that: both films are funny, laugh-out-loud funny'.

Much the same could be said of the rare British hit, *Four Weddings and a Funeral* and *Notting Hill*. You could analyse them in terms of what they have to say about commitment and love in the 1990s. But in reality they are very funny scripts that apparently took many rewrites before being considered ready to be filmed.

Manipulating the audience

Despite the fact that they get it wrong so often, studio executives know exactly what they want – bums on seats. A great script – something rare – can deliver a perfect dose of yearning. But it is easier and safer to resort to a happy ending. After all, the real bosses in Hollywood are not the studio executives; they are the shareholders.

Creativity in this business is about remaking reality; diffusing or refracting it through your eyes and your mind, applying the discipline of the craft to get the audience to see your new version of reality. But the audience will not find new insights unless you manipulate them, unless you plant information whose significance will not be immediately obvious, indeed which they may not even notice initially. Later on, it will dawn on them that black is actually white, and this revelation will enable them to get a sense of satisfaction from what you have written. Good writing will fulfil the writer's part of the contract.

Good writing does not always lead to a sale. If the reader of the script is stimulated, the script may not suit his or her needs, but if the reader sees a spark, then it might have served its purpose. From that may come work. The most common cry from script editors, professional readers and producers is that they can never find enough good writing.

You must try to make every script, or every treatment, work for you on two levels. It represents the story you are telling, and it represents you as a storyteller. Agents probably make more submissions of calling-card scripts than anything else. These are scripts which may never be filmed but which exemplify a writer's ability within the structure of a known format. To impress producers who are scanning the writing of perhaps a dozen or even twenty writers every week, a script has to be exceptionally good to be picked out from the rest. That is why you should never be satisfied with what you've done. You should always want to improve it.

So take hope from this cry for good scripts. Don't interpret every rejection as proof that you know better than they do. If a particular person doesn't like what you have written, then take it at face value. Try to learn from it. They may be wrong. Move on to the next person and, more importantly, move on to the next piece of work. If two or more readers have the same negative reaction, they may be right.

Improving your creativity

There are many aspects of your professionalism as a creative writer that you can learn and improve. Being able to conceptualize an idea and articulate it doesn't necessarily have much to do with whether you can write well, which is why pitching is so important.

You also need to know how the system works, and who is both important and accessible to you. If you come up with an idea for a story, but you know no one in the industry, there is not a great deal you can do with the idea or with a short pitch. This is where being able to network, and having occasion to spend time with people in the industry, pays off. You will also begin to notice the difference between how stories are told and the stories themselves. The best stories and ideas often come from people who can't write. Such people sometimes make great producers or script editors.

Steven Spielberg is unquestionably very creative, although there's not a lot of originality in *Duel, Jaws, Close Encounters, ET* or even *Jurassic Park*. The stories themselves are tried and tested.

His creativity lies in the way he tells the stories, in the extent to which he makes them so accessible, that literally millions of people all over the world enjoy them. His craft is to give enough viewers a very powerful experience. Writers need to be able to do this for every individual member of the audience.

Pascal Lonhay, the writer and script analyst, described this process as follows: the story should lead the viewer through a vicarious experience that makes the viewer feel as if he or she had participated, witnessed and were involved in it themselves.

If that's creativity, it's not surprising that it's difficult to do well. Being able to make an audience react, even to the extent of creating physiological responses, involves great sensitivity and imagination. The truth is that most scripts are not very good. James Park, in a seminal article entitled *False Starts*[5], argued that the decline of the British film industry lay with its scripts.

He catalogues a number of unsuccessful British films and goes on to describe them as follows:

> The makers of such pictures don't seem to have asked themselves the crucial question: will we care about the characters and empathize with their experiences? Again and again, the people at the centre of the story are so casually introduced and their emotional trajectory so loosely explored, that there's no hope that the audience will get inside the characters' feelings. The writers of too many recent British films seem to stand outside their characters, clinging to the belief that the clever intellectual connections they make between scenes, or the significance of the message they think they're espousing, will mean something to an audience.

The problem lies partly in the fact that film has traditionally been more of a director's medium than a writer's, in terms of the power on the set. Hollywood now seems a little more inclined to the view that the key thing is the script (rather than the scriptwriter), and a couple of speculatively-written scripts have reached the heady heights of $3-4 million (Joe Eszterhas's *Basic Instinct* and Shane Black's *The Long Kiss Goodnight*).

One of the problems about creativity is that the process of creating is beguiling. There's something very satisfying about feeling that you're being creative. However, it's easy to be complacent, and difficult to be objective. How do you make ruthless choices when you're feeling so good about every word you've just put down?

If you are unable to be objective – or find someone to be objective for you – your creativity may be more of an indulgence than you would like to admit. And once you have pushed the script to the point where it is as good you can make it, but it is still not good enough, what next?

The passage of time can improve it, often by providing distance between the writer and the work. But feedback is usually the best way to move it forward, and this is where the way you handle yourself and encourage criticism can make a difference. We sometimes find ourselves saying to clients, 'The script is *terrific*. What you've done is a *big* improvement on the previous draft'. But what does this praise really mean? It does not necessarily mean that it's now a really good script. Before, it might have been a bad one. It certainly doesn't mean that it is as good as it could be. It may only be as good as that writer can get it.

So what's needed to enable that writer to make it better? If I've gone through five drafts with the writer I may not be able to help further. We may now have to look to a producer, another reader or a professional script analyst. There are producers we trust, whose judgement we trust, but will the writer be open to even further input? And how does anyone know when further changes will damage the tone or texture of the script, even if they finesse the storyline?

There is a saying: 'Writing is something that everyone except writers finds easy to do'. Good writing is about much more than getting the right words down on the page. Coming to terms with this is one of the things that distinguishes the professional writer from the amateur.

Notes

1 John Lyttle, *The Independent*, 12 November 1992.

2 *The Guardian*, 'Ars Brevis' cartoon.

3 Character 'backstory' is the historical background of a character pre-dating the beginning of the action in the script or novel. Without knowledge of the characters' backstories it is very difficult to develop three-dimensional characters.

4 *The Guardian*, 8 August 1994.

5 James Park, *Sight & Sound*, the magazine of the BFI, Summer 1990.

3. The Writer as a Business Person

Generally, successful writers treat what they do as a business. It is a profession. Unfortunately, many people write for other reasons, ranging from passion and the enjoyment and challenge of creating a world, from self-expression to vanity, from political commitment to easy money. So let's start by looking at motivation – not character motivation, that's what you can get from creative writing courses. I mean the motivation of the writer.

For writers, there is a very basic question to ask: why am I writing this? Writers should know what it is about writing that makes them willing to compete with thousands of other writers. I don't know how many scripts are in circulation in Britain, but it is estimated that there are about 50,000 actively circulating in Hollywood at any one time.

Some writers write for pleasure. Some writers write, they say, because they have to. They have something that they must say. There is a driving compulsion to put words on paper. Some of these make wonderful, committed, passionate writers. But theirs can also be a myopic obsession, leading nowhere. Do you know the expression 'to kill the darlings'? Usually the 'darling' in question is a scene or line in a script that the writer loves and won't allow to be cut. This is sometimes the result of a short-sighted obsession.

Scriptwriting is often seen as a route to something else, directing in particular. After all, if you can create a film in the reader's head, doesn't that give you some claim to be able to put it on the screen? But writing when your real intention is directing seems odd to me. It may be the best way in, as a novice director, though it is not likely to produce the best writing. If you are so set on directing, why not find something to direct which is written by a better writer than you? Why do something yourself if you can find someone better to do it? If the answer is because you can't find anything better to direct, I don't believe you have looked hard enough. If you can't find something at a price you can afford, then you probably haven't tried hard enough. It is possible, with real dedication, to negotiate around most things.

Conversely, if what you have written is good enough for a better director than you, perhaps you should sell it. You will eventually get to direct, assuming you have the talent, if you can write that well, and are determined enough about it. But if your script is of no interest to anyone else, should you be wasting your energy raising the money in order to direct it? Perhaps there isn't much choice. But it's not a great way to start. It may be because your vision is genuinely ahead of its time, and there is no one else around who can see what you can; you have to go it alone. I applaud that attitude, even if I can't always respond to the piece of work.

For many first-time directors or producers this might be the only way to break in. But do not risk devaluing your reputation. Think about how other people see you. If you get a good reputation as a writer, producers, script editors and agents will talk about you. You become sought after, which makes it somewhat easier to get producers to agree to buy what you want to write.

Creative Relations

Your reputation is made up of more than the sum of what you write. It is how you interrelate with the other members of the team. And I am not talking about teamwriting. That's another thing altogether. I am talking about the people you should be closest to: the development person or script editor, the producer or director, and your agent. How you enable them to do what they want, to achieve what they need, will determine how they see you.

I don't want to minimize the inherent conflict within these creative relationships, because there is much potential for disagreement. Some of the conflict should have been preempted by the negotiated and signed contracts, and some of it can be avoided by your ability to manoeuvre, negotiate and pitch. Achieving what you want is more likely if you set up the 'preconditions' well, namely that you are a serious, businesslike writer, easy to get on with, knowledgeable about the industry, and with the interests of the project and the team at heart.

When there are clearly opposing views on how the script should be written, what happens depends on the particular circumstances and the balance of power in the team. Always try to see the conflict from the other person's point of view before you dig your heels in. If, having heard them out, you still believe you are right, and they cannot change your mind, find constructive ways of getting your way. Your choice of what to write about is critical. Being successful means having good judgement, something that usually comes with experience.

Priorities

After lack of talent, the single most common reason for scripts being rejected is the choice of subject and central character. It is often said that writers should only write about what they know. The reality for most writers is that they simply don't have exciting enough lives. If you have actually had very interesting experiences, it certainly does help. But if you consider the sources of writing income for most writers at the beginning of their careers, it is not from the original ideas that they feel passionate about. However, those ideas or scripts may have been what got them the work in the first place. There is therefore often an ambiguity in what you should concentrate upon. But most writers' first regular income comes from writing scripts where storylines have been provided – usually for TV serials.

Writers need to be flexible, unless they have a very particular voice. And they need to have staying power, or a day job. Then they can go on until someone listens to what they have to say and likes it enough to do something about it. Young writers with a passion for the cinema must follow their passion, but the discipline that comes from writing long-running series episodes usually sharpens the talent as well as building up the bank balance. Writing as a career is not usually based on one piece of work.

This is where the short-term/long-term problem comes in. It is a problem that confronts most writers at some point. This can be a nice problem, if you have two commissions and you have to work out how to take both, even though you probably can't deliver both on time. But many writers are forced by financial circumstances to concentrate on the short term, and it is possible to become dependent on writing series episodes, particularly if you are good enough at it to be in regular demand. Your original ideas can end up being left in the bottom drawer.

Only you can decide your priorities. But you should do so with the full knowledge of the facts, and of the industry. Friends in the business, fellow writers, your agent, can all help explore the options with you. Being businesslike is really common sense. For example:

1 *Evaluate priorities.* Do you really want to do this project? Or is it that you need the money? Will you be able to deliver? If you have too much on, will you deliver an acceptable draft on time?

2 *Schedule your time* so you can take on more than one thing. Always try to build in margins of time. If you can't deliver on time, let those to whom you are contracted know as soon as possible. Find out realistically what their deadline is: can you meet it? If you know you can't, give them every opportunity to get someone else in to write it who can deliver on time. That may even be necessary if the first draft is an original piece of work by you. Usually they will find a way of compromising. But in rare cases it is too late for that and too much is riding on the script being ready by a particular date. So be generous; it is simply a matter of being professional if you are not to let them down. It will do your reputation a world of good.

3 *Always make follow-up notes*, copied in to your agent if you have one.

4 *Know how to present your work.* If you don't know the accepted formats for page layout, look them up in the many books on scriptwriting. And please get a decent printer for your computer. The type generated by cheap dot-matrix printers is horrible to read and tends to make those who see it extra-critical of your work, if they read it at all.

5 *What's your attitude like?* For example, you have written a spec script which you are in love with. You want your agent to sell it, the producer you have shown it to buy it. But did you discuss the idea with your agent or the producer first? It might be a lousy idea in their opinion, in which case you are risking rejection and antagonism over what might be a poor script based on a bad idea. Be businesslike and ask for criticism early on. It is not your child. Remember: 'It's only typing!'

A writer who chooses to spend months writing something, knowing that he or she is at a disadvantage, and does little about it, is not being professional.

Your Attitude and your Career

When I talk about the need to understand your role in the business as a whole in order to see what you can do to improve your position in it, I hope it has become clear that this has very little to do with the art of screenwriting, but much to do with your career.

One of the first things to remember is that writers are always in competition, not only with each other, but with the thousands of other writers they will never meet, names and careers they do not know exist, in towns and cities they may never go to. If you only have the aspirations of an amateur, that's OK. There is no reason why you have to break your back to succeed, if you write just because you enjoy it. But if you want to succeed, to be taken seriously as a writer, or as someone who works with writers, it helps to understand something about the business you want to be in, for example about the contracts you sign, the taxes you pay, indeed even the rudiments of the word processor you may be using. Unless you understand the business you are in, even if rather superficially, you will be at a disadvantage.

Agents obviously prefer working with writers who are very businesslike. I suspect that most producers feel the same. Unfortunately there are many agents, script editors and producers who are not really that good at reading scripts properly. Serious writers prefer working with producers or script editors who are, themselves, informed and professional.

Nonetheless, every writer is different. There are those who simply cannot and will not be organized. If their writing is magical one puts up with it. But laziness is too common a failing. And so-called originality is often an excuse for laziness.

Be Prepared

Too few writers regularly read film and TV trade papers. It is the easiest and least expensive way of finding out who is doing what, and to whom material or ideas should be sent. It is the best value money can buy for writers. Keeping up with changes in personnel can only be done by regular reading of the trade press. Simply knowing that someone is about to move is valuable information. In their 'old' job no decisions will be being made by them; but they will probably want to see new material in their new job despite the fact that people tend to take favoured writers with them when they move.

There are other changes apart from job moves, such as new slots and new opportunities, ratings and box-office figures, and so on. You need a working knowledge of them all. There are also changes to do with multiple ownership, multinational companies, new systems of delivery, whether satellite, cable or interactive, deregulation and privatization.

You may wonder why you need to know about this. But how else will you be able to talk to the other players if you can't talk their language? You don't have to know much, just enough to bluff. Otherwise every conversation will have to be about the weather or about your ego, your work, your interests. The fact is, the other person is probably more interested in their work, their interests and their ego.

If you get a chance to meet an important producer or script editor, you should not waste the meeting. If all you can do is pitch your ideas, you will miss an invaluable opportunity to get information from them. You want insights and clues as to how to improve your chances of making a sale or getting a job. So you need to be able to talk about what concerns them. They are as anxious for success as you are. And you might be able to give it to them. So find out what they think will work next year, not this one. It is no good hoping that next year's flavour-of-the-month will coincide with what you have just spent six months writing.

If you are going to be serious about narrowing down the options for what you write, to give yourself a better chance of being successful, it also helps to know the salespeople, the people out in the field. I go to film and TV markets and to booksellers' conventions, to meet the sales executives. They don't buy themselves, but they tell me things the editors or producers don't, often things the 'buyers' seem unaware of. And at MIP (the international television market held in Cannes in April), the Cannes Film Festival or the Edinburgh International Film and Television Festivals there is a wealth of valuable information waiting for you, all for the price of a drink or a meal. If you worry too much about the cost of that meal, then you probably do not value your time properly. Cost your time as a business person; the real cost of writing one script over six months, or a novel over a year, is such that a trip to Cannes or Edinburgh is a small investment. As is the cost of a private script analysis.

This is not to say you must go to Cannes or Edinburgh to be a professional. But certainly not to read the trades is unprofessional. If you can't afford your own subscription, use your library or join the British Film Institute and use its library. This is a business that is always changing, so you need to know what is happening to take advantage of it. The really smart writers are those who see the shape of things in the near future and write material that creates the new benchmarks.

Really great writing, for example the British TV thriller *Edge of Darkness*, or the TV series *Prime Suspect* or *Cracker*, did create new benchmarks, a sudden realisation on the part of everyone else that there was an audience for excellence in that genre. And the usual substandard clones followed.

Getting Paid

Where do writers fit into the business financially? How much should writers get paid?

The old rule-of-thumb – still a good one – is that the proportion of the budget attributable to the script and underlying rights should be approximately 4 to 5% – half to the script, half to the book if there is one to be adapted. If there is no book, and no other underlying rights, it does not mean that the script gets the 5%; it would still be about 2.5%. If the book author is very famous, or the book is in the best-seller lists, then it might attract 3% and the scriptwriter, if not well known and with little track record, only 2%.

You should also be aware of what in Britain and the USA are known as 'Writers' Guild minimums', and you should be aware of scriptwriters' earnings versus novel writers' earnings. It may surprise you to know that in general there is more money to be made out of writing novels than there is from scripts. For a start, there are many more novels published per year than films or even drama episodes.

You can also sell a novel over and over again, as long as you don't sell world rights to any one publisher. If your publisher controls your world rights, your novel can still be sold in many different territories, but the income will be set against your advance from the previous publisher and you will only receive payments on an annual or six-monthly basis (depending on your contract).

You have to be fairly thick-skinned to survive in the business as a writer, perhaps more so than if you had followed any other career path except acting. Although producers and directors can't do without writers, they are ready to dump them when they think the time has come. Every writer who has had a movie made, has either had the experience, or certainly knows of it, whereby once the script has been sold, the producer, the production company or the director takes it over and it ceases to be the writer's film.

Collaborations and Rewrites

Lynda Myles, who produced *The Commitments* said, 'There's no point in becoming a screenwriter unless you understand collaboration. Because there's no such thing as a writer's film. Especially since any director worth his salt is going to impose his own vision on a screenplay.'[1]

William Boyd, who wrote the first script for Richard Attenborough's film *Chaplin*, said, 'If you make a film for a Hollywood studio then at some point the prospect of someone else rewriting your script will loom. It's like a knee-jerk reaction on behalf of studio heads: if in doubt, hire another writer. No one would dream of saying to a director, "you're brilliant at car chases but lousy at love scenes, so we'll get someone else in to do those". But in Hollywood they don't hesitate to send for a script doctor...'[2]

A script doctor is, in fact, usually another writer. Europe does not have many script analysts. These are script doctors who can analyse a script, identify what's wrong and suggest what should be done. I believe that, in many cases, the original writer should do the rewrite. But I also believe that very few producers or directors are really capable of briefing the writer in such a way that the writer can or will make the changes necessary to lift the script to a higher level.[3]

A re-writer will often throw out the good stuff just because they want to impose their own ideas. Instead of training everybody in the business to read scripts, the knee-jerk reaction which William Boyd refers to is really an admission of failure on the part of the person making the decision.

Of course, writers can't always write good scripts. And a writer who's come up with a script that doesn't work but is as good as he or she can get it does eventually need to be replaced. Writers must be prepared to accept the realities of the business, with all the problems of getting scripts produced. If they can't, then they should write for another medium.

If your passion is to write for the screen then try to improve the odds in your favour. Learn to manipulate people in the industry, just as much as you manipulate your characters. Accept that you are going to write scripts which you are paid for but which may never get made. You have to learn how to survive in what is known as 'development hell'.

If you have the talent as well as application you can earn substantial sums of money. You can also gain the satisfaction that comes from knowing that your work, often so personal and intimate, is appreciated. Ideally you want both, because appreciation alone doesn't pay the mortgage, or send the kids to a better school. So I am going to make the assumption that you actually want to be more businesslike, more professional and that you want to make money. If you don't, well...why are you reading this book?

1   James Park, *Sight & Sound*, Summer 1990.

2   James Park, *ibid*.

3   There are also organisations like TAPE (Television Audience Programme Evaluation) in London and Script House in Berlin, both of which cover film as well as television.

4　Writing Treatments that Work

The best way to sell something is to make it easy to buy. Speculatively written scripts, which involve little risk to the producer, might therefore seem attractive to a writer trying to break in. If you have written a 'spec script' and are not asking the producer or broadcaster to put high-risk money up front, it might make it easier for them to buy it. The truth is that 'spec scripts' are seldom sold and even more rarely produced. There are always more reasons to say 'no' to a spec script than 'yes', and many more unwritten scripts are commissioned than written scripts bought.

How can you increase the odds in your favour? How do you help them to buy your script? Can you help yourself to write it well? One answer to all these questions is to be able to write a good treatment. This helps not only because you can secure a script commission on the basis of a good treatment, but you will possibly write better scripts if you have worked the story out before you start writing.

Having a treatment is also the best way to know something about your project before you come to pitch it (more on this later). But you might find yourself pitching in order to get a commission to write a treatment. And delivering a successful treatment is then the only way to get the script commission.

These two skills – writing treatments and making verbal pitches – are closely related. They can occur in either order. Both can be crucial in getting you the script commission. Most writers don't seem to like writing treatments. It may be because they don't feel confident about writing them and because many believe that they are not good at writing them. It is also because of the ever-present danger of 'the treatment trap'. When writers get commissions to write scripts, but first have to write a treatment, they often fall at this first hurdle.

The Treatment Trap
Most producers who want a book adapted, or provide some sort of storyline for the writer, will want to see how the writer will treat the story. Hence the producer needs a treatment, and until satisfied with this stage of the development work, the producer will not usually be willing to invest any further money in the script. The producer may have chosen you because of previous scripts you have written. In other words, it is your scriptwriting talent that has won you the commission, not your treatment-writing ability. But unless you can write a good treatment you may not get the chance to write the script.

Part of the problem is the lack of adequate time and finance available for the writing of the treatment. Writers usually get paid 10% to 20% of the total script fee for the treatment. To do any justice to yourself and the treatment, this usually takes significantly longer than 20% of the total time you will spend on the whole job. It can take as much as 60% to 70% of the time.

Treatments need to be manipulative selling documents that every writer should be able to write. We have a couple of clients who are so good at treatments that they even get to write them for other people. Ironically, the 'other people' are mainly producers who are trying to raise money to commission scripts from other writers.

Sometimes you will even be writing a treatment in competition with other writers. Producers have no obligation to accord you exclusivity, as long as they are paying you. Whoever comes up with what the producer wants will get the job.

Fitting the Bill

There isn't just one way to write a treatment. So how can you be sure that what you write will be the approach that is acceptable to the producer you are dealing with? You must talk to the producer, at length if possible. Here is a checklist of some of the things that you should know or ask. It is not an exhaustive list, and is in no particular order:

1 What is the track record of the producer; what are his or her strengths and weaknesses?
2 Who is the director, or the likely director (if there is no clear answer, ask for a shortlist of the sorts of directors that the producer would like)?
3 What is the budget? (This is useful information to have before you start writing, although unless you know a little about budgets it will not mean much to you.)
4 Is any development or production funding committed to the project from sources other than the producer, and if so who is/are the investor(s) and what do they hope to get out of the film? If there are coproducers, what are their needs? (If they are from abroad they may have different expectations from our own.)
5 Does the producer have any casting ideas? This knowledge is useful but not essential, as casting is often not possible until later. But it can help give the characters 'voice' if you and the team have an idea who will play the roles.
6 Who does the producer see as the target audience for the film or TV programme and, if the latter, in what slot is it likely to be transmitted? (After 9pm you can usually use riper language and be more explicit. If you have no idea what time your programme is likely to be screened, how can you know your audience?)
7 What other films or programmes can the producer liken this one to? Shorthand may be used here, eg 'a cross between *Jagged Edge* and *Basic Instinct* but on a smaller scale'. This usually tells you more about the producer's expectations than about the film you are hoping to write, but it can be a valuable insight into the kind of treatment that will make the producer happy.
8 If the project is an adaptation, which parts of the book or which characters or relationships should you concentrate on or leave out? (If this elicits a blank look, and the answer is 'I am paying you to tell me', ask the producer what they particularly liked about the book, or why they think it will make a good movie.) If you really do not think it is filmable, I suggest that you learn the difficult but important skill of saying no. A lousy movie is not going to advance your career. If you really need the money, then try to make it a good movie, even though the odds may be stacked against you.
9 Finally, you might confirm who the central character is, even if it is obvious. It is essential to know from whose point of view the story will be seen. If you do not agree, then discuss this rather crucial question until you do agree. Don't be afraid to do this. Remember the mantra:

- whose story is it?
- what do they want?
- and how do they get it (or what nearly stops them from getting it)?

You can't go far wrong in approaching the writing of a treatment or a script if you have really clear answers to these three ubiquitous questions.

Sometimes the producer will provide you with a very clear idea of exactly what he or she wants. That's the good news; the bad news is that you then have less room to manoeuvre. In other words, if you don't deliver more or less exactly what was asked, you might be fired.

Being Professional

Getting the basics clear from the start will help both you and the producer. Sit down with the producer and have a long meeting (or lunch) to discuss these points. Then send the producer a letter confirming all the points that were agreed. As you should always take a notebook and pen and make notes during such a meeting, the letter is easy. You empower yourself by taking the initiative; you gain additional control and you become more attractive as a professional writer.

If you have a co-writer who wasn't there and/or an agent, send a copy of the letter to them. Put 'cc' on the bottom of the letter so that the producer knows that you have done this. That way, when things go wrong (as they often do), you have a record of what you agreed that you were paid to do. This can be very helpful in getting the money if the project falls apart.

Good producers do not only want treatments or scripts. They also want a writer who can think, who can articulate, who can take a problem that exists in the story and find a solution. So you are not just selling some sheets of paper. You are there to solve problems for the producer. This is not to say that the sheets of paper don't have to work for their living. At times there is no one to speak up for you except your words on paper. At script conferences or editorial meetings, the producer or editor who has been championing the story makes the pitch. Then it is everyone else's turn to comment on it.

'Oh no, not another serial murder story!', or 'The last film set in Egypt bombed, let's avoid the area altogether'. They have probably not even read your lovingly prepared treatment, yet they can make crass superficial judgements. That, I am afraid, is their prerogative.

But this is exactly why you need to be a real player, and you need to know more than just what you want to write and how to write it. Treatments, synopses or outlines can save you a great deal of time and work. Once people know how well you write, there is every chance that they will give serious consideration to a proposal from you.

If you believe that no synopsis can do justice to your idea, you may have to write the whole script before showing it. Find out what works best for you. Keep in mind the fact that if the original idea is yours and the producer has not bought it then you still own it. But this, like almost everything else regulating your rights and earnings, will be determined by the contract you are going to sign, which is why it is important not to sign any document in the flush of gratitude at being offered too little to write something. Be businesslike. Serious producers will respect you; they may not like you for being businesslike, but you have to decide whether you want to be liked, or whether you want to make money. Some writers manage to do both by being courteous, strong-minded and by delivering successful work.

Let's assume that you have been paid some of the money for the treatment but not all of it. The idea is your own, and the contract is a fairly standard one. Yet no further money is forthcoming even though it is due. The producer doesn't seem to like what you have delivered and is avoiding your calls.

To get your money, you can send registered letters and call constantly. But in the end, you may have to go to court. You are unlikely to be able to sell the idea or your treatment to someone else without repaying the producer, even though the producer has not paid you in full. If the treatment is based on a book or on someone else's idea, then you need to be even more careful. So you may do a lot of work, not get paid much for it, and have nothing at all to bargain with at the end.

What you have to worry about, if the producer rejects your treatment but clearly loves the idea, is that the producer will go off and find another writer to do the same sort of thing. If it is your idea, you may be protected by the law regarding breach of confidentiality, which we will look at later.

Given the amount of work that usually goes into well-written treatments, it is worthwhile being properly protected.

How to write a treatment or synopsis

A treatment for a film, or a synopsis for a novel, should perform a number of functions. The document is used to persuade a producer or a publisher to purchase rights in the work. A well-prepared presentation, which creates a sense of confidence in the reader and a belief that the writer is in control of their characters and storyline, is more likely to result in a sale.

A second, but equally important function, is to help the writer organise his or her own thoughts. With treatment in hand, the writer can discuss more clearly with the editor, agent or producer what he or she intends to write. It is always necessary, at some point, to talk about what you are writing, and if you can do so well, the chances are you will save yourself time and gain very useful feedback from professionals in the marketplace. For all these reasons, careful preparation of a proposal for a book or a script is important.

There is one additional reason for spending what may seem like a disproportionately long time preparing a treatment. You should not be concerned only with making a sale. You should also be concerned with making a good deal and a successful film or programme. Or your producer (who should now own the rights to the treatment) can use it to raise the finance as a prelude to making the film.

The level of the deal, whether for a script or a novel, will not only determine the probable level for your next deal but may also influence the amount of time, personnel and money that the producers or publishers will invest in your project.

If they pay a very substantial sum to buy the rights to what you are writing, they will need to work harder to justify it and to recoup the outlay. Purchasers will often spend additional money to make sure that they achieve this.

There is a danger of writers being the victims of a publisher's or producer's exaggerated expectations. Having spent a huge amount on the advance for your novel, or a Hollywood-sized fee for the rights to your script, if the publishers find the book doesn't sell or the producer can't raise the finance on the script you've written, you might begin to be perceived as a loser.

It's often easier for agents – rather than writers themselves – to manipulate the prices paid for treatments or scripts, because we tend to know what has been paid for similar work. If you are going into a negotiation without that kind of inside knowledge, you are at a disadvantage. I'll discuss later on how to get some of this knowledge. When you are writing a treatment you should bear in mind the all-important questions: why do people read, or watch television or go to the movies? If you know the answer, you are well on the way to being able to write a good treatment.

A treatment should demonstrate a number of things, namely:

1 That you know what you are writing about.
2 That you know who your characters are.
3 That you know what market you are writing for. This is particularly important if you are writing a genre book or script. Do you know the conventions of that genre as well as the fans do?
4 Finally, that you know how to present an analysis of a story you have not yet written to an editor or producer in such a way that he or she will believe in your ability to transform the project into a script or book. The people you are dealing with should also want to buy what you're writing, because they advance their careers by doing so and the companies they own or work for will make money out of your work.

A treatment needs to be carefully structured in order to achieve all this. I would suggest that it is broken down into four sections. There is a reason for this, and the order of the sections has its own logic as well. However, there are no absolute rules here. This method has worked well for many of our clients, but there are other ways of structuring treatments that also work well.

Section One: The Introduction

This should be a brief statement about the programme, film or book, written in the style of the jacket copy of a paperback. In other words, it should not attempt to tell the whole story, but picks on the most salient selling points. It may simply put the central character in the context of the genre. This is where you sell, not tell, the story.

While this short statement (anywhere between 5 and 20 lines) must grab the reader's attention, it is important to remember that there is a danger of overselling your work. The longer, descriptive synopsis or full treatment that the prospective purchaser will hopefully read later, must live up to the short 'hard sell' description. In other words, don't claim that what you are writing is the greatest love story since *Gone With the Wind* if there isn't very much about the love story.

A useful approach to writing this 'hard sell', is briefly to describe the premise, the central character and the key dramatic incident. This will hopefully pique the reader's curiosity, leaving them wanting to know what happens next. It is also possible to use a short extract of dialogue as a teaser. Look at existing book jackets or film posters for examples. Spend an hour in a big bookshop reading book jackets (especially in the best-seller section), or go to a multiplex cinema and read every poster carefully. Ask yourself why they are 'pitching' the film in the way that they are.

The choice of title is also very important. If you can't come up with a really good one, put in the best you've got and, if necessary, put the words 'working title' in brackets after it. The title should create an immediate desire on the part of the reader to know more about the story. Your existing knowledge of the story can be a hindrance to your coming up with a title that will work for someone who knows nothing about the story. If the title only has significance once you know the story, it is not the best title.

Section Two: Character Biographies

There should be short biographies of all of the major characters (between five and twenty lines each). It is essential to make clear who the main character is, and what motivates him or her. There is no excuse for ambiguity here. If you don't know or are not sure who the main character is, you have a fundamental problem. His or her ambitions and weaknesses, as well as their potential for change, can be mentioned.

If there are two or three main characters, make that clear. But also make clear through whose eyes we see the story. In an ensemble story, where there are several main characters (eg *American Graffiti, Peter's Friends, Four Weddings and a Funeral*), this does not apply so rigorously. But even in stories like this, one or two characters will usually stand out from the group.

Do not describe too many elements of the story in these short biographies. Give the reader psychological and personal insights into the characters, describe in an impressionistic way what they look like (for example, tall or short, not 'six foot one-and-a-half inches'). Describe one of their characteristic attitudes to life. Think of someone you know very well and then write ten lines about them. It's much the same.

For your own purposes, it may also be worth writing five or ten pages of a full biography of each of your main characters, to get them to come to life. But do not impose this on the reader of your treatment unless he or she either asks for more detail or buys your treatment, in which case it will be a pleasant surprise.

For minor characters, five to ten lines is usually enough. If there is a large cast of characters in a script, you don't have to describe every single one of them in your treatment. A Hollywood executive is reported to have said during a pitch meeting with a writer, 'Don't confuse me with details'. By not being too specific in your characters' biographies, you enable the reader's imagination to flow. Too much detail slows people down.

Use broad strokes in writing treatments. You are offering suggestions. If the reader of your treatment is given just enough detail, he or she will fill it in. The more their imagination can grasp the picture you are painting with words, the stronger that picture is likely to be, and the more likely they are to see the movie in their mind's eye.

Section Three: Statement of Intent

This section is rather idiosyncratic. If your book or script is based on a real event then say so, and describe your sources. If it is based on real experiences you have had, then describe why you want to write about them. In other words, why this project is special for you, and you for it.

If there is any personal, factual or other background, then provide this information. It will help the reader 'place' the story in relationship to the writer. It can create a frame for the picture you are about to paint.

Section Four: The Storyline

The reason for breaking the whole document up into four sections in the order suggested above, is that by the time the person reading the document gets to the storyline, he or she will have already absorbed a great deal of the relevant background material. The storyline is therefore likely to have greater impact on the reader than it would otherwise have had. If they read the storyline first, which some people do, the rest of the material you have submitted will still be impressive.

The storyline should be a narrative, flowing, relatively brief description of the story of your novel (usually called a 'synopsis') or of your script (usually called a 'treatment'). It is different from a 'step outline' (see Chapter 5). In reality, it is a proposal for the storyline. It is seldom possible to write this in sufficient detail to feel you are doing it justice. Don't worry. It is inevitable that when you actually write the manuscript or script you will make changes; this, too, is normal. Everyone in the business understands it. But if you make very extensive changes to it (known as 'moving the goalposts'), you should first check with whoever is paying you.

You should also show awareness of any gaps in the storyline. If you do not know how every step of the story will develop you can state in a covering note that there are choices still to be made. It is neither necessary nor possible to know every detail before you start writing.

It is particularly important for the synopsis to convey 'emotion' not just 'plot'. This is something that most writers fail to do. It can easily be done by making clear why the characters are forced to behave as they do, and what the impact of events on them – or their impact on events – will be. You can even assert that a particular scene or incident will be 'very emotional'. This is, after all, a document of intent.

It is also important to convey to the reader that you are willing to discuss changes and to do rewrites. There is no doubt that revisions and rewriting are as important as the writing of the first draft, yet few new writers recognize this or put enough effort into it.

Your synopsis (or treatment) should read like a summary of a book you have just read or film you have just watched. It will have a greater sense of immediacy if it is written in the present tense (for example 'The book or film starts when...'). There should be no biographical descriptions of characters or details from the background to the story because they have been given in the earlier part of the document. In other words, this section should actually mirror the pace of the novel or script.

The fact that the novel or script does not yet exist is irrelevant. Editors, agents, publishers and producers are professionals. They understand the problems of trying to state what it is you want to write before you've done it. Or at least they should!

An additional section: a few scenes

You can add a further section containing a few scenes to give a sense of your writing style, a voice to your characters, and strengthen the impact of your treatment. There are different views on whether your chosen scenes should be the opening ones, or perhaps something very dramatic from the climax. My preference is for the opening scenes. For a start, they should be exciting. You have no excuse for a boring opening. If you really want to include something from a later stage in the film or book, do so by all means. Identify the scenes clearly and never send in random unconnected scenes. Writers who pick a few pages at random from different sections of their work to show how versatile they are (which is not uncommon), achieve the opposite effect.

Length

A user-friendly treatment (or synopsis) is usually between ten and twenty pages long. It is difficult to do justice to a well worked-out story in less. Two to three pages is a pitch document, not a treatment. Forty to sixty pages is probably too long. Once you have a commission, or have made a deal, then it doesn't matter how long your working document is, but a forty- or sixty-page selling document – in prose – will take longer to read than a script, and few producers or publishers will be impressed by such verbosity.

Conclusion

Because your work will be going into a highly competitive marketplace, to short-change yourself on the treatment or synopsis can be costly. Word for word, page for page, it is as important as the finished work, even though it will never be seen by the public.

I normally assume that a really good treatment will have gone through many rewrites before it is ready to go out. The reason that I am willing to work on spec with clients to get this document into the best possible shape is because it can make a significant difference to the size of the deal. The buyers of treatments are in a business that involves speculating in buying rights in unwritten material. You are also in that business. Artistic sensibility needs to be tempered by a manipulation, if you are to write great treatments!

Laying out the document in these four or five parts will help the reader understand your intentions, feel confident about your ability to achieve those intentions and hopefully predispose them towards wanting to buy your work. Don't forget that writing is a highly manipulative process. Words are selected in order to create responses in readers, whether the reader is someone who has just purchased a copy of your book from a shop, or is a script editor who may be sufficiently impressed to want to commission a script from you. And creating that impression should be your primary intention.

5   The Step Outline

Confusion sometimes arises in distinguishing between treatments and step outlines. The previous chapter dealt with the treatment which is your description of how you propose to treat the various aspects of the story for a script. In this chapter we look at the step outline which addresses itself to the detailed *structure* of a film. It is important to understand the difference between these two documents. It is advisable to work through both treatment and step outline before you write the script or manuscript.

If one of the main purposes of a treatment is to enable the writer to pitch the story, a step outline enables the writer thoroughly to explore the story and see that it works. Producers therefore usually prefer narratively written treatments for the purpose of raising finance, rather than the more step-by-step approach of a step outline.

There is no single correct way to write a treatment or step outline. Here are some suggestions for you to think about. Whether you find your own method or use someone else's, make it effective. Remember to be manipulative: the purpose of these documents is to sell a story.

The Structure

I am going to describe a three-act structure, which generally applies to feature films but can also be applied to TV films/plays or series episodes. It does not usually apply to serial episodes which often end with a resolution or climax of one of the storylines plus an equally important cliffhanger which leads to the next episode.

The step outline should mirror the structure of your proposed film. The acts should be identified clearly. You can preface it with a couple of paragraphs on the world of the story – its location, atmosphere, the people who give the place its particular dynamic. Follow this with a paragraph on each of the principal characters – their age, appearance, but more importantly their ambitions, strengths, weaknesses and their potential for change.

What follows is a classic analysis of the structure of a step outline based on the approach used by Clare Downs and Pascal Lonhay, the script analysts at EAVE.[1] Most books on writing screenplays have more detailed analyses of screenplay structure, as do courses like Robert McKee's excellent story structure course.

The First Act

Start each act on a new page, telling the story in the tone, style and mood of the film, having first asked yourself the following four basic storytelling questions:
1   Whose story is it? What is there about the main character that makes him/her ripe for this experience?
2   How is his/her 'undisturbed routine of life' set up? (This helps an audience get to know the main character, how the character thinks and acts in the world before the event that triggers the main action of the film.)

3   What is the catalyst, the event that starts the story, that throws the main character out of balance? (This is also called the 'point of attack' or the 'inciting incident'.)
4   What is the main tension of the story which will be established by the end of the first act? (The main tension is often established at the point of no return, when the main character makes the decision to pursue what he or she wants.)

The First Act should be about 25 pages in length in a fully developed feature-film script. It may be no more than two pages in your step outline.

The Second Act

Having set up the essential information on characters, location and what the story is about in the First Act, the Second Act usually develops the story through the problems and obstacles faced by the main character. These problems generally build to a first and a second culmination within the Second Act. There are no hard and fast rules here. These are just rough guidelines and if you know what you are doing and why you are doing it, you can break the rules or guidelines, as long as it achieves a desired and desirable effect.

In a fully-developed 100-minute-long feature-screenplay, the Second Act is around 60-70 pages. It usually takes over an hour to develop the main tension to the second culmination at the end of this Act. Because it is such a long Act, you usually need two high points to propel the story forward – these are known as the culminations.

The first culmination should be around the middle of the Second Act. This is the first time that the tension between desire (springing from the main tension) and danger (the obstacles that are thrown up along the way) reaches a peak.

The second culmination is the point at which the forces which create the main tension are fully confronted and resolved. The subsequent twist gives a new tension to the final act. This is not a formula, it is just reasonably common.

Sub-plots are very useful, as they can help push the story towards either or both of the culminations.

The Third Act

The final act must have a final resolution, which you reach through a crisis and a climax. The crisis deals with which decision the main character must make to take the final action of the story to the point where he or she gets what they want – this is the climax.

The Third Act can be from ten to twenty-five pages in length in a fully-developed feature-screenplay. Ten pages is on the short side. Generally speaking, the Third Act is about the same length as the First Act (about two sequences of 10-12 minutes each). The Third Act should give meaning to the whole story. It is shorter in action films, longer in psychological, character-led films.

Scene Progression

As I mentioned above, the main function of a step outline is to break down the story, scene by scene, so that the writer and producer can analyse its structure, and juggle with the scenes to establish the most exciting way to tell the story.

Some writers put each scene on a separate card and pin all the cards to the wall so they can move the scenes around and see what effect that will have on the structure as a whole. Other writers draw flow charts and graphs for the characters.

You need to examine your choices carefully. For example, do you tell the story chronologically or not? Are the scenes visually interesting or very dependent on dialogue? Are you communicating with the ears of the audience as well as with their eyes?

All this helps to make sure that the structure works before you begin to write the first draft script. Four or five short sentences should adequately cover what each scene is about.

As you start to decide how to describe each scene, ask yourself these questions about each and every scene:

1   Whose scene is it? Does the scene belong to the appropriate person?
2   What does he or she want? Why can't they get it or how do they get it?
3   How does this scene move the story forward? Can I still tell the story without this scene? Why is it necessary?
4   Does the scene reveal something important about the character to the audience? If not, how can I make it do so? What could I introduce?
5   Is the chosen location the best possible one for making the scene as dramatic as possible? What are the alternatives?
6   Have I told the story in this scene visually (which is necessary) or aurally (which is usually less effective)?

And Bear in Mind...

A useful question to set up in the First Act is: what is the worst thing that could happen to the main character? If there is to be a happy ending, the second culmination at the end of the Second Act stresses that the main character is close to failing. The resolution shows how he or she succeeds. If there is to be a tragic ending, the second culmination stresses the hope that the main character may succeed after all. The resolution shows how the character fails.

Another way of thinking about the development of the structure of a story is: how do you want the audience to feel when they leave the cinema? Once that is known you can check to see if the shape of your Acts does lead naturally to the ending which will result in the audience having the reaction you intend.

As with a treatment, a full presentation of a step outline can be accompanied by a couple of scenes with dialogue, to show how the characters reveal themselves as well as to indicate the balance struck between the visual and the spoken.

Beware of your own familiarity with your characters and your story. If it is too internalized, you will tell the story in an ineffective shorthand. Remember, you can never expect your readers – whether film professionals or members of the public – to make great efforts to understand complex plots or confusing characters. A well worked-out step outline will make writing the script easier; it will also result in a better script.

Note

1   EAVE stands for the European Audiovisual Entrepreneurs, one of the EU MEDIA programmes. It consists of a series of pan-European producer-training workshops.

6   Markets for Your Work

European culture is so rich and diversified and there are so many languages and such complex regional variations that the development of a centralized, industrially-oriented, film industry in European countries, such as exists in America, is not possible. The size of the individual domestic markets in Europe is insufficient to sustain economically viable film industries.

The European film industries may also have been hampered by the existence of dominant and self-perpetuating cliques of elites. Because film finance in Europe is so difficult to come by, those who have greatest access to the money are those who tend to get their films financed. They are also dependent on the subsidy system which is so prevalent. Take the subsidies away and film-making in some European countries would almost grind to a halt.

Because of the inability of the industry in most European countries to build up any real momentum, with the exception of a few companies, the financing and making of each film is like having to reinvent the wheel. Many film-makers spend more time trying to raise finance than they do making films. So the film industries in Europe are not generally profitable and European films don't compete well with the better-developed and often higher-budget American films exported to the European markets.

A Conflict of Interests

Since the end of the Second World War, Europeans have had access to an endless stream of American films and TV programmes. We became comfortable with images and values of American life. As Europe regathered its strength in the 1950s and attempted to inject life back into its movie industries, the emphasis was on culture, not commerce. Meanwhile, European audiences were willingly seduced through watching the subtitled or dubbed programmes that were readily available from America.

The increasing quantity of imported programmes shown throughout Europe probably does have some effect on our national cultures, perhaps by diluting them. At the same time, there is little doubt that being exposed to other cultures can be enriching. There is also no doubt that an accessible and open media has a democratizing effect on any society.

A fragile peace exists between the EU and the USA over GATT and the exporting of American films into Europe. European politicians frequently seem to feel the need to be protectionist, however. This is understandable, but it is ultimately a futile and misguided attempt to prop up the European film industry, which gains no long-term benefit from this. Profit-oriented subsidies or private investment schemes would have a far greater long-term beneficial effect. So would a change in attitude towards stimulating better script development.

Instead of this, however, there is a fairly constant complaint that the Americans dump cheap programmes into our markets. While they certainly do this, European audiences are not protesting. So while we shouldn't necessarily let the inmates run the asylum, we should perhaps consider why the Americans make films that are so popular all over the world. It might help to ask why they can afford to sell their films and TV programmes so cheaply. They do have a large, linguistically unified, domestic market, so their budgets can be higher than ours. But that alone does not explain why more than half the revenue of their films is earned from their export markets.

The answer lies, simply and starkly, in the way they tell their stories. What should European writers do in this situation? What should the writer choose to write and how should he or she write it? I do not believe that we should get too involved in arguments about saving the national culture by blockading imported programmes and films. The question to answer is what should the writer or producer be aware of in planning to write and sell a script or raise money for a production?

In other words, what is the market you are aiming for? If you need to appeal to markets in addition to your domestic market, you need some understanding of those markets.

The American Market

In any comparison between American and European film- and programme-making, one thing is clear: a century ago, America was going through the process of absorbing in countless people of other nationalities. They became Americans over a period of time. Yet foreign languages, and other cultural manifestations, still remain today. There are Little Italies, Chinatowns, as well as Polish, German and many Hispanic neighbourhoods.

The fact that all those families from these countries chose to emigrate to America meant, to a greater or lesser extent, that they were willing to become American. However, to expect people living in any of the countries of the European Union, for example, to somehow subjugate their national or regional identity, is absurd. Making films which are less culturally specific will not increase their appeal across borders. Removal of economic barriers does little to remove cultural barriers and prejudices – in fact it can raise them. Cultural specificity is not as important as accessibility and universal themes in making films work in diverse markets.

Most films and programmes that are successful outside their country or region of origin are culturally specific. These include *The Last Picture Show, My Life as a Dog, My Beautiful Laundrette, Thelma and Louise, Annie Hall, Jean de Florette, Howards End, The Crying Game, Four Weddings and a Funeral, Trainspotting, The Blair Witch Project* and even *Kindergarten Cop*. In other words, it may be a mistake to look at the content in the hope of determining the likelihood of a film appealing to a widespread audience.

So what is it that makes some films more successful abroad, if it isn't the cultural content? I believe it is largely the way the story is told in the film. This does not only mean the structure of the film, although clearly structure is a large part of it.

The way a story is told includes such things as the way the characters are set up, the use and extent of dialogue and visual narrative and the extent to which the story offers a positive experience. Why did American movies evolve differently from those made in Europe, despite the fact that so many leading writers, directors and studio heads in Hollywood between the wars were European immigrants? It was precisely the multinational immigration into the country which had a marked effect on what films they made and how they chose to tell the stories in those films. Their audiences, whose English was not always fluent, also had a great sense of optimism, which they brought to their viewing of movies. For the new waves of American citizens, hope sprang eternal, while in Europe two world wars seemed to leave audiences in deep, pessimistic depression.

Yet it is clear from the worldwide sales of tickets to American films that in virtually all countries there are enough people who want positive messages from their visit to the cinema. These audiences have had good experiences watching American films and this makes them susceptible to the appeal of new ones.[1]

The constant comparison of Hollywood with film industries elsewhere in the world can be instructive if one is able to learn from the differences. Is there a difference between a European script or an American script? No. There are good scripts and bad scripts: this is not a useful distinction.

The cultural differences between most of the European countries and the stylistic differences between writers and directors in different countries is considerable. Europe is about diversity not homogeneity. Further, it is not enough for the subject matter to be European or the locations and cast to be European to overcome a bad story or a good story badly told. Producers sometimes seek stories that will appeal to audiences in more than one country. The danger in this is that they are likely to satisfy no audience.

European writers, producers, directors and critics complain constantly about the invasion of American movies and American television. The cinema owners and distributors don't worry about it too much because it's where they make most of their money. In English-speaking countries outside the USA, American films take in excess of 80% of the box office. And American television takes about 40% of Europe's TV screen time.

This is why Hollywood is like the Holy Grail for so many scriptwriters. They feel that if only they could come up with something which would appeal to Hollywood this would dramatically change their careers. The fact is that Hollywood is not really interested in what the Europeans are doing. There are exceptions, notably talented Europeans who've gone over there and have made it in Hollywood.

Don't think that just because you can write in English it's going to make it easier for you to write successfully for the United States. Our cultural and educational heritage mitigates against it. The way we use words, the way we cut scenes, the importance that dialogue has for us, put us at a disadvantage when it comes to competing with American writers for American money. Trying to imitate the style of American movies usually fails because the imitation is a pale one without the craft, discipline or conviction and because the script is usually underdeveloped.

A senior Australian producer was briefing a group of young Australian producers some years ago on their first outward-bound trade mission to Hollywood. They were excited at the thought of going to the heart of the international film industry. He brought them down to earth a little by pointing out that for Australian producers the American market represented only 2% of their box office. The figure will have gone up since then, but the point remains valid.

Despite films like *The Crying Game, Four Weddings and a Funeral* and *The Full Monty* the same is more or less true of British movies and even more so of Continental European movies which have to overcome American (and British) audience's unwillingness to watch dubbed or subtitled movies. You'll often hear that American movies take over 55% of the world's box office. That may be true. But for any single country in the rest of the world exporting films to America, that market represents a negligible amount of their overall box office.

You will be made to feel very welcome if you go to Hollywood to pitch scripts or stories. For a scriptwriter determined to make it in the USA, spending some time living in Los Angeles is invaluable. The development executives and producers appear really eager to hear new ideas. But Hollywood is governed by fear of failure, fear of missing out on something big, which is why it is such a conservative place. As the distinguished critic Pauline Kael said, it is the only place in the world where you can die of encouragement.

While European cinema is more idea-driven, America is star-driven. Where we are concerned with fostering creative expression on the part of writers and directors, they are concerned with fostering the satisfaction of the audience.

I would not encourage European writers to try to break into the American market unless they are prepared to go and live in the US for a while. In any case, I think they would be better focused by becoming really successful in their home market first. That is more likely to get them taken up by the Americans.

The lessons to learn

Films that are successful generally have certain things in common. There are some fascinating statistics which go a long way to explaining the differences between American movies and European movies:

- The average American movie contains approximately two-thirds of the dialogue of the average European movie.
- The average American movie requires some 600 subtitles; the average European movie requires around a thousand.
- The average American movie scene is approximately half the length of the average European scene.

American movies also usually play up emotion and sentiment; we criticize them for it. But think about why they do it: it's because all the evidence suggests that this is what the largest audiences go to the movies for. Why do you think that Hollywood will pay $4 million for a script and $1 million for a rewrite? It's because there's so much money to be made out of the movies. Rewriting is far more common and extensive in America than in Europe because investing in development has been shown to produce profits. That does not mean that the decision to rewrite is always a good one, nor is the decision to bring in another writer rather than persevering with the original writer. Regarding films as products that must 'pay their way' tends to impose commercial demands on the creative personnel.

When you are told that another writer is being brought in to write your script, it is seldom a pleasant experience. You might be able to lessen the chances of that happening to you if you have thought through the above statistics, and asked yourself the following questions:

- Have you been given enough opportunity to rewrite the script yourself? Did you negotiate that into your contract?
- Have you been given enough editorial feedback from the script editor or producer?
- Do you think that the producer doesn't really trust you?
- Is this because you haven't really got to know the producer well – in other words have you let yourself down by lack of networking?

These considerations are part of the normal business life of scriptwriters. They result in part from the high level of gambling that accompanies the decision-making process producers go through when making films.

Just because the American market is so large, you do not necessarily improve your odds by aiming for it. Over 600 films are made in a year in the European Union, as opposed to about 400 in America. Yet the American films take 80% of the EU box office, and the bulk of that goes on relatively few films, usually with high budgets.

The assumption that if only Europeans could make films with equally high budgets they would also have big hits is erroneous. Size of budget is one element, together with immediately recognizable stars and a great script (or even just a good script). A big budget European movie without the script will fail. But small budget European movies, with brilliant scripts, like *The Crying Game* or *Four Weddings and a Funeral* were a huge success. Hugh Grant was not a star before that film. It is worth repeating that the script was rewritten many times.

We should be filled with admiration for the American film industry. Not because their films are better than ours. Not because their stories are more interesting. And not because they reflect better cultural values, but because they are succeeding in a competitive market where we are failing. We can compete with them more effectively if we choose to, but only if we respect the audience that goes to the cinema.

Whatever the story you wish to tell, tell it in such a way that it will be accessible to the widest number of viewers. This means having to tell it visually. There is no alternative. Verbal or aural information is a much less efficient way to communicate. You have to appeal to those characteristics of audiences which we know to be dominant, namely their wish to have emotional experiences, their wish to feel rather than think when they go to the movies.

If you ask why so many movies fail or why so many bad movies are made, I'd put it down mainly to ego, the ego of writers, directors, even bank managers. Nor would I omit the egos of agents either.

Far too many people in the industry behave as if making a film is an end in itself. I can understand why a writer feels good to have sold something. But if, under a little pressure, the writer admits that the script isn't a very good one, should the writer be feeling so good about having made the sale? Is it really going to benefit his or her career in the long term?

I am not against art-house movies. I think there is a very important and valuable role for cultural films as there is for theatre and opera. We all know that without subsidies opera houses would close. And in a Europe without subsidies the film industry would disappear in its present form. However, it might also re-emerge leaner but healthier.

If you removed the subsidies, it would change the way films are made. We would have to compete more seriously with the Americans. Some people would see this as lowering our cultural standards (the lowest-common-denominator effect). Since much of what is written, funded by subsidy money, is not geared to any particular audience or market and since most subsidy systems appear to be relatively 'uncritical', we have two extremes. The sensible answer is to aim somewhere between the two. By encouraging more editorial and development work on scripts, our cultural integrity would not be jeopardized and our films would compete better. The result might be to greatly strengthen and promote our cultures.

In other words, subsidies in Europe are not the all-important cultural lifeguards many politicians and film-makers seem to think they are. To some extent they have the opposite effect. Less energy spent chasing subsidy money, and more on storytelling might be a way to improve matters. It will be interesting to see how effective the new Berlin-Brandenburg Film Fund, which started in 1994 under Professor Klaus Keil, will finally be. He has stated categorically that funding will only be available to films that can demonstrate they are commercially viable and have an audience in view. I believe other film funds will have to follow suit.

To further understand this point, comparison of the rewriting approach used in, for example, American sitcoms with the more 'auteur' approach in European sitcoms, is instructive.

A different approach

Caryn Mandabach, the Executive Producer of shows such as *The Cosby Show*, *Roseanne*, *Third Rock from the Sun* and *Grace Under Fire*, described the process in the following way.[2]

After the first draft script is delivered (which won't be the first draft as the team of highly-paid writers will have worked on the storyline and the actual script for some time), the producer gives editorial notes.

Only then, when the producer thinks the script is in reasonable shape, does it go to the cast for the *read-through*. The next day, after hearing the read-through, the writers start another rewrite. This rewrite will change approximately 50% of the first draft script! The writers expect this. They know that if the standard of the show is to be maintained, they need the criticism to help them dump the 50% that has not reached a high enough standard. They can learn from listening to the read-through

After the rewrite is delivered, it goes back to the cast for the first rehearsal. Producers and writers watch carefully while the the actors rehearse holding copies of the script. It becomes clear that some scenes still have room for improvement and need rewriting: 25-30% of the script will change after this rehearsal.

At the second rehearsal the network executive may come to watch – a new set of eyes helps. They may even recast someone at this point. In general, a further 10% will be rewritten after additional criticism, leaving only the final polish. A gag writer might also be brought in on some episodes to 'punch up' the dialogue.

It is difficult not to generalize when comparing what the Americans spend on development with what is spent in Europe. But the implications of the difference is clear, irrespective of the exact figures. The global percentage spent on all aspects of development in the film and television industries of America is probably somewhere between 7% and 10% of the total audiovisual budget. In Britain this figure is generally thought to be 2%, and on the Continent closer to 1%.

It all comes back to the way you tell the story. If there is any lesson to be learned from America, that's it.

Europe as a Market

What else can we in Europe learn from the audiovisual dominance of America? And how should Europe as a market be perceived?

It has been argued that in Britain and I think, by association, Europe as a whole, we seem to have a creative environment that is not conducive to producing consistently successful cinema scripts.[3]

Can one sustain the argument that the European film industry has failed because there are very few scripts around with sufficient vision and craft to become truly successful international movies? I think the answer is yes. Writers need training both on and off the job. Investment in the training of writers in Europe is minimal. There are few professional or industry-oriented three-year courses. Three years is considered the minimum for most university degree courses; there is little evidence to suggest that less than three years can provide adequate training to attain a professional level in scriptwriting. Europeans tend to regard writing with a respect bordering on awe; instead we should be toughening up our writers for the competitive world outside.

It is not primarily the writers who are at fault, it's the industry and the people who are running it. It's producers and directors, script editors and agents. They are the ones who should be providing the feedback and they must take a great deal of the responsibility for the state of the industry's scripts.

This is a bleak outlook for writers because the European industry shows little sustained signs of industrial lift-off, not only because of the success of American 'cinema imperialism', but because the players in our industry, including writers, do not seem able to escape their own cultural elitism. It comes down to the fact that we rarely make films that are both culturally specific and easily accessible.

This is why the American industry has such a highly developed craft of storytelling. It has to make sure it connects with its audience because that audience is so mixed and so broad. If Europe invested half as much as the Americans do in development and in scripts, Europe might create an industry worth investing in. And writers who passively complain about the status quo without joining the writers' associations, and lobbying for better conditions, are just as culpable as the people who attempt to exploit them. By encouraging criticism throughout the relationships that writers have with agents, script editors, producers and directors, the team will benefit from a better result.

For scriptwriters in Europe, fluency in a second language can open doors to commissions. In general, fresh commissions are always easier to obtain than sales of 'spec' scripts that a writer has already written. This is partly producers' ego and partly the fact that in a particular country good producers know what their sources of television, film and banking finance will invest in. It makes sense therefore for them to look for the talent to write the scripts they need, rather than hope to find an 'off the peg' script that will fit.

Countries like Germany, which have a relatively large domestic television market, and where there is intense competition between the networks, are using established writers from the UK and USA to write to order in English. The scripts are then translated into German. As everywhere else, German audiences prefer watching German actors and actresses playing German characters and speaking in German. (The audience seldom knows or cares who the scriptwriter is, or what their nationality is.)

The emphasis on domestic stories and lack of fluency in English makes these countries relatively difficult to access. Southern Europe is even harder to get into. Scandinavian countries are fluent in English, but they have a significant number of talented local writers and their small market-size makes them harder to access for non-Scandinavian writers.

If you do want to find work outside your own country, you can try sending calling-card scripts with detailed CVs and, for countries like France, Portugal, Spain, Italy and Greece, if you can speak and read the language, some information about your linguistic abilities. This is useful rather than vital, but if you are fluent, write the covering letter in the language of the recipient. Names and addresses of production companies are readily available from specialized publications like *European Filmfile*[4] or from the MEDIA Desk of the European Union in your country (only available in EU countries). It also helps to familiarize yourself with what is on their screens. It is worth getting a satellite dish or cable with the full range of European channels if you are serious about breaking into these markets.

All the main trade papers – *Variety, Screen International, C 21, Broadcast, TV World, TBI, Moving Pictures* – have copious amounts of information about what people all over the world are watching. Read them. It is worth repeating that there is little excuse for being unprepared whatever market in the world you choose. The information superhighway will no doubt make it even easier to obtain market information, and Internet and e-mail already have networks of particular interest to writers.

Finally, there are a number of key international trade fairs – MIP, the Cannes Film Festival, MIPCOM, MILIA and the AFM amongst them – which are worth attending. They are extensively written up in the trade press.

The UK Market

Television in Britain is an effective training ground and is a relatively good market for writers. Soaps, series and serials are where writers usually get their first commission. There are also a growing number of scriptwriting courses available in higher educational institutions.

It is relatively easy to identify programmes which use new writers. Firstly, publications ranging from the trade papers to magazines like *Writers News* and the *Writers' & Artists' Yearbook* provide valuable information, the latter including a brief guide to writing for television.

Secondly, writers' groups, such as the Screenwriters' Workshop and dozens of regional groups have seminars, lectures and meetings at which new opportunities are discussed.

In general, the script editors on long-running series and serials will also provide information, including copies of 'bibles'. They sometimes select groups of prospective writers for induction days at which the writers meet producers, directors and cast, and visit the sets. If you are taken to work on *The Bill* you are encouraged to spend time with the police, even driving around in the back of police cars!

The single play, which was the training ground for new TV writers in the 1950s and 1960s, has been replaced by *Film on 4* and series of BBC-TV films. There are therefore still opportunities for new writers to see an original script filmed, but the competition is so great that the chances of breaking in with a film script are very small. It is advisable, therefore, for new writers to polish their craft on series and serial episodes, where the opportunities are greater and the support system for writers is well-established.

The story for the feature film industry in the UK is not quite so happy. There are over a thousand independent production companies (not all trying to produce theatrical films). But with little government finance and an unprofitable industry track-record, investment from private sources is poor. So getting your first feature script sold, never mind made, is difficult.

The increase in cinema audiences in the UK over the last few years has been as much in attendance at American movies as at our own. For British writers, TV movies are therefore more of an opportunity than cinema films, but you still need to draw attention to yourself. Short films are another way in.

The main British producers' association, the Producers' Alliance for Cinema and Television (PACT),[5] produces a membership guide which is a useful way of finding out what kinds of films and programmes its members have made and are making. A copy of the guide is available from PACT. It also gives the names of the key people in each company so you can write to them by name.

The broadcasters each have departments dealing with drama, children's programmes, factual programmes, as well as light entertainment (usually responsible for situation comedy) and so on. Some names can be obtained from Macmillan's *The Writer's Handbook*, or in more detail from a publication called *Contacts*.[6] Because of the relatively high turnover, as staff change jobs, it is best to check before writing to someone you don't know. It is always preferable to address letters to individuals, with their correct position, rather than to 'Dear Sir/Madam'.

Conclusion

It is better to concentrate your main effort, however, on your local producers, be they broadcasters, independent producers, in feature film or in television. If you do not have an agent, much might depend on who you know and how well you know them. That's why networking is important.

Research the markets. The information is readily available from:
- the trade papers
- books
- publicity material from broadcasters

- writers' associations and their newsletters
- writers' groups

By the time you know what you want to write, and have prepared your treatment and some script, you should also know where the market is. It is chicken and egg. You (or your agent) need to identify an individual to whom to send it, so you should also prepare your pitch and negotiating strategy.

Notes

1   Martin Dale, *Europa, Europa*, is illuminating on the American cinema industry. A recent publication by the EU, in a document hopefully entitled 'Audiovisual Policy: Stimulating Dynamic Growth in the European Programme Industry' (MEDIA II 1996-2000) points to the decline in the competitiveness of the European audiovisual industry compared with that in America: 'In the space of ten years, European films have lost two-thirds of cinema audiences in Europe, with their market share falling to less than 20%. European films have been the worst hit by the drop in cinema attendance, which has been particularly drastic in Europe (from 1.2 billion spectators to 550 million in fifteen years).

'The number of hours of television broadcast by European stations has more than doubled since 1988 (from 500,000 hours to the current 1,000,000 hours) without any corresponding increase in the production of European works. All this means that the Community's audiovisual trade deficit, which with the United States is already some $3.6 billion, continues to grow larger.'

2   At a PILOTS workshop for the development of long-running series. PILOTS stands for Programme for the International Launch of Television Series. See 'Friedmann' in Bibliography.

3   James Park, ibid.

4   Published by European Film Production Guide Ltd, 30-31 Great Sutton Street, London EC1V ODX, tel 0207 454 1185 fax 0207 490 1686.

5   PACT, 45 Mortimer St, London W1N 7TD, tel 0207 331 6000

6   Available from an organization called SPOTLIGHT at 7 Leicester Place, London WC2H 7BP, tel 0207 437 7631, fax 0207 437 5881.

7 Life's a Pitch

There are times when it is more important to sell the story than to tell the story. Pitching is one of those times. Pitching is the selling of a story or idea for film or television by describing it verbally. We have all done it with varying degrees of success, but not everyone realises that there is more to it than just a few well-chosen words.

Pitching is when writers, script editors or producers have to get up on stage and perform. Because we do not work in a 'pitching culture' in Europe – this applies both to those pitching and to those receiving the pitches – there is not enough preparation for this performance and too little importance is placed on it. Whether you enjoy pitching or not, your career as a writer will benefit from being able to do it well.

Pitching is important for the simple reason that good projects are too often rejected because the 'buyer' loses confidence not in the story but in the person pitching. The result? A rejection.

There are specific preparations that you can make to improve your verbal pitching. Writers and producers rarely put as much effort into preparing themselves as they do into preparing the descriptions of their projects. But you are part of the pitch, and you can easily let yourself down.

Once you understand why so many people pitch badly at really important meetings, you can do something to prevent yourself from doing so. Most of us have had the experience of coming out of an interview or meeting knowing the answer to a question that we couldn't answer in the room. This can be prevented.

You can find out how to tell when to stop talking, or when to change direction. You can learn why it is more important to sell the story, and how to stop yourself being inexorably drawn into telling it. You can also learn how to control the direction of a meeting to get what you want to out of it.

Why is all this so important? Because the film and television industries thrive on 'confidence'. If someone has confidence in you, you are half-way there. Much of what is said in the industry is simply not true. For example, the sentence 'I have a deal' often means no more than 'I have had an optimistic conversation'! Industry insiders are inured to this; there is a lot of scepticism to overcome with your verbal pitching.

Many commissions result from one-to-one meetings with producers and commissioning editors. Having read your calling-card script or seen something you wrote on television, you are invited to meet them or your agent sets up the meeting. The conventional wisdom is that you should be able to make your initial pitch in less than one minute. This is not all you will say about the project (unless the listener hates it!). If someone likes your short pitch you will undoubtedly be asked for more information. Personally, I prefer to offer them a written document next, although sometimes you are asked to talk about it.

The Succinct Pitch

What is the best way of getting the succinct pitch to work? Everyone has a different approach. What seems to work reliably is to distil the essentials of the project down to the minimum. For example:

1   What it is about. You do not need to tell the story, just indicate what sort of story or programme it is.
2   Why it will appeal to audiences and to which audiences will it appeal.
3   If you are the producer, where you hope the finance will come from.

Pitching therefore involves 'packaging'. It is something writers and producers and film-makers do without necessarily calling it that. But to be able to do this successfully you need to know your way around the players in the industry.

The package

The term 'packaging' reaches its ultimate expression in the methods used by the biggest Hollywood agencies to bring together their own clients (producer, writer, director and stars) in a 'package' which they take to a studio to wholly finance. The package is so bankable that the studio cannot (or does not) refuse, whatever the budget. Or it may be that the studio is so anxious to get one of the elements in the package that they take them all. This is the ultimate deal-led approach to financing; it has some advantages but many disadvantages.

An obvious disadvantage is that the script is not always given the priority it ought to receive, since packages tend to be vehicles for stars rather than writers. The result is that many films with star-studded casts either flop or are dreadful but still popular. In both cases, more attention to the script would have benefitted everyone.

For a writer, particularly at the beginning of a career, the package may consist of only a calling-card script, a CV and a covering letter explaining why you have written this particular script. Packages like this shouldn't be sent in cold, according to some agents. Agents, producers and script-editors are always looking for new talent, but a large parcel landing with a thump, unannounced, on a desk, is not the best start. First find out if they are willing or interested in reading your material. In effect, make them ask for it. Psychologically, it can make a difference.

Once you have assembled your package, you need to be able to sell it and yourself. This will, at some point, involve verbal pitching. An essential part of your preparation is to have written out several pitches of different lengths for your project. The idea is not that you will recite one of these in a wooden tone, but that you will have the confidence to do justice to the project in under a minute or, if requested, at greater length. The point is that you must start with a punchy, succinct, easy-to-remember description. The benefit of this is twofold. The person listening to you will know that they can easily pitch it to someone else (which means it will be easier to sell to the public) and their interest will grow so that they start asking for more information.

Three words are better than four

It is often thought that the shorter and more memorable the initial pitch line the better.

Don't worry if you find it difficult to come up with something as good as 'We are not alone' (*Close Encounters of the Third Kind*), 'In space no one can hear you scream' (*Alien*), or 'Jaws in Space' (also *Alien*). These are usually poster slogans, not initial pitches. A story concept or short pitch usually encapsulates the central character and the key action of the film: 'This is a story about a man who did something...' You should be able to reduce almost every proposal to that formula: 'This is a film/play/novel about X who Y.'

A log-line is different from a story concept or full pitch. It is usually very brief, and is designed to catch the eye. Log-lines are what gets viewers to watch TV shows every evening. They are specifically written to appear in the daily or weekly TV guides or evening papers, or on the posters of films.

Famous feature film log-lines include 'There are two sides to this love story' (*Kramer vs Kramer*), the notorious 'Love means never having to say you are sorry' (*Love Story*) and 'You don't have to assign him to murder cases – you just turn him loose' (*Dirty Harry*).

Apart from making it easier for the tired executive to remember your pitch, you need to impress with your passion for the story. If you don't care about it, it is unlikely that anyone else will. Passion is important, which is why if you go in with five or ten ideas it begins to look as though you are promiscuous or fickle and not interested in a serious, long-term relationship.

Remember that a major Hollywood studio could receive up to 50,000 pitches or proposals a year, yet they can only make ten to twelve movies. This is why writers have a relatively low status. In Europe the ratio may not be as extreme, but there are clearly an enormous number of ideas floating around the desks of the industry over here. Our agency alone receives over 120 applications per week from writers who want to join the agency (this does not include material submitted by our 160 clients) and the bigger agencies must receive more than that.

So competition for pitches to be heard is tough and pitching is one activity that can always be improved, whereas if you have no writing talent there is not much you can do about it. So if you are able to pitch well it will help get you onto the first rung of a very long ladder. Again, flexibility – being prepared to pitch to any length, whether fifteen seconds, one minute or an hour – is desirable. And be prepared to do it without notice, you never know when you may get introduced to someone who could say 'Yes'. I once heard an impromptu pitch by a man standing at the men's urinal in the Majestic Hotel during the Cannes Film Festival. I stood washing my hands, filled with admiration for the producer. It may not have led to a deal, but he had initiative.

Basic Pitching Guidelines

At the end of this chapter I will list a number of specific points which can usefully improve the way you pitch, but here I would like to mention a few general guidelines:
1 Keep it short. You can always expand at the invitation of those you are meeting, but brevity will prevent you from being boring, which is the most common quality of pitches.
2 You need to let them see the story or film in a few deft strokes.
3 Have a back-up, in case what you are pitching isn't suitable.

If you remember these points (and the fact that a pitch is not a story, so you should not go into detail), you will avoid the biggest pitfalls. If you can pitch to someone who can actually say 'Yes' to you directly so much the better, but it is not always possible to do this, because most people who can say 'Yes' sensibly hide behind 'gatekeepers' whose primary function is to say 'No'. However, the bottom line is that a good pitch may get you a deal, but it won't necessarily get you your film made. If you are very adept at coming up with 'high concepts' (ideas for films that can be easily grasped), good at articulating them and persuading people that they're worth doing, but you are not a good enough writer, then perhaps you should be a producer. There is not much point in pitching yourself as a writer if you can't write. Further, you must always have good material ready to follow up your pitch meeting.

There are some differences between feature films and television when it comes to pitching, but what's important is to remember that in general stories are about characters with whom audiences can identify. This is not simply because audiences want to experience the lives of those characters but because the audiences want to gain insights into themselves. You must be able to get an audience to invest its own emotions in a character, so that the audience experiences (rather than only observes) what the character is going through. It is this vicarious form of experience that is the key to success. For documentaries, the audience's motivation for watching is obviously somewhat different. However, the essential question can still be asked: why would someone want to watch this film or this programme?

Whether it is a feature or an episode of a soap opera that you are pitching, you need to enable the listener to relate strongly to your characters. You also need to remember that for the purposes of packaging and pitching you are the centre of attention. Your opportunity to pitch may be over a drink or in a script-lined office, but it's up to you to go out on that stage and be the star of the show. The stage is crowded with others out to impress the same limited sources of finance. Being able to present yourself and your project well is nearly as important as having a good script. Many of the worst films you've ever seen were financed because they had a brilliant pitch and were an attractive-looking package.

Do not underestimate the importance of the way in which you pitch. Learn about body language, learn to negotiate, read books about techniques of selling and closing deals. The fact that these books may not have anything directly to do with film or television is not important. They have everything to do with your skill as a player in the business.

There are a number of basic points against which you can test your pitching preparations. These are:
1 Yourself
2 The buyers
3 Non-verbal communication
4 Handling meetings
5 The pitch

These checklists will cover most of the points you should be aware of before you go into a pitch meeting.

Checklist 1: Know Yourself

1 What is your perception of how you pitch? Do you speak fluently and with conviction? Think about it for a moment. Find out how you sound – use a mirror, friends, a videocamera or tape recorder.
2 Much more effort usually goes into the preparation of projects than into the preparation of the pitch. So prepare yourself. What reaction do you normally bring out in others? What is your perception of your strengths and weaknesses, particularly as a negotiator or team member?
3 Learn negotiating techniques because the art of pitching certainly involves negotiating. It involves your reacting to the reactions of those you are meeting. These techniques are well articulated in dozens of books.
4 Learn to relax. Breathing exercises, a good night's sleep before you go in and a healthy dose of fatalism will all help your performance on the day.

When people are very nervous, oxygen is redirected to the muscles so they can see and hear better but don't necessarily think or speak more clearly. The brain 'appears' to decide, in a 'fight or flight' situation, that you don't need continuous logical thought as much as the ability to run or hit! In order to counteract this, make sure you breathe deeply and properly to get more oxygen to the brain. When you have come out of a meeting knowing you've pitched or dealt with the questions really badly, although you had all the information to deal with them well, a possible cause might have been lack of oxygen to the brain.

Checklist 2: Know the Buyers

5 Know who you are meeting, their names, positions, track records. Offer a business card to each person you are pitching to, so that you get theirs.
6 Know what they've done: how well it performed, what their specific role in it was.
7 Know what they want.
8 Know what they can pay and have paid in the past.

Checklist 3: Non-Verbal Communication

9 Shaking hands is important, but don't do it too hard, especially if you are male and the other person is female. And don't seem limp or timid.
10 You give out and perceive signals from a very early age. Body language is something you ought to know something about if you want to succeed. There are no books about body language in film and television pitch meetings, but there are many about body language in general, so read at least one.
11 Try to have direct eye-contact and make open gestures. For instance, sit with your arms open rather than folded tightly across your chest.

12 Leaning towards someone, not away from them, is more likely to make them feel you are engaging with them.
13 Mirroring their behaviour and body language can also be subliminally flattering. It's not usually done consciously, but it's interesting to observe. Watch couples trying to pick each other up at parties to really see mirroring in practice!
14 Making notes about what they're saying will give them a sense of being important and of being taken seriously.

Checklist 4: Handling Meetings

15 Establish rapport at the very beginning of the meeting by asking the person(s) you are meeting questions about themselves, their company, their films or programmes, their country. It's perfectly OK to spend at least the first five minutes doing this – in other words, get them to pitch themselves to you. It breaks the ice and gives you great leads and cues.
16 If you don't both have the same mother tongue, make sure you speak slowly and clearly. Speaking slowly tends to lower the voice and this increases the apparent authoritativeness of the speaker.
17 Encourage criticism and frankness. Start by emphasising that you really want them to tell you what they think.
18 Do you know how to control the direction of a meeting? It's done using intelligence, perception and the ability to think fast on your feet. If you are bad at it, get someone else who can do it to accompany you.
19 Do you know how to be a good listener?
20 Do you know how to be a perceptive watcher? Can you observe while you are talking and listening? In other words, can you stand back a bit while in full flow?
21 If they ask difficult questions, keep your integrity by saying you'll get back to them later with an answer, rather than 'improvising' and possibly being caught out.
22 Don't react negatively to criticism. Say, 'That's interesting and I'll certainly think about it', even if you think it's not interesting or just plain stupid. Be cool.
22 Finally, remember that you are not a one-story writer or producer.

Checklist 5: The Pitch

23 Passion and clarity are the two most important qualities in your pitch. This is particularly true in a longer pitch, where it is more difficult to maintain passion and clarity.
24 Know in advance how much you want to say.
25 Learn to be aware if you are running over time. Know when to stop (do this by watching and listening to them).
26 Don't over-sell.
27 'High concept' means something easily grasped. Can you find a way of putting your project into those terms?
28 The pitch should sell the story whereas the treatment should tell the story. Don't confuse the two. Never get into the boring 'and then...and then...and then' storytelling rut. It's deadly to listen to.

29 Remember the three 'rules' about pitching:
- a) what is it about? This breaks down into three sections:
  - i who is the main character?
  - ii what does the main character want? (and what's stopping him or her from getting it?)
  - iii how does he or she get it?
- b) why and to whom will the story appeal?
- c) where do you think the finance will come from?

30 A lousy story and a bad pitch can sometimes still get you a result if the people you are dealing with think you are someone they can work with.

A Last Word

I think it was William Goldman who once described Hollywood as being 'about your next project'. Never lose sight of the rest of your career. So don't put too much emphasis on this one project. Do not look or sound desperate – i.e. don't plead. Always try to open doors for yourself. You are part of the pitch. It's what most writers and most producers forget as they invest all their available time in working on the story.

In the end, the pitch and the treatment will be in the past. Remember, the story is not as important as the way you tell it. A mediocre story in the hands of a great writer will be more successful than a great story in the hands of a mediocre writer. Everything will ultimately depend upon the script.

8 Criticism and Rewriting

You have pitched an idea or a treatment, even a finished script. You will receive feedback. Some of it will be insightful; some of it will be negative. Distinguishing between useful and constructive criticism on the one hand and useless destructive criticism on the other hand is vital. If you believe in the truism among experienced writers: 'Scriptwriting is rewriting' you will be more receptive to criticism in general. If you actively encourage criticism of your work, you will get it. Nearly everyone likes to stand in judgement. Hopefully, it will be constructive. If it is not, the fact that you were able to ask for it will probably mean that you are capable of politely ignoring unhelpful and negative criticism. Use those notes and comments that are helpful, and in the process you will find that it is possible to maintain productive working relationships, even when there are disagreements.

Handling meetings and handling written editorial notes involves the ability to finesse other people. As long as your rewritten new draft is better than the previous one, you have succeeded. Unfortunately, however, rewrites are not always improvements. So how can a writer get the best notes, the most instructive feedback, in order to produce the best rewrite?

For a start it is important to recognize that lack of criticism does not mean that the script does not deserve criticism, or that it cannot be made any better. Even if you are told by a script editor or producer that you have written a great script, and fulsome congratulations are all you hear, tell them – however daunting this may seem – that you know it can be better and that you want it to be better. If necessary, find other 'readers' to give you feedback. Ask for a professional and independent script editor or analyst if your production company isn't giving you enough feedback. Then listen to what they have to say, and think about why they are saying it.

Let's assume that you receive some criticism or suggestions. Firstly, are you sure you clearly understand what has been said? Misunderstandings are so commonplace that it is worth checking. If necessary, rephrase the criticism in your own words: 'Do you mean that...?'

Secondly, the reader might not really know how to phrase the objections, although there is something that he or she is unhappy about. A reader's inability to articulate does not mean that you should ignore what is being inadequately conveyed.

Thirdly, sometimes people criticise scripts or manuscripts because they feel that they need to impose a little of themselves on the work, either just to show that they have read it, or because their ego requires them to assert their position in the hierarchy. Writers should never be surprised by the effects of ego.

After you leave the meeting at which the rewrite was discussed, and before you start the rewrite, send a fax or email to the key person at the meeting, just confirming what it was agreed you would do. Always copy a note like that to your agent if you have one. Producers or script editors should also send follow-up letters of confirmation to a writer after a meeting, describing in a brief summary what was agreed. The two versions will sometimes differ, which proves the value of the confirming note in ironing out misunderstandings before rewriting begins. And because rewriting is usually to a relatively tight schedule, time wasted can be serious.

Even if you only write up your 'meeting notes' for your own sake, they will be a useful *aide mémoire*. I often wonder about people who sit in meetings for hours without taking any notes at all. Perhaps they all have photographic memories?

During the meeting and in the follow-up letter, the writer should react calmly to the notes, suggestions or criticisms and offer to consider them carefully. If the writer thinks that the suggestions will not work when the rewrite is sent back, a covering letter should explain why the writer chose not to follow particular points. It is advisable to acknowledge that as the reader/producer felt there was something that did not work in the treatment or script, the writer has come up with a solution (although it might be a different one from that suggested).

In other words, in the relationship between writer and critic, give reasons, and you may well persuade them of your point of view. Or if they really believe they do have a point, they may elaborate on it in an attempt to persuade you.

There is another tactic which can be useful if you want to change your mind (and not lose too much face). Tell whoever sent you the notes that what they were saying wasn't clear to you. However, you might have to bear some of the responsibility for not listening properly, if you did not make it apparent the first time round that you did not understand the point that they were making.

It is better to show yourself as flexible rather than rigid. People in the industry prefer working with writers who know their own minds, but who are not afraid to admit that they were wrong. Pretending criticism doesn't exist will only bring it back to haunt you later. Listening is an activity. You would not like to think that the audience for your film was not listening to your dialogue, so you should make an effort to get behind the comments that are being made about what you have written.

It is natural to want to hear praise for your work. All writers want recognition in some form, financial or otherwise. Very experienced writers can need criticism as much as novices. However, the better-recognised or established writers become, the less comprehensive is the criticism they tend to receive. This is not, alas, because they are necessarily better writers now than they once were.

It is a problem of sycophancy. It is difficult for others to be as critical to writers who have become very successful, precisely because both they and their audience change. They were probably once open to criticism, and may still think that they are. But there are sometimes subtle changes in the dynamics of relationships with writers who have become very successful. They begin to announce their intentions differently, they narrow down the scope for criticism, sometimes unwittingly, and they can become resistant even to good ideas if they develop too strong a sense of omniscience.

If the producer or publisher paid hugely for the writer because of his or her track record, it's difficult for a script editor or agent to seem to criticise the writer's abilities. So agents or editors can also be responsible for inflating the egos of the writers they work with.

If you are closed to criticism, you may never know what brilliant insight someone might have offered you. Think about it from the point of view of another writer whose script you have been given to rewrite. How will they feel about the changes you choose to make? Are those changes really improving the script, or are you marking your territorial possession on the script? To what extent are the changes primarily the result of your ego?

When you receive a copy of one of your scripts, after another writer has rewritten it, take several deep breaths and think about what you might have done to his or her script, before you read yours. You will probably hate it, even the really good bits that are better than yours were. And you will no doubt find bits that you think are worse than yours were. But c'est la vie. Whether you accept it or not, rewriters feel they need to put themselves into the script, and they have no greater a monopoly of perfect insight than you do.

Will you lose control of your script?

What happens when your script editor tells you that another writer is being brought in to rewrite your script? Firstly, you should have made sure that your contract entitled you to prepare at least one rewrite yourself. It is reasonable to be allowed this, even if your first draft is a mess.

You are also reasonably entitled to get detailed notes from the script editor or producer, outlining what they don't like and how they want it changed. Just saying that they don't like it is not acceptable and you should push for more information.

This information is important. You have to navigate a route between doing what you think will create the best possible script and what they want. The two things are often different. Do you give them what they want even if it is, in your opinion, a bad way to tell the story?

Your ability to control the conditions of a rewrite depends on many things, including:

- your relative power (if you are a beginner you will have little);
- how much time there is to do the work (if very little, then do what they want or drop out after having one go at persuading them; if you have lots of time try more than one rewrite);
- whether you have the ability and talent to do what is being asked of you (many writers find themselves out of their depth; it can then become a damage limitation exercise by the producer);
- whether there is enough money left to pay another writer (which may mean that you can offer to do it for less and therefore keep some control over it).

The politics of the relationships between the players over rewrites could fill a book on its own. It is often the most fraught time in the creation of a script. It is not surprising that it is so tough to get right.

William Goldman, one of the most highy-paid rewriters, was asked whether he had even been hired to fix something that seemed perfectly OK.

I was asked to fix *Aliens 3* which I had not seen. I read it and it seemed to me just as dorky as *Aliens 1* and *2*. I didn't know how to fix it. I mean it's... how do you fix *Aliens 3*? So I turned it down and then I got a call saying would I talk to the Director? Of course, I'll talk. The Director calls and he said, "You're not going to work on the movie?" "No, but you're just going to be great." He said, "But let me explain to you the philosophical implications I'm going to put in the movie". And as soon as I heard those words, I knew the movie was in deep shit. If I had been the studio and had heard those words I would have fired the Director that day because once you're thinking philosophical implications for *Aliens 3* you know the movie's going to run over budget (which it did), you know it's going to be a disaster (well, not a disaster but there will not be an *Aliens 4*, let's put it that way). End of story.[1]

Goldman was then asked if he had ever read something that was so good that there was no point doctoring it? He answered: 'No, no never – that will never happen. There's something you have to understand about screenwriters; it's like politics, it does not call forth the best people. Graham Greene, whom I think is the greatest writer of the century in English, did write screenplays, and you know that William Faulkner would go out and fiddle with Howard Hawks. For the most part, really good writers just don't write screenplays.' No one said it was easy. And it was also Goldman who said, 'No one knows anything.'

If the material is good enough (and readers have varying standards – an option does not mean it is a good script) it may survive the hazardous journey past committees of faceless people until it reaches the magical 'first day of principal photography.' No one really knows the fall-off rate, but it is probably more than 1000:1. In other words there are at least 1000 completed, polished, loved scripts around for every one that gets made. Maybe it is closer to 2000:1. However, this is no reason to stop writing. It is a reason to be demanding of all the help you can get.

Rewrites involve compromise. And with all compromise it helps to negotiate well. That means getting as much of what you want, while they think they have got much of what they want – we'll discuss this fine art later on. Be passionate about what you do. Write it with the conviction that it will be perfect. But if it isn't, in the eye of a reasonable beholder, well... change it.

Realising that no script is ever perfect, or ever finished, is also a good way to keep sane. It helps you deal with criticism, with rewrites and with stupid people, without necessarily costing you too much. You will eventually be judged by what is produced based on what you have written. While you may have little control over the actual production or direction, you owe it to yourself to provide the best script that you can. Rewriting is one of the ways of achieving that.

Note

1   Quoted with the permission of the Scottish Film Council, organizers of the annual Movie Makars scriptwriting workshops in Inverness.

9   Script Editing and Script Reports

I was surprised when I first heard that a top script editor on a network series in the States could earn $400,000 a year. The same person in the UK or on the Continent might earn £30–50,000. This should give you an idea of the influential role script editors play in America and the importance attached to this aspect of script development.

In the States, a script editor usually starts out their career as a scriptwriter, producing scripts on spec until one or two get sold. Spec or calling-card scripts get written both for existing shows and based on original ideas. If, for example, you write a *Roseanne* script on spec you send it to others who might recognise the qualities in it, and want to hire you, perhaps to write something completely different. It is you, as much as your scripts, that are being offered for sale.

The likelihood is that the *Roseanne* producer won't read it for legal reasons: if they do they probably won't want it because it won't be anything like the storylines they are currently working on or, even more frustratingly, it will be too much like a script they have in development already. It is very easy to see why writers can become paranoid. You have worked up a great episode, a different angle, something that stands out. It may have taken you weeks or months. And based on the briefest of verbal descriptions you are told that they already have something like that so your effort is of little interest to them.

Do you take this at face value? Do you fear that they will steal your idea and give it to one of their pet writers? Can you protect yourself? The answer is there is not much you can do about this situation. Don't even waste the emotional energy caused by the bad feelings that creep in every time you think of the production company. If you do you are on the beginning of a slope that becomes so steep you will hate writing, feel that you can't trust anybody and that there is a conspiracy against you.

In the UK, script editors have considerable power and responsibility; on the Continent they are less common but they are increasing in number. For example, some of the broadcasters have well-trained script editors who play a positive role in ensuring that the scripts suit the broadcaster's needs for audience and advertisers. Here the script editors are the focal point for the writer, as they should be.

Gaining Confidence

Scriptwriting should be a team activity, even if the writer seems to be left on their own for much of the time. Once you are working for a producer or broadcaster you should have a script editor to work with, who might also be the producer. What you need to do is to get to know this person really well, because he or she is your point of contact. Lunches, drinks, movies, parties all help in the bonding process. You need to be active in making yourself part of the team.

Let's assume that the script editor or producer likes your calling-card script. There is a reasonably good chance that you will be invited to go in and pitch a few storylines for the show. In the States it is more likely to be verbal pitching. In Europe you will probably be asked to write a couple of one-page ideas, particularly if it is for episodic television.

For a pitch meeting, you could also be asked to come up with as many as ten one-liners. For example, Sergeant Cryer in *The Bill* lets someone go who was suspected of committing a crime, because the man was so plausible. The episode shows how he deals with letting his colleagues down. This is the barest of ideas, at this stage completely undeveloped. This may be rejected by the script editor, but it is a starting point and you will need many of those.

If the producer and script editor like your ideas and your writing, you have a reasonably good chance of getting a commission, as long as there are still slots to be filled. It is tough being told that you are good enough but all the scripts for the next series have been allocated.

Once you've been commissioned to do an episode, if they like it and the way you responded to editorial notes and meetings, and you kept to agreed delivery dates (especially for rewrites), and if you get on well with the whole team (which can include script editors and other writers as well as the producer, executive producer and the director(s)) you are likely to continue getting commissions.

In the States, after a reasonable number of episodes for one show you may be suggested for another show. And you may then move upwards to a script-editing job. Eventually you can earn as much as $10,000 a week doing this – far more than in Europe – and you'll probably still get to write a few scripts for the show over a season, for which you get paid in the normal way. Once you are on staff, however, much of your time will be spent reading scripts that come in for the show and rewriting or restructuring them.

At the top of the ladder is the 'showrunner' or writer/producer, who is responsible for developing ideas for a show, pitching them to broadcasters or production companies and then putting the whole show together, picking the writers and the script editors, and producing the scripts.

Most showrunners become producers, or what are called in American jargon 'hyphenates' – writer-producers. The double salaries they get by acting in these two capacities artificially inflate the development budgets, but the results tend to outweigh the investment risk the network or production companies have to take. When they get a hit it pays for all the shows which were developed or piloted but then dropped.

This differs from the situation in Europe where most of the people who become script editors do so as a step on the way to doing something else. They don't seem to want to be script editors, but it's one of the first jobs a broadcaster offers to recent university graduates or people getting into television for the first time.

The new script editor often starts working on scripts written by people much more experienced than themselves. Working on the script of a feature film is different from an episode of a soap, but there are a number of similarities. The checklist below of what script editors do is not exhaustive but will give you some idea of the extent of their work.
1   Finding writers. This involves networking with writers' groups, meeting agents and reading unsolicited scripts. If an announcement is made that a new series is looking for writers or an existing show is going into a second series, the script editors on the show get buried under submissions.

9. Script Editing and Script Reports

2 Script editors make recommendations to their producer (who is usually their immediate boss). These recommendations could be to try a different writer, or alternatively to go after established writers. Together, the script editor and the producer allocate all the episodes for the forthcoming series.

3 The script editor is the liaison between the writer and the production team on everything from delivery dates to notes for the rewrites, as well as on what it is permissible to include in the script (how far can the writer go with bad language or explicit sex, for example).

It is unusual for writers of episodes of a long-running series to meet the producer or director (unless the writer is present at the filming or taping of the show). Script editors have considerable power with regard to writers, especially on series and serials. Series usually consist of a number of self-contained episodes, with some continuing main characters and some continuing storylines. A serial or soap always has a core of the same central characters and storylines generally stretch over a number of weeks or months.

4 If the series has a 'bible' (a detailed description of the world of the series, the location, characters and storylines) the script editor is often the writer of that document. If the original idea came from a writer, the two of them may jointly prepare the bible.

5 On some series and serials there are separate 'story-liners', who are responsible for providing the episode storylines which the writers then follow. This is particularly important when it comes to the long-term development of continuing characters. Conflict and disagreement between story-liners and script editors is not uncommon.

6 Once a storyline has been presented to the prospective writer of that episode, the writer has some leeway regarding the details of the episode, but far less room to play around than he or she would have had in an original one-off. This is why writing series and serials is not as easy as writers often think. The script editor is responsible for briefing the writer with the storyline elements and, once the draft script has been delivered, the script editor is responsible for the initial editorial feedback to the writer, particularly if more work is needed on the script before the script is presented to the producer.

7 Once the script editor is happy with the script (which does not mean that it won't need further work), he or she presents it to the producer or the editorial meeting. The editorial meeting is held regularly if this is a long-running series or serial, or even a mini-series. On a one-off programme, such meetings will usually be ad hoc. The changes required as a result of that meeting are then communicated to the writer by the script editor.

8 The script editor is usually responsible for managing the flow of scripts, in their different drafts, so that the cumbersome and expensive production process is not held up. This is one reason why writers need to take deadlines seriously. Delays can cost considerable sums of money, and a reputation for being late does not get writers highly recommended.

9 In a long-running series team, it is the script editor who provides the information to the writer on how many and which sets can or must be used in an episode, and which characters can or cannot be there. They also check the running time and

continuity of the first draft script and advise on cuts or additions that are needed. At first or second draft the script is also checked for legal problems; this is usually the responsibility of the script editor.

10 The director is sometimes the last of the key players to come onto the team, particularly on a long-running series. Once the writer, script editor and producer have agreed on the script, it is the script editor's job to find out what changes the director wants and to mediate between the director and the writer. The script editor should be on the side of the writer at this point. Directors, despite a reputation for throwing their egos around, often come up with improvements.

At every stage there is room for conflict. The extent to which a script editor will fight for (as opposed to against) the writer may depend as much on the personal relationship between the two of them as on the qualities of the script in question. That relationship, and the writer's relationship with his or her agent, can be the two most important in the writer's professional life.

11 Any information the writer gets about casting, production details or visits to the set usually come from the script editor in TV. On a feature, visits to the set may be arranged by the film's publicist. The right of a writer to be consulted on casting, attend filming, see the rushes or the rough cut may need to be negotiated into the contract.

Script Reports

Script editing and script analyses often go together and are sometimes the responsibility of the same person. Freelance script editors are the people usually hired as 'readers'. Whether they then get employed to work with the original writer, bring in new writers, or rewrite the script themselves depends on how good they are thought to be by the producer. Whoever does the rewriting, it is usually based on some kind of report or analysis of the treatment or script.

Script reports tend to form the basis of any rewriting that is requested or commissioned (the latter is usually paid for). They take a variety of forms but fulfil essentially the same function. A fairly typical script report will usually contain the following:

Title of script
Writer's name
Reader's name
Date received
Date completed
Storyline: (This can be one to three pages long and is usually a straightforward summary of the story of the script or manuscript. It can also be taken from a published book which is being considered for adaptation.)

Comments: (These can also be one to three pages long, and can take different forms. In some cases the analysis will be an overview of the material being considered, looking especially at its suitability for the company considering it. So for one producer it may be inappropriate and therefore be rejected, whereas it might be right for another producer. Rejection does not necessarily mean that a piece of work is bad.)

Comments can include some or all of the following (this list is not exhaustive):

- does the plot structure work?
- are the characters well drawn, sympathetic, easy/difficult to identify with etc?
- does the dialogue read well?
- is it original?
- is it authentic, does the writer know the subject matter and locations, is it convincing/credible?
- did the reader enjoy it, or what didn't he or she like about it?
- to what audience will it appeal?
- what other films or programmes can it be compared to, and how favourably?
- if there is a budget, is it realistic?

Some script report forms have a series of boxes which the reader ticks. Unless most of the ticks are in the 'excellent' or 'good' columns, the executive for whom the report was written won't even read it. The checklist boxes might look like Table 1.

	Excellent	Good	Fair	Poor
Characterisation	❏	❏	❏	❏
Dialogue	❏	❏	❏	❏
Structure	❏	❏	❏	❏
Originality	❏	❏	❏	❏
Uniqueness of Setting	❏	❏	❏	❏

Table 1.

Writers often find that when they are asked for a meeting to discuss the script. Executives will have only read the report, not the script. In such circumstances don't show that you are offended, however offended you might feel. Be thankful that the company has paid for a report to be written which, we hope, the executive has actually read (probably while you were waiting in reception!). You gain little from showing them up.

Sometimes there is also a summary of the reader's analysis (which is also used by busy executives). An example of this summary sheet follows below. The reader may have to complete one or more lines of comment. This summary is for convenience; it does not confuse with too many details, though it can also focus the writer clearly on the strong and weak points of the project. It is rare for writers to be given copies of these internal documents. This is a pity, as they are often the most honest assessment available.

Analysis Summary

General Impression   *Remarks*
    Characterization
    Dialogue
    Structure

Originality of story
Reading enjoyment
Script presentation
Credibility & Characterization of Main Protagonist/Antagonist
Name of Protagonist
Name of Antagonist
Other major characters
Plot Quality
Credibility of plot
Structure of plot
Climax setting
Use of turning points
Use of sub-plots
Plants & pay-offs
Visuality of plot
Uniqueness of settings
Strength of ending
Commercial viability
Special Values ...   .
Suggestions for a Rewrite   ...   .
Further Documents/Actions Required   ...   ...
Reader's Recommendations   ...   .
(eg to reject, ask for spec rewrite, commission a rewrite, take an option etc)

These analysis documents vary, but they cover largely the same points on which your work will be judged. Read through your script while bearing them in mind, to make sure that you get there first, so that if the general view is that there is something wrong with your script, you have a rational answer prepared.

If the criticism is made available 'for the writer's eyes', it is often toned down. There is little that can be done to prevent this, except building up such a good relationship that you do get told the truth. You also need to ensure that the 'reader' or script editor knows that you really do want the truth.

Most editors, whether of scripts or books, place great importance on the willingness of a writer to take criticism. For example, it can make a significant difference to what a publisher might pay for the advance of a book by an author they have not worked with before if the publisher knows that the author will rewrite and rewrite and rewrite. So do yourself a favour and learn to take criticism – however painful.

For writers, the most important person in this area of their professional lives is their script editor. For novelists, it is the editor too. But whether you are given the full benefit of their editorial abilities and experience will depend to some degree on you. No one likes editing a writer who is resistant, reluctant or ungrateful. So you can influence the quality and quantity of the editorial work you get. In the career paths of many writers this is sometimes the ingredient that makes the difference between success and greater success.

10 The Psychology and Physiology of Emotion in Audiences

Consider the question 'Why do people go to the movies?' (or, for that matter, watch TV or read). Entertainment and education are the most common explanations. But self-exploration underlies the experience. As Frank Daniel says, when an audience is looking at the screen, they are really looking at themselves. Joseph Bronowski's famous analysis of early cave paintings suggested that, for the early hunters, looking at drawings of threatening creatures was one way of learning to cope with the fear they caused in the hunters in the real world.

Richard Walter puts Bronowski into a media context:

> In the caves' security the hunters could allow their emotions to simulate those experienced in the actual hunt. In complete safety they could wallow in fear. Later, in the hunt, recalling the cave experience they could successfully steel themselves against surrendering to their panic, which, thanks to the caves, was now familiar to them. A film is a life simulator enabling modern men and women to rehearse their emotions, to experience desperate, painful sensations in an environment of total safety.[1]

A fundamental desire of the movie-goer is to experience emotions. There is a similar, though less all-embracing, process involved in reading. By its nature, reading is more reflective, and it allows the reader greater control of the speed at which the story unfolds. Film, and to a lesser extent television, attempts to control all the sensory inputs available to the audience.

The darkened auditorium, the inhibition on talking during the movie, the surround-sound and the big screen all play their part in enveloping the audience so that nothing interferes with the film's ability to manipulate the audience.

But what takes place in the minds and bodies of the audience? And can such knowledge help you write better scripts? I believe that it can, and that the single most common cause of unsuccessful scripts and unsuccessful movies is the result of ignoring the audience.

Being an Audience

As people sit in their comfortable cinema seats, indulging in oral fixations – sucking on a straw, pushing handfuls of sweet tasting food into their mouths – and looking up at the larger-than-life faces and bodies, what else are they doing?

For a start, there is a certain amount of mirroring behaviour. Actors on screen have great charisma and audiences find it easy to relate to them. As long as we are involved with the characters and the story, we may mirror the behaviour of the actors by tapping our feet, singing under our breath, clenching our fists and grinding our teeth. When our hero is battling against great odds, we will flinch or tense up as the blows are traded, and so on.

Depending on the kind of film we are watching, our reactions will vary. For instance a horror film might give us cold, fear-motivated sweats. These are reactions that are physical – not consciously controlled – as we watch the flickering screen.

Because we project ourselves into the films that engage us, we become the objects of our own gaze and for a while, unknowingly, we are transported by the medium of the actor. We can then vicariously experience extremes of pain and pleasure, which would be unendurable in real life, safe in the knowledge that at the end of the movie the lights will go on and everything will be normal again.

A dream, which is a similar experience in some respects (except that one is the writer and film-maker as well as the audience) does not give one the safety-valve of being aware, while watching/experiencing the dream, that it will come to an end. A nightmare is usually more scary than a movie.

Being an audience is potent. If one is not identifying with the persona on screen, one might identify with the object of their attention. So girls in the audience watching Daniel Day Lewis or Richard Gere feel themselves to be the object of his interest and sexuality. Why shouldn't the weak feel strong, the thin feel fat and those who think they are ugly or unloved feel beautiful and loved? And if we can choose to enrich our lives with positive feelings by being an audience, why not also explore the dangerous, the forbidden and the taboos of our society?

Most scripts seem to pay too little attention to the audience/star relationship. Writers don't make the characters sufficiently easy to access, so the audience doesn't get involved or care, and the experience of going to the movies is disappointing. Word-of-mouth about the film is then poor, as are the reviews.

An audience which gets bored and thinks of other things, rather than what the writer or director want them to, is not being controlled. Writing should be a leveller. If it is an effective film, we in the audience can all feel the power of the film (or TV episode). That is precisely why we read or go to the movies or watch TV. It's also why we listen to music.

We find out who we are by comparing ourselves to other people, something which is not easy to do in real life. That is why movies are such a valuable way for society to look at itself (and why censorship is so short-sighted). We find ways of improving our inner lives, expanding the life we live in our imaginations, enriching ourselves.

Scientists have now been able to identify, with some precision, the physiological and chemical changes that take place in the body, as we undergo different sorts of experiences, in 'real life' or in the cinema. It is not surprising that movies, television, radio and books make up such an important part of so many people's lives.

Creating a World of Involvement

What is involved, for the writer, in creating a world for a viewer or reader? How can the writer ensure that the viewer or reader will relate to the characters and the world portrayed? And is it more important for the viewer to be involved emotionally than intellectually?

Far too little attention is paid to this in scriptwriting courses and books. It is not easy to explain the interaction of brain and nerve processes that make up the biology of emotion. Nor does this interaction seem to be thought relevant enough. Let me explain why I say this.

What makes characters involving for the audience? Why do films with strong conflict perform so well worldwide? The answer will go some way to explaining why the vicarious experience of powerful, moving emotions is a primary need of audiences all over the world.

If writers become more aware of how audiences react when confronted with certain scenes, they can use that knowledge to increase the audience's involvement in the film. The key to the experience of viewing involves 'anticipation' and 'expectation'. The ability of our minds to relate what we see to the future enables us to 'put ourselves into a character's shoes', and to experience emotions, including those that come from physical experiences like pain (eg, being shot) or pleasure (eg, kissing one's screen idol).

What happens when we feel an emotion? The chemical and physiological reactions that take place are fascinating and revealing for the work of the screenwriter.

In *The Oxford Companion to the Mind*, emotion is described as:

> ...any discrepancy, any interruption of expectations or of intended actions produces undifferentiated visceral (autonomic) arousal...thus, riding on a roller-coaster produces serious disturbances and discrepancies between our expectations and current feelings of balance and bodily support. Whether the ride is seen as joyful or dreadful depends on what we expect about the ride...and whether we feel in control of the situation. Some love it, others hate it.[2]

The popularity of the horror movie as a genre, whether *Frankenstein*, *Friday the Thirteenth*, *Silence of the Lambs* or *The Blair Witch Project*, is the result of the public's positive wish, and perhaps need, to scare itself. Self-induced trances in countries in which voodoo is practised, or self-induced hysteria at pop concerts, are to some extent similar in the effect that they have on the individual. We seek from life more than we would otherwise receive. Films, TV and books are among the most common ways we can get it. So what can the writer give to us? All the books on screenwriting talk about the importance of character. Unless there are characters that readers or viewers cannot help but care about or be involved with, the book or film won't be as successful as it could be. The means to achieve this is called 'empathy'.

A definition or description of empathy is revealing: 'The feeling of "belonging to", associating ourselves with, or "being carried along" with something. Thus, a golfer may feel that he is almost soaring into the air with the ball when he hits a good drive.'[3]

As a spectator, I have certainly felt such a feeling while watching the ball hit by a golfer I was rooting for, soaring towards the green; when his opponent hit a good shot I felt no such feeling. I have felt the same watching most sports including boxing and wrestling (which I dislike but am still affected by) and countless movies. But if we accept that it is desirable for a film to stimulate emotion in audiences, we can immediately see why conflict is so vital to the film's success.

The Technology of the Brain

The brain is, not surprisingly, the key to the emotions. It is part of the nervous system which, together with the cardiovascular system (blood) and the endocrine system (hormones), make up the complex physical and chemical network we need to understand if we are to make sense of our emotions.[4]

The surface of the brain is the cerebral cortex. This is where the higher-level processing of information happens and probably gives rise to consciousness. Embedded deeper in the brain is an area that includes the hypothalamus. This deals with the basic emotions – pleasure, fear, anger, and so on.

Nerve cells in this area, when receiving electrical impulses from other cells, prompt the release of the chemical known as phenylethylamine, or PEA. This is colloquially known as 'the happiness drug', one of whose derivatives is what we call 'speed'.

When this washes over the other cells of the brain, negative thoughts are, more or less, inhibited. Positive and relaxing thoughts are encouraged and at the same time various physical processes are slowed down, like the heart rate and blood pressure, which are reduced to a less stressful level. Watching a movie can bring about a feeling of elation and well-being. Several stimulants are released whose effects are similar to those of illegal drugs.

When we are emotionally depressed, signals from the hypothalamus will put stress on other parts of our bodies. In this way, illnesses such as high blood pressure can be caused. These are referred to as psychosomatic illnesses because their only causes are in our 'minds' (read brains).

It is important to understand that much of this effect is beyond our control. The autonomic nervous system acts and makes decisions by itself, regulating our bodies in a way that is programmed to maintain a balance. Two branches of the system work in concert, one opposing the other. When we are relaxed, the parasympathetic branch keeps energy-spending down to a minimum and concentrates on essential functions like the digestion of food. If you are sitting calmly in a chair reading this after a meal, it is the parasympathetic nervous system that is in control.

If you hear a window in the next room smash, and you think that someone has broken in, you will, without thinking about it, move into what psychologists call 'fight-or-flight' mode. You will be prepared in an instant to defend/attack or to run away. This response is the result of your sympathetic nervous system becoming dominant.

A number of physiological changes take place in your body. The endocrine system releases hormones from glands to increase your heart rate, enlarge the size of your pupils and make more sugar available in your bloodstream. This gives you an immediate surge of energy to fight or run.

If you then discover that the window was broken by a bird or a child's ball, then your parasympathetic nerves, triggered by the realisation that you are not in any danger, signal your organs to slow down.

Blood vessels constrict in order to lower the amount of blood your heart needs to pump and if this braking process is very sudden you may even faint (extreme relaxation).

One of the hormones released during 'fight-or-flight' is adrenaline. It is released into the bloodstream and travels around the body affecting the cells it reaches, altering their activity, speeding some of them up, slowing others down. In this way, it stimulates the release of sugar (from the liver) for energy, the pupils dilate to allow better vision, and so on. It is the body's way of instinctively bringing into play all the natural resources that are essential to fight or flee.

Most of the instructions telling the organs to release hormones into the bloodstream, come from the nerve cells in the hypothalamus. And it is not only fight-or-flight that is affected. The reproduction of milk in the breast, the timing of menstruation, the control of the breathing rate, as well as the toning of muscles for action, are all controlled by the hypothalamus.

When we choose to see a horror film or a thriller we usually have some idea of what we are letting ourselves in for. The way films and books are marketed helps condition us to expect or anticipate certain experiences. So, why do we want to feel and experience what we would generally call negative emotional states?

The Bronowski explanation is part of the answer. We want to prepare ourselves for difficult or dangerous experiences in the real world, or we 'want' experiences at arms' length, such as killing or raping (which most societies 'forbid' by imposing sanctions). Wanting to see a film like *Thelma & Louise* does not imply any wish to rape or murder or even any enjoyment of such acts; it is a way of exploring our own and society's reactions to rape and murder.

Chris Vogler, a story consultant in LA, described the process as follows: 'A story is a model, a metaphor for something else. The story-teller puts out a metaphor and the audience looks at it and each one compares his or her own life to the story and the characters. Stories have a healing function. The Greeks invented drama in the first place to deal with the pressures of living in a society. It was created to purge the emotions of the audience which had become poisoned by living in a group.'[5]

Cinema and emotion

Cinema, television, theatre and books are amongst the most widely-accepted ways of having these vicarious experiences. We actively choose – by standing in line and paying money – to have the experiences of fear, sadness, aggression, anger, lust and, of course, love. The cinema is like the prehistoric cave. And as in the cave, we can release stored-up feelings or emotions, or have experiences that are missing from our lives or forbidden to us by society.

It is socially acceptable to cry during a sad film, and our fear of Freddie during *Nightmare on Elm Street* is limited by the knowledge that we are not in real danger. The experience of most movies is that the good guys win. At the end of the film we feel better than we did before or during it. This 'uplifting' feeling is partly the result of chemicals being released into our bodies, like the feeling of well-being associated with the eating of chocolate.

Music must be mentioned here because it is undoubtedly of great importance to the success of a film. The theme music for a film like *Jaws* is more emotive than any scene in the movie without music, because it creates immediate tension or suspense. If the central character, with whom we have become emotionally involved, has a need or a goal, and there is an obstacle or gap between the character and the goal, we – the audience – can be made, by clever scriptwriting, to feel suspense. This is mediated through the intellect and is relatively complex. One bar of appropriate music goes straight to the viscera and can cause tension and suspense.

So what actually happens to create the feeling or state of suspense? We experience 'feelings' sitting in the cinema, while watching the character on the screen portraying similar feelings. We are sometimes in possession of information that the character lacks, so he or she may be unaware of the fact that the villain is just around the corner with an axe. We suffer the greater anxiety.

Our nervous and endocrine systems prepare us for fight or flight, despite the fact that we are fully conscious of the fact that we are sitting in the darkened auditorium of our local cinema with our loved ones watching a movie and eating popcorn. We feel scared, tense, stressed or whatever. A good writer or director will, like Robert Ludlum in his thrillers, sense when the stress reaches a peak and not let it go on too long.

Ludlum is particularly good at leading the reader to expect something dramatic to happen, to the point that the reader virtually anticipates the occurrence. At this point something completely different, but even more credible, happens. In other words, the writer needs to get the reader or audience to use what Coleridge called 'the willing suspension of disbelief'. If the writing is so good that the audience has little control over its feelings, then the audience will leave the cinema satisfied.

When the characters reach their goal, or simply reach safety, stress levels drop, there is a surge of energy in the body and the 'happiness chemicals' rush through the system. This is the moment of enjoyment, of relief and release. It is not that different from the feeling of energy and well-being that occurs after a session in the gym, starting with exhaustion and ending up energized.

If the suspense in the movie continues for too long, the audience may start to get uncomfortable, to fidget. If the suspense is released too early it will not get the rush of energy and well-being that it came to the cinema for. A balance must be achieved to gain maximum effect.

Maintaining suspense

I do not want to suggest that writers take a medical degree before attempting a script! But so many of the scripts offered to agents and producers are so weak that it is clear that the more understanding writers have of the nature of audiences, the more likely it is that they will write well for audiences.

Getting the act structure right is important, but it is not so important that writers can ignore other aspects of their craft. Injecting suspense and anticipation into a script is the equivalent of printing money. Joe Eszterhas's work in *Jagged Edge* and *Basic Instinct* is a case in point. He knew that if he wrote a sufficiently good script on spec, he could then auction it, because he knew that more than one prospective buyer would want it. (Auctioning properties is explained in Chapter 13.)

The easiest way to focus on building suspense and anticipation is to ensure that there is conflict. You also need to have a protagonist with whom the audience can empathize and care about. You can then trigger anticipation in the audience's mind, and while they are trying to anticipate, they are in suspense. That's when breathing, pupils and pulse all change.

If the audience can actually anticipate exactly what is to come the film will lose its suspense because it will become predictable. Expecting a killer to be hiding behind a door which a helpless protagonist is approaching (eg a blind young woman) is suspenseful because although the audience anticipates it, and therefore fears it, there is no way of knowing exactly what is likely to happen.

If the tension reaches its peak just as the protagonist is about to open the door, but the viewpoint changes and we suddenly realise that the killer is stalking the protagonist from behind, we will be surprised and there will be an even greater rush of adrenaline.

The audience's involvement with a character will depend on the choices that the writer gives the character. Making a likeable protagonist suffer greatly in his or her attempt to escape from a fate worse than death makes it easy for audiences to identify, to empathize, to care. If the protagonist escapes with no difficulty in the first few minutes you do not have a movie. Lessen the obstacles the protagonist has to overcome, play down the villainy and strength of the antagonist, and you immediately short-change the audience and shorten your writing career.

You can help your career by attempting to come up with original ideas that are 'high concept', plots in which there are high stakes, an antagonist the audience fears, who seems for much of the time to have the upper hand. Then you will be well on the way to creating a commercially successful movie.

You always need a well-chosen and well-portrayed central character with whom the audience will identify emotionally. What that means is that the audience will experience the emotions you want them to, rather than just watching the character experiencing emotions.

By being aware of what emotions you wish to arouse in your audience, you will focus more clearly in your selection and depiction of characters, plot points, twists and reversals. The likelihood is that you will write a better script.

Notes

1   Chair of the Scriptwriting Faculty at UCLA, in his book *Screenwriting* (Plume/Penguin, 1988).

2   ed by RL Gregory (OUP 1987).

3   *The Oxford Companion to the Mind.*

4   I am indebted to Terry Kelleher, who was studying the biology of emotion at Jesus College, Oxford, for a 'medical' analysis of this process.

5   Lecture at the 1994 PILOTS workshop, published in a second volume of lectures on long-running series by the MEDIA BUSINESS SCHOOL.

11 Ratings, Share and Audience Research

Audiences have the same aspirations, anxieties, dreams and passions as writers. Writers aren't a breed apart. And unless you give the audience the chance of having the experiences that they want to have, they are unlikely to feel that you have fulfilled your part of the deal. So how can you achieve this yet still write what you want to write?

The process is no different for a director or producer when it comes to choosing the story and deciding how to tell it. The most common failing on either their part or the writer's, however, is to think that because it seems to be a good idea, it will work. The idea still needs to meet the audience's needs. Telling a bad idea well, as I mentioned earlier, will almost certainly produce a better script than telling a good idea badly. Good storytelling works because it connects with the audience.

In the triangular relationship between writer, characters and audience, the primary relationship the writer should have is with the audience. The most common and most pervasive mistake made by writers in Europe is to indulge in their relationship with their characters to the exclusion of their relationship with their audience. Hence relatively uninvolving and inaccessible scripts.

Although it is another generalization, the discipline imposed by the system in America tends to force writers to take more trouble with their audiences. This is partly because there is much more money to be made in that market, and also because it is usually assumed that whatever is produced should make money. The American model is generally true of commercial television networks in other countries. The programmes exist to deliver audiences to advertisers who buy time around or during the programmes. Public service television, which does not usually carry advertizing, has a different remit and can afford to be more educative at the expense of entertainment. Whether this makes for better television depends on who is making the value-judgement. Most television programmes, like most novels, are not intended only for oneself!

The Analysis of a Particular Audience

I am going to look in some detail at the audience analysis for one TV movie. The film, called *Hostage*, was shown on a Saturday night on ITV, the commercial channel. It is a thriller, based on a novel by Ted Allbeury called *No Place to Hide*. The script is by Arthur Hopcraft, it was produced by Tom Kinninmont of Independent Image, directed by Robert Young and starred Sam Neill and Talisa Soto.

The shoutline of the poster for the film (which had some theatrical exhibition in countries like Spain, Germany and some in South America and a substantial video release) was: 'He came to destroy her family. And she fell in love with him.' It might have been even more effective if it had said, 'And he fell in love with her.' The 'shoutline' is similar to a log-line or pitch-line, but usually occurs on a poster accompanying a picture.

Sam Neill plays John Rennie, a British Secret Service assassin. He is a dedicated, unquestioning machine, serving his country in the name of national security. When a senior defence analyst is taken hostage by terrorists in Argentina, Rennie has the task of rescuing him.

He is ordered to kidnap the children of the terrorist leader, to bargain for the Briton's release. The plan goes wrong. First Rennie sees the kidnapped children suffering. Then he and a member of their family fall in love. So he acts against his orders. Back in London Rennie is now seen as a liability, and becomes a target for British security. He is forced to go on the run.

The broadcast of the film was considered to be a success. After consolidating the figures for video-recording, the audience for the film was estimated at 9.2 million. This was the equivalent of a 47% share of the total audience available at that time. Since ITV did not normally beat the publicly-funded BBC on a Saturday night, they were very pleased with the performance of this film. *Miss Marple* which was being shown on BBC1 at the same time got a 42% share.

While writers and programme makers usually think in terms of a finite number of viewers, reported as ratings, ITV companies and advertising agencies are also interested in 'share' – the proportion of the audience available at that time which a particular programme pulls in.

A programme might get a 25% share if shown at 8.30pm, during prime time, but a 30% share at 10.30pm (even though the 10.30 audience could be fewer in number). It is important to be aware of this distinction. Except in public service television, the people who ultimately finance the production of what you write are usually more concerned about audience share than about ratings.

Scriptwriters and producers should have more than a minimal understanding of audiences and what they watch. When you think about what to write or a programme you want to produce, do you think about what slot the programme might be best shown in? Would you know how to find out how audiences are analysed, or what advertisers are looking for?

Here, therefore, is a brief look at one programme. This sort of detailed information isn't easily available, although the trade papers do regularly provide a range of data on audiences.[1]

The figures below give you an indication of how the film competed, in other words, who watched it. It was important to the producer to know how the film performed for several reasons. One critical reason had to do with whether the broadcaster would finance a sequel. If the film did better than expected, then a sequel was likely to be given the go-ahead.

We will look at figures for London and Yorkshire. Figures like this are available for every region in the UK. These detailed analyses are prepared by specialist research companies and by advertising agencies. What the advertising agencies are looking at is the breakdown of the audience according to the advertisers' definition of social and economic classes as shown for London and Yorkshire in Tables 2 and 3 .[2]

The production company, Independent Image, used the research figures to argue convincingly for a sequel. The broadcaster agreed and offered to put up a sum of money.

The summary of the research provides an interesting insight into the way that the broadcasters think, and therefore the way that producers and writers need to think.

1 *Hostage* has highlighted two things: home-produced quality drama can outperform some US imported productions and one doesn't have to sacrifice a programme's appeal to the lighter viewing sections of the population in the quest for high audiences.

2 *Hostage* was the top single drama shown on ITV during 1992, attracting 9.2 million viewers to the channel during peak viewing time on Saturday night. Its popularity extended across all age and social groups. It was the top drama for 16-24 year-olds and the third most popular drama for ABC1s across all channels for 1992.

3 When compared to TV films, perhaps more akin to *Hostage*, again the programme's performance was excellent. It was the second most popular programme when ranked against US TV films, both for all individuals and ABC1s. It was the third most popular programme in comparison to US TV films for 16-34 year-olds.

4 Because of the greater appeal of home-produced drama and TV films in comparison

London

Audience	TVR	Conv	All Week Average Conv	+/-
AB Men	15	79	64	+23%
ABC1Men-35	13	67	62	+8%
Housewives with children	22	113	100	+13%
ABC1 Adults	14	75	73	+3%
Women in full time work	16	90	81	+11%
Adults-25	8	44	78	-44% [3]

Top 10 Programmes for AB Men

	Programme	AB Men TVR
1	News at Ten Monday	21
2	News at Ten Thursday	17
3	Airplane 2	17
4	News at Ten Tuesday	15
5	Blade Runner	15
6	**HOSTAGE**	**15**
7	The Bill Tuesday	15
8	The Bill Thursday	14
9	Silver Streak	13
10	LA Law	13

Table 2. Breakdown of information on the London audience

Yorkshire

Audience	TVR	Conv	All Week Average Conv	+/-
AB Men	15	85	66	+29%
ABC1 Men -35	7	40	68	-41%
Housewives with children	21	104	83	+25%
ABC1 Adults	17	100	83	+20%
Women in full time work	16	91	71	+28%
Adults -25	12	70	72	-3%

Top 10 Programmes for AB Men

	Programme	AB Men TVR
1	Coronation Street Wednesday	21
2	News at Ten Monday	17
3	Coronation St Friday	16
4	Colombo	16
5	Dirty Dozen: Deadly Mission	15
6	**HOSTAGE**	**15**
7	The Bill Tuesday	14
8	Coogan's Bluff	14
9	News at Ten	13
10	Coronation Street Monday	12

Table 3. Breakdown of information on the Yorkshire audience

to imported productions *Hostage* is only the fifth most popular UK TV film. It has a much tougher time trying to outperform UK films than US ones.

5   *Hostage* proved itself a considerable asset to the fragile ITV Saturday night schedule, attracting an extra 1.3 million viewers, which is above the average for this peak-time slot. It raised the ITV share of the audience to 46%, happily outperforming *Miss Marple* on BBC1.

6   Unfortunately it was a one-off rise in audience rather than part of a growing trend. Another film the following week, *The Grass Cutter*, saw the audience drop back to just over seven million individuals and a 36% share of viewing.

7   Interestingly, three out of the five top performing programmes in this slot were ITV-produced drama, a further indication of the merits of producing high-quality popular drama within the UK.

8   *Hostage* not only attracted large audiences but the kind of audiences that advertisers want to buy. Compared to the overall profile of ITV, Hostage attracted a much lower percentage of DEs and over 55 year-olds than normal.

9   Quality action-adventure dramas appeal not only to viewers from all walks of life, but particularly to the younger sections of the population and the ABs, those with disposable income. Not only will these dramas help to attract light viewers of ITV

Home-Produced and Imported Single Dramas

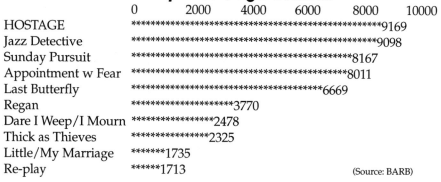

	0	2000	4000	6000	8000	10000
HOSTAGE	**9169					
Jazz Detective	***9098					
Sunday Pursuit	**8167					
Appointment w Fear	***************************************8011					
Last Butterfly	********************************6669					
Regan	******************3770					
Dare I Weep/I Mourn	***************2478					
Thick as Thieves	**************2325					
Little/My Marriage	*******1735					
Re-play	******1713					(Source: BARB)

Table 4. Top performing ITV Dramas in 1992 (all the individuals viewing, in 000s)

Average Share of Audience by Channel

		0%	10%	20%	30%	40%	50%
HOSTAGE	ITV	*********************************46%					
Miss Marple	BBC1	****************************41%					
La Dolce Vita	BBC2	****4%					
Encounters	CH4	*1%					(Source: BARB)

Table 5. Competitive Programming.

away from other channels, but will also help attract light viewers to television per se, hopefully turning television viewing on a Saturday night back into an appealing way of spending the evening.

The figures highlight the significance of AB MEN. This is, for advertisers, perhaps the most interesting category. AB MEN spend money. The significant figure is that the All Week Average Conversion was 64 for AB MEN but the film actually achieved a 79, an extra 23% higher. For AB MEN it was the sixth most popular programme.

Hostage did reasonably well with ABC younger men (under 35). It is above average by a small amount. It did above average with everyone in London except under 25s, because on Saturday night they tend to go out.

If you look at Yorkshire it is only slightly down for younger people, which probably tells you that there is less going out among kids in the regions. Note that the AB MEN count is also high – 29%. Although again, it does not score well with younger ABC1 MEN. The category of housewives with children does well, but they are not a premium audience for the advertisers at this time of the evening. On the other hand, women in full-time work are good news for the advertisers here, because they tend to have disposable income.

AB MEN in particular are a big target on a Saturday night. It is interesting to see what AB MEN were watching in the north of England – *News at Ten* doesn't rate higher than number 8 or 9. The top programme with AB MEN in the north is *Coronation Street*, which doesn't even make it into the top 10 with AB MEN in London. One probable reason for this is that people who are AB in London are not home early enough to watch *Coronation Street*. They may be home in time to eat by 7.30pm, but unless they watch TV while they eat they will miss it.

The main piece of information that the producer can use, and that the advertising people consider important, is that the score for AB MEN was very good. Advertisers will pay a premium for advertising around a programme that can deliver that sort of audience. An ITV company, armed with these figures, will expect to get more than the average for the ad slots it can sell around the sequel.

Delivering Goods

A writer who writes a show that delivers the hoped-for audience will be in a stronger negotiating position. Which is why you should never be complacent about whether a particular script is as good as it can be. It can always be improved. Writers don't have easy enough access to information on audiences. The ratings and box office charts published in the trade press are invaluable, but they don't go into the sort of detail that will help refine the choice of story and the way in which that story is being told.

Even an unsophisticated understanding of audiences is better than none at all. One hears commissioning editors talking about wanting programmes or programme strands that will appeal to, for example, 'the upper end of the market'. Know the socio-economic implications of that. Certain programmes have more appeal for audiences with higher levels of education or greater disposable income. Talk to editors in terms that show you understand and even share their aspirations and needs. And be aware of the audience's aspirations: young teenagers want to watch shows about older teenagers, and so on.

The commissioning editor will have a brief to fulfil. A writer or independent producer who shows that he or she really understands the requirements of the proposed programme will be more attractive to work with.

It is apparently possible to calculate, by using sophisticated research, what the audience for a particular programme would have been if the programme had been transmitted at a different time or on a different day or even in a different month.

It is not enough to think that you want to write about something just because it interests you. You must think about how you will communicate it to your audience, which means having some idea of who that audience is. In my experience, even when writers appear to be thinking about their audience, they often do not tend to target it accurately enough.

It is also important to remember that broadcasters are not only interested in the gross figures, the ratings. You might not be happy when your programme is to be transmitted at 10.30pm instead of 8.30pm, because you know that you will get fewer people watching at 10.30. A commercial broadcaster might do this because it could win the slot with your programme at 10.30pm, but lose the battle for 'share' at 8.30pm. By putting another programme on at 8.30pm they could win that slot, thus winning both, despite the fact that your programme achieves a smaller audience than if it had been scheduled for an earlier time. By clever scheduling a programme controller can increase the revenue from advertising. Since commercial channels make their money from advertising, this is clearly important for them.

Similar processes of evaluating audiences exist in virtually every country. If you are writing a script aimed at an American or German audience, you need to know something about the ratings, the audiences and what the TV decision-makers in those countries need from a programme. This information is available in all the TV trade papers.

It sometimes helps to think about the decision-makers as your first audience, and the general public who might watch as the next audience.

Think about what story you want to tell. What else is there on television like it? Who are the audiences for those programmes? Find out what the ratings for those programmes are.

Think of several ways of approaching the story. Which will be most surprising, have most impact, be most original? In other words, which will reach out and 'captivate' your audience?

In all probability, audiences have hardly changed over thousands of years. It can be argued that in pre-literate times storytelling used similar forms and structures to those used today. Stories, as far as we know, have always had beginnings, middles and ends, or to put it another way, a three-act structure, because they work better. This could be the result of the way the human brain and the nervous system works.

It is easy to say that the cardinal sin in screenwriting is to be boring. But it is difficult to know when you are being boring. The premium on hot scriptwriters is so high precisely because so few writers can be exciting all the time.

Audiences are prepared to pay for their willing suspension of disbelief. They want to see whatever will enable them to expand their lives, to fulfil their dreams and wishes, to experience the out-of-reach or the forbidden. For the audience, going to the cinema or reading a book is a form of narcissism, of self-exploration.

It can be the same for the writer. Self-exploration may be the dominant motivation to write. The craft lies in making one's own self-exploration as a writer accessible to others, by expressing the very feelings or fears that large parts of the potential audience want to explore too. *Poltergeist* and *Ghostbusters* help us make sense of the supernatural. These experiences also appeal to our desire for the incredible and our attraction for the unknowable. Unless you believe in reincarnation, you can only die once. You can never, therefore, 'know' what death is like. Hence its popularity in books, films and TV drama.

I have never seen a ghost; I am not even sure I believe in them. But I still want to know what to make of them. Whether or not you have ever fallen in love, you will want to know exactly what it feels like for someone else. We are forever measuring ourselves and our experiences against others. It is how we define ourselves, how we come to know who we are. That is one of the reasons we like watching movies.

Conclusion

Getting that emotional and physiological reaction out of your audience is easier if you write visually because people tend to believe the evidence of their eyes, rather than what they hear. If you did not believe in ghosts yet saw one walk though the wall in front of you, you are far more likely to believe it than if you were told that someone else had seen it.

Audiences operate on many levels at one time: remember Jon Boorstin's analysis: brain/intellect, heart/emotion, gut/viscera.[4] We don't even have to ask why people like to have new experiences, or why they go back to experiences that they have enjoyed. Nor are we surprised that they prefer positive experiences to negative ones.

Watching a massacre or a rape may not seem at first sight like a positive experience, and in a pornographic film it won't be. But from the safety of the cinema, films like *The Accused* or *Thelma and Louise* are positive experiences. The morality of their stories creates a context in which we can judge what is right and what is wrong. If we are also emotionally involved with the characters the films have an even greater impact on us.

Some horror films lack a moral element to their story, but may satisfy an atavistic desire for violence in audiences. This may create commercially sucessful movies, but leaves something to be desired. The best suspense films enable us to examine our consciences and our values, to find out more about ourselves precisely because we are able, using the flickering screen and our imaginations, to put ourselves into situations that we hope never to experience, as well as those that we want to experience.

Notes

1 For these figures I am indebted to the production company that made *Hostage*, Independent Image, and to the broadcasters, Tyne Tees.

2 Social and economic class categorization:

Grade	Social Status	Type of Occupation
A	Upper middle class	Higher managerial, administrative or professional.
B	Middle class	Intermediate managerial, administrative or professional.
C1	Lower middle class	Supervisory/clerical and junior managerial admin. or professional.

3 **TVR** – this is the audience as a percentage of the total population in a group.

Conv – 'conversion' is a rather complicated way advertising agencies have of assessing whether their ad campaign spending is reaching an acceptable number of the target audience. Advertisers have a finite amount of money to spend on a campaign. Assuming that they decide that their target audience is men with a bias towards ABC1 men. The ad agency decides which spots to buy, around or during particular programmes.

The number of people who watch television is very carefully monitored (this can be done with great sophistication). The agency and their clients will know how many people in each of the categories watched a particular programme and the ads (eg how many ABC1 men, women, housewives with kids, etc.). The maximum number of ABC1 men possible is 100% – this is called a '100 rating'. If the ads reached a rating of 80, that would be a '80% conversion', which would be considered very good by the advertiser.

All week average – this is the average conversion over the week. If a programme gets a higher figure than the all week averge that is also thought to be good.

4 Jon Boorstin, *The Hollywood Eye* (HarperCollins, 1990).

12 Interactive Multimedia

Of all the new markets the most exciting, confusing and important is 'interactive multimedia' (IMM). The excitement and confusion stem from a combination of two things: IMM involves the latest technology, and it is growing so rapidly that the newest products are out of date by the time they are available in the shops.

It is important to discuss IMM because we are on the brink of the most significant communications revolution since the printing press and the moving picture. The changes will affect all sectors of the communications industries, from writers and producers to lawyers and agents. Like the gold rush, there are fortunes to be made, and lost. But IMM is so new that it is not possible to be categorical about the implications for writers.

In order to see where writers fit into the brave new world of IMM and how they can make money in it, let us run through some of its basic elements. This is only a rudimentary survey, but it will hopefully enable writers and those who work with them in the traditional media, to decide a) whether IMM is relevant to their ambitions or needs, and b) where to get into it.

I will start by an overview of the technology and terminology of IMM, and look at the prospects for growth. With that background established, I want to look at two areas of particular relevance to writers: firstly, the development of interactive fiction (known as 'hyperfiction'), a genre that calls for many of the skills of good scriptwriting and one which may attract writers accustomed to the interaction of words and images in a TV or film environment, and secondly, the negotiating and contractual issues thrown up by IMM, which writers need to be aware of in order to protect their rights.

Because there are so many novel points of view on IMM and it is still such an unexplored territory, I am going to select comments from a wide range of people who are now active in this field. I am dubious about the extent to which one can draw clear-cut conclusions, though I am sure there will be work for informed writers in the next few years. After that it might quieten down. Who knows? Let's hear from some of the experts.

Technology and Terminology

Some book publishers have moved fast to embrace IMM opportunities for recycling both text and artwork from existing non-fiction books. From encyclopaedias to language learning, cookery to *The Joy of Sex*, CD-I or CD-ROM discs have duplicated what exists in book form, but with the added attractions of sound, movement and easy search facilities.

The new technology has initially been determined in part by finding ways to improve the accessibility of large amounts of information (though so far the main application and driving force has been games). Writing about MILIA (the International Illustrated Book and New Media Market) in Cannes, Bruce Marshall quoted a speaker from one of the seminars:

12. Interactive Multimedia

As readers, we graze, browse or hunt. Grazing is reading whatever comes along – a novel bought at the airport for reading on the beach. Browsing is scanning information space, a newspaper, say, with no explicit target. Hunting is looking for specific information, as in a reference book. The new media best serve the hunters.[1]

We all know what is involved in the printed media, in movies, TV and video. IMM merges aspects of all these, including interactivity, to become a form of 'electronic publishing', the publishing of digital information that can be read by a computer.

The two most popular formats are compact discs (CDs) called CD-I and CD-ROM. CD-I (the 'I' stands for 'interactive') combines sound and vision, is moderately interactive, and is viewed on a TV screen. CD-ROM (the 'ROM' stands for 'read only memory') can hold vast amounts of data (text, sound and vision) that can be stored in a computer and retrieved with great precision and ease. All of this comes under the umbrella phrase 'electronic publishing', which utilizes digital technology. What precisely is digital technology? Geoffrey Adams gives this definition:

> ...digital technology...involves the conversion and storage (even the creation) of original works in "endless strings of noughts and ones". To a microprocessor it does not matter whether the work is initially conceived as words, music or visual images; they all take the same form once consigned to the computer, which may be a word processor, a CD player or – in future – a television set.
>
> There are...two principal characteristics of digital information: an infinite number of copies can be made without any loss of quality (and a work or performance has a potentially infinite lifespan) and it can be manipulated, altered, sampled, mixed, combined – with relative ease.[2]

The development costs of these discs are far higher than for even lavishly-illustrated printed books, but they cost far less than movies. Alan Buckingham, Managing Director of Dorling Kindersley Multimedia, in the early days one of the more active IMM publishers, says that the reason for the high development costs is simple: as an example, he cites one of their titles, *The Way Things Work*. This has 70,000 words, 1000 illustrations, 1500 pop-up windows, 300 animations and video clips, and an hour of audio. All of which require permissions fees. More recently DK have cut back on titles and staff.

The average cost of developing a CD-ROM is put at between £200,000 and £300,000.

> ...from signature of contract to finished disc takes eight to twelve months, and the gross return per unit (to publishers) is twenty to thirty percent... worked out on an average selling price of $50 which converts (illogically) to £49.95 over here. It means a publisher must sell between 30,000 and 50,000 units to break even.[3]

From the simple old-fashioned, text-and-illustration-only book, to the multiplicity of illustrations, sounds, moving images, text and interactivity, it is easy to see the novelty value. But in all probability the majority of CD-Is and CD-ROMs purchased in the first flush of acquisition of the hardware will be little used and quickly forgotten. In fact, the high sales figures for some CDs are the result of them being given away as inducements to purchase the hardware. This is called 'bundling'.

The Birth of a New Industry

At present, we are in the honeymoon phase of IMM, but there is little doubt that it is here to stay. The big prizes will no longer go to those who rush out book-based discs into the marketplace, but to those who come up with innovation. According to the Optical Publishing Association there were about 17 million machines equipped with CD-ROM drives or players by 1996. The OPA goes on the say that recent studies '…have shown how interactive learning is a more powerful experience than passive reading or playing…people retain only 10% of what they see, 20% of what they see and hear (the multimedia advantage) and 80% of what they hear, see and do (the interactive edge)'.[4]

Carol Robinson, an American who writes about the interface between publishing and the interactive world, suggests that the most effective CD-ROMs will probably be produced by creative teams who also have experience with learning theory. She quotes *Fortune* magazine as saying that

> Many of the businesses of the year 2000 will deliver not just services but experiences. According to this line of thought, the flagship companies of corporate America in the 21st century will not be Intel or Microsoft – but Walt Disney or Time Warner. Today, entertainment represents the second biggest US export after aerospace.[5]

Writers, producers and software developers will all have to come to terms with the new technology, but underneath lies something that is not that far removed from the way we watch movies. Furthermore, the underlying reasons for watching and 'playing' are similar. Frank Daniel describes the process of sitting in a darkened cinema, looking up at the screen, as 'looking at ourselves'. Apart from the enormous educational value, what has made cinema and television such a dominant force for entertainment throughout the world – the need for vicarious experiences – will also apply to IMM, in addition to its educational pleasures and benefits.

Peter Kindersley of Dorling Kindersley believes that 'interactive media meets the human need for freedom of exploration where we can search for patterns out of our existing world, and that it is this need which is the driving force behind new media, even more than the new technology.'[6]

While this revolution is taking place in our homes and in the high streets, the reach of cable and satellite is spreading and the promise of interactive TV is closer. Books and movies, which traditionally share our leisure time with conventional television, will undoubtedly face increased competition from IMM. Movies may receive some financial boost from video-on-demand through telephone cables and the TV set, and this may make up for the anticipated drop in rentals and sales of video cassettes.

The new delivery systems will probably increase the total usage of material created. But whether traditional publishers and film makers can get enough added value out of already existing material to compete with custom-created material, is uncertain.

What is certain is that IMM publishers have been scrambling to recycle whatever they can. Rex Weiner, writing in *Variety* describes what is taking place in Hollywood:

> Seeking to squeeze more bucks from film libraries, Hollywood studios are rummaging in the vaults for old movies on which to base new interactive entertainment. But not every classic may be suitable.
>
> Ted Hoff, head of Fox Interactive, says he is primarily tapping the film production pipeline and trying to get a jump on the 15- to 18- month CD-ROM development process by reading scripts when films are 'greenlighted'. What you don't want to do is just re-purpose a film. People want to explore with interactive. You have to give them stuff they've never seen before. Let them go behind the scenes. Give them a sense of discovery.[7]

Carol Robinson identifies the genres that publishers believe can be more easily converted into IMM. For anyone wanting to break in, finding a way of presenting one of these might be a starting point: travel, cookery books, gardening, how-to, reference, biography, diet, financial, science fiction, children's literature and adult games (where there is some learning involved).[8]

Fiction and IMM

But what about fiction? The applications for reference materials and games are clear; their adaptation to IMM uses conventions with which we are all reasonably familiar. Fiction, on the other hand, poses problems scriptwriters are not used to. Writers and developers of computer games will have an advantage here.

Can IMM provide opportunities for writers and script editors to use their experience and talent in a new medium? Can these opportunities match those currently presented by commercial novels, popular movies and TV drama?

Robinson, who surveyed leading book-publishing industry figures, says that many of them do not think that fiction lends itself to the new media. Or is it that they cannot see the way in for themselves? Peter Kindersley does not agree. He believes that 'even the novel will become interactive, and therefore more experiential. However much one exhorts scriptwriters to give audiences experiences – emotional, physiological and intellectual – it is clear that IMM offers something closer to an experience of the real world; much of the time one is reacting to one's environment, which one can also to some extent influence'.[9]

Robinson quotes Scott Walker, of Graywolf Press in the USA, who predicts that interactive fiction and multimedia narrative will be a new genre coming out of this technological revolution. Domenic Stansberry, editor of a fascinating new magazine *InterActivity*, reviewing the state of hyperfiction art, cites titles from multimedia producer Broderbund: 'These books resemble high-tech pop-up books. The reader can flip pages, listen to a text narration and activate animations by clicking on objects.'[10]

In adult hyperfiction, the reader can choose the feelings of the protagonist as well as what to do next. No one thinks that hyperfiction (a hybrid of film, fiction and computer games) will replace narrative movies or novels, but those who are most involved in multimedia think it has a future.

Phyllis Grann, the publisher of Putnam, is quoted as saying that they 'always respond to quality and readibility when making selections for book titles. And the same will be true for the new media.' Robert Abel, who produced IBM's Columbus agrees that 'the best multimedia will come down to who tells the best story'. Or, perhaps, who tells the best story in the best way.[11]

In an article in *InterActivity* entitled 'Searching for Interactive Fiction', Connor Cochran describes the current state of the art:

> Here in the last decade of the 20th century, another new artform is being born: Interactive Fiction. Just as with motion pictures, the bouncing baby of IF is a hybrid mix of cultural and technological breeding stocks: one part computer, one part video, one part digitized audio, plus a fuzzy blend of contradictory story-telling traditions appropriated from novels, films, role-playing games and television. Mother to this infant is the CD-ROM, while the would-be fathers are legion – a diverse batch of artists, techies, and businesspeople, unified in their urge to live up to (or at least profit from) the field's astronomical hype. So what is Interactive Fiction? Is it a brand new form of art that will eventually change the world as much as movies have? Is it just another techno-fad, the cyber equivalent of chrome tailfins and the hula hoop?

Cochran goes on to suggest that every creative medium

> ...has three sets of constraints: technical, cognitive and structural. And each one of these constraints has an impact on the three-way relationship that exists between artist, work of art and audience. The artist/artwork/audience equation is easier to visualize. Most people think of it as a line, thus:, artist – artwork – audience. But, it's...really a triangle, with each vortex of the triangle having its own unique relationship to the others.

Cochran examines seven programmes sold as Interactive Fiction. Only two fulfilled the particular criterion he felt was needed for it to really be interactive fiction. They were the only ones that offered him a sensation he has never had from a movie, a book or a play.

The two were the award-winning *Myst* and the children's programme *Grandmother and Me*. Why were they different? 'They invite you to explore, not to solve a puzzle or win a prize, but just for the sheer fun (kids' version) and intense focus (adult version) of trying to figure out how the world works and what your place in it is. The two programmes offer people...a chance to shift one vortex of the triangle and trade the passive role of audience member for the active role of artist.'

The two brothers who created *Myst* are interviewed at length in *InterActivity*. They describe how they developed the best-selling CD-ROM: 'One of our ideas when we first started out was we wanted to

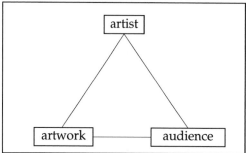

'... people think of it as a line ... But it's a triangle'

make the game very much based around your senses. So when a player played, they had to rely on their real senses. Their hearing and sight.'

Writers and IMM

Writers will clearly have to learn new skills (including teamwork) if they are to succeed at IMM. It is relatively easy to select sound bites from an existing text. That is really an editorial process. Creating from scratch will be far more difficult and potentially far more remunerative.

A detailed understanding of and feeling for the technology will undoubtedly help. The writer will not only have to do the traditional writer's job, but he or she will also have to be able to think analytically like an editor, visually like a film director, and aurally like a composer, to take advantage of all the opportunities offered.

Most script writers already feel that they do not have enough power in relation to the director or producer; according to American literary agent Richard Curtis, with the technological changes taking place in the industry, 'the role of the author must without question become subordinated to that of the producer'.[12]

Whether this will lead to an increase in writer-producers is too early to say; the fact that they became the dominant figures in long-running TV series in America suggests that the same thing will probably happen in IMM. Where the creative decisions must be carried through to the rest of the team, the people capable of taking those decisions have the chance to take control. Only financiers are in a better negotiating position. In Britain, at Dorling Kindersley, in-house teams make the scope for freelance or spec writers small:

It is important for authors to appreciate the degree to which these titles are made by teams with whom the author relates. The team is much bigger than an old-fashioned editorial team and the author's role in multimedia is to be one of the members. For authors who want to break into this field, the most important thing is to get thoroughly familiar with the technology and with the published titles. A prospective multimedia author would do well to talk to a programmer or software developer to see how an idea can use the power of the computer. It is as important to know what the limitations are as to know what marvels you can achieve.[13]

There are courses in writing for IMM. One of these is given by Paul Gray, a Hollywood script analyst and teacher.[14] He describes his course as follows:

Scripts for interactive feature films have to meet different demands than traditionally narrated films. Within the framework of a given plot the scripts must provide several possibilities for the active spectator to choose between different options. All of them must come back to the original storyline. Therefore interactive feature films based on a different dramaturgy and new narrative structures must take into account the spectator as an "acting film character". The traditional narrative conventions do not meet the necessities of interactive feature films, but the new medium hasn't established new ones yet.

How can one integrate the spectator as an acting character in the narration of the film? What happens to his wish for identification? What does the dramatic structure of interactive films look like? Is it possible to build up a dramatic tension in a way that is independent of the decision of the spectator/player? How many options should one offer? When should the options be offered? How can you create a set up that works for every option/choice of the spectator? Is a more-or-less linear "tree-structure" a solution for scriptwriters, or is it preferable to connect elements to non-linear networks?

Gray's lectures and workshops focus on questions like:
- the role and psychology of the player/spectator as a key character or as a developed role player
- the psychology of involvement
- the structuring of events, of plots and of the dramaturgy
- the changes in narrative structures and dramatic conventions
- actual examples

In other words we need to abandon (to some extent) what we take for granted when it comes both to the types of story that we try to tell in the IMM formats and also the way we choose to tell them. While we conceive ideas or write for IMM drama we must not lose sight of the fact that we will always have a co-writer, the player using a computer and the digitized computer program. Even more than ever before, the 'writers' must put the 'readers' first. Janet Winkler, Director of HarperCollins Advanced Media, believes that 'interactive media form the basis of entirely new businesses that are not simply by-products of our traditional businesses'. She also thinks that 'with interactive media there needs to be a new way of thinking about content and it will have to be more revolutionary than the process of adapting books for movies. With interactive media the user decides where to start and what to do. The product needs to be created in such a way that it can enhance the power of the user.'[15]

Protecting your rights

What can writers or creators do about protecting their rights in IMM? We need to distinguish between those who have created a work for another medium entirely, like a book or film, and those who are working directly into IMM. The latter need to take care, as at the early stages of development and exploitation it is difficult to predict the revenue from a new program. Producers will often emphasize the high development costs and risks (which there certainly are) at the expense of equitable remuneration. Undercapitalized independent film and TV producers do it all the time.

There are various ways the cake can be cut. The editor of *The Electronic Author* suggests that authors might get 5% of the 20-30% which publishers get of the gross. At approximately £40 the publisher could get £8-12 per unit, the author 40-60 pence per unit. If the disc sells 20,000 units, the 'royalty' to the author could be £8-12,000 (assuming that lower royalties are not paid for high discount bulk sales to wholesalers).

In the case of an innovative and original IMM work, there is a reasonable chance of negotiating a better deal with higher starting royalties and a sliding scale, so that once the publisher has recouped the development costs the author would get an increasing royalty percentage.

Serious problems stem from the fact that new uses, not properly covered by the original agreements, are being found for old material. The cost of underlying rights can be high. This can result in the new writer's share being whittled down. This may not be unfair, but the principle of sliding scales can still be usefully applied.

Rex Weiner writing in *Variety* describes the situation as '...a tangle of rights and residuals. Any full-motion video clip from any movie requires permissions and triggers residuals to actors, directors and screenwriters.

Hollywood's talent guilds are watching closely several pending lawsuits by writers against companies reusing their published work on CD-ROM. The outcome could affect how studios go about tapping vintage titles for interactive entertainment.'[16]

Another *Variety* story, headed 'Rights squabble begins over new media explosion' gives more details:

> A Federal Judge in Manhattan's Southern District Court is hearing a case brought by several freelance writers against the *New York Times, Newsday, Time* and a number of database companies. The writers argue, among other points, that they were not compensated for their work when it was redistributed on CD-ROM, databases, online services and other electronic media.
>
> According to Martin Garbus, a copyright lawyer in New York, many screenwriters and playwrights have not secured the rights to their work being used on media that didn't exist when the work was originally sold.
>
> The cases will help clarify how screenwriters, for example, are compensated for their scripts, which are increasingly finding their way onto database services.
>
> Increasingly, lawyers and agents are drawing up covenants that protect clients' rights in the electronic age. But just as five or ten years ago even the most sophisticated lawyers were unaware of how lucrative CD-ROMs or databases would be, few can guess what rights will need to be protected in the next century. To be sure, these issues are hardly new. At the dawn of television, when broadcasters aired old movies, actors were outraged that they were not compensated. Similarly as cable TV and home video developed as ancilliary markets, moviemakers squabbled over rights.
>
> The stakes could be huge. Under copyright law, an adverse ruling forces defendants to return any profits and possibly pay legal costs and damages.
>
> Regardless of the outcome of both cases, deal making for rights is going to become far more cumbersome as lawyers and agents maneuver along the infopike.[17]

On the question of how writers in the other media (books and scripts) should protect their work and their income when it is used in IMM, a great deal depends on their original contracts. A number of organizations in the UK are paying close attention to the whole area of revenue for writers from the media. They are therefore well-positioned to be effective in the field of IMM. These include the Authors' Licensing and Collecting Society (ALCS), the Society of Authors (SOA), the Writers' Guild (WG) and the Association of Authors' Agents (AAA).[18]

The ALCS publication *Authors in the Electronic Age* provides valuable ammunition for authors. Whether the contracts are for works in printed form, electronic form or a combination of the two (which can be 'parallel and equal'), they may be drawn up differently:

> ... authors and their agents will wish to secure the integrity of the text, the right to equitable remuneration, credit in electronic form and a measure of control over the forms of republication. Most authors are likely to deal with folio (print) publishers among whom there is a growing tendency to introduce policies demanding electronic rights whether they have any intention of exploiting them or not. Publishers should be able to demonstrate how they propose to develop rights before being granted them.
>
> The author's optimum (negotiating) position is to avoid passing blanket control of all electronic rights to publishers because it is vital to define exactly what rights are being negotiated in any individual case. It is not appropriate to lump electronic rights under a general Subsidiary Rights Clause, since, in many cases, they may become equal rights (equal in stature to the original book rights) or may even overtake volume sales.
>
> At the same time there is a case for including the right to electronic exploitation where the text will be a verbatim, unabridged and unadapted version of the printed work but not where the text is combined with other media.[19]

The Society of Authors advises its members to negotiate the following in order of preference:

1   Retain all electronic rights (along with other rights not specified in the contract); failing which,
2   Grant the publisher first refusal on particular and specified electronic rights with each use being subject to the author's consent and on terms to be agreed; failing which,
3   Grant specified electronic rights to the publisher subject to the following:
   a) If electronic publishing is to be by the original publisher, the advance, royalties, electronic publishing and other terms must be agreed before production and release for publication, with the publisher meeting any additional cost of material such as music, visuals, etc.;
   b) If the publisher wishes to sub-license any electronic rights, the terms for each licence (especially its duration) should be subject to the author's approval and the gross receipts income divided at least 80:20 in the author's favour;
   c) All enquiries received by the publishers concerning electronic rights should be referred to the author for due consideration and approval;
   d) Electronic rights should revert to the author if not exploited within X years of first publication;
   e) All rights under the contract should revert to the author in the normal way when the work is out of print even if an electronic version is still available (eg in a database);
   f) The author's work should not be altered in any way (except in format) and the publisher should agree to include such a condition in any sub-licence.

The licence term should be of limited duration, say three to five years from release, to enable authors to renegotiate on successful titles or to avoid being locked into an unsucessful technology.[20]

Many writers will perhaps feel daunted at having to insist on these terms in the face of a large corporation offering them the chance of a lifetime to see their work realised in IMM. Even if the writer really needs the money, it is very advisable to negotiate as far as is possible, which is usually further than writers think possible at the start of the negotiation.

We will look in more detail at tactics in the chapter on negotiating, but it bears repeating that there is almost always room for improvement, that the other side may be as nervous as you are and that they, too, may be bluffing. So why give away your work for less than it is worth in the marketplace? And anyway the points mentioned above by the Society of Authors are perfectly reasonable.

The Association of Authors' Agents (AAA) argues that without clear answers to these questions it is impossible to assess what electronic rights are worth – another reason why blanket clauses disposing of all electronic rights are not appropriate.

The AAA suggests that all negotiations should take account of essentials that can be expressed in the following questions:

1 What languages will the work be published in?
2 In what territories will it be published?
3 What is the length of licence (see above)?
4 Is there a minimum sales target?
5 What is the retail price and will payment be on a royalty basis? (Payment calculated on price received – or the wholesale price – can dramatically reduce an author's royalties.)
6 Will the text be an unaltered version of the original (and if not will abridgements be subject to the author's approval)?
7 If substantial changes are made so that the result becomes a 'derivative work' who will own the derivative version?
8 What safeguards (if any) will the product offer to render the text unalterable by the user?
9 What is the liability where text can be edited by the user and then copied on?
10 What percentage of the whole project does the text represent?
11 Precisely what platform is being requested? (Platforms can be databases, CD-I, CD-ROM etc.)
12 What is the approval mechanism for transferring to another platform?

ALCS takes issue with the argument from publishers that

> they can act as the author's agent in steering through the confusing multiplicity (of platforms). This would hold good if it were not for the fact that publishers are increasingly forming joint ventures with hardware and software houses who are locked into particular technologies. This may mean that an opportunity for a different technology is lost to the author.
>
> In open systems, such as databases, ALCS makes the important point that there is 'at present, no readily available protection against duplication of material (electronically or on paper) once it has been distributed to the user.

At a conference in Harvard on the implications of new technology for copyright, the US Registrar of Copyrights, Ralph Oman, noted that '...every plugged-in consumer is a potential author, a potential publisher and a potential infringer – all at once or at different times. Everyone will have the capacity to manufacture copies of works of perfect quality...Vast libraries of information, today encapsulated in books, music, films, etc, will be available "on-line" and virtually on demand anywhere in the world.'[21]

Geoffrey Adams, reporting from the same Harvard conference, noted some progress:

> Solutions have been found over time to the problems presented to the copyright system by technological advances...(and)...some of the new forms of control already developed: levies on blank media (tapes) and hardware; collective licensing arrangements for photocopying; the introduction of a rental right (at least for sound recordings and computer software).
>
> Moral rights will have to be re-assessed in the light of the relative ease with which digital information can be adapted, translated, mutilated and parodied. Technology may also be harnessed to support the administration of copyright. As one speaker pointed out, techniques already exist to enable the software that searches out and retrieves material to check whether the user has a valid licence to do what he wants to. "Smart cards" are available to assist authorisation and to permit the automation of royalty payments...

One of the more contentious issues in negotiating rights sales from books to film producers and studios is the producer's blanket assertion that IMM rights must be included in the purchase of the other audiovisual rights required for the financing of a film. Studios say that acquisition of these multimedia rights is essential and is a deal-breaker. But in reality there are relatively few movies that will make it into CD-ROM. In most cases, when a blanket negotiating tactic is used one of the reasons behind its use is 'CYA', otherwise known as 'cover your ass'.

Employees of large companies, especially if they are lawyers, worry about their jobs. They do not want to lose them. So any weakness on their part in a negotiation – whether the point being negotiated is important, or justified – must be avoided. Their bosses do not need to be reasonable or fair in shouting at them, so it is usually easier to dig their heels in and make you look like you are the one who is being unreasonable.

For writers or software developers creating original material specifically for IMM, many of the negotiating and contractual points are similar to those in conventional book, film or TV contracts. The same negotiating principles apply. An advance should more than cover the realistic cost to you of the time/work required for you to deliver; you should receive a royalty so that if the sales are exceptional you will not lose out; the royalty should be on a sliding scale, and so on.

Protecting yourself

If you are forced to grant IMM rights to your book or script, then the contract should, as recommended by the AAA and SOA, specify how and when you get paid, for how long and when the rights come back to you, and there should be a clause imposing upon the acquirer of those rights the obligation to exploit them, preferably by an agreed date. If they are not exploited by that date they should automatically revert to you.

12. Interactive Multimedia

If you are able to retain the rights, you might have to be prepared to pay the publishers or production company a share of any revenue you get from exploiting those rights. They could argue that the film or book, for example, will have been instrumental to some extent in creating demand for the IMM rights.

Many writers are being paid salaries as part of teams. Others are being paid flat fees for specific editorial work on an IMM package. The 'buyout' principle usually applies to the fees – but you should get paid a reasonable amount (calculated on the basis of time and effort and expertise) and try to get 100% on top of that as the buyout figure.

Because the future is still so unclear, all parties to any negotiation will try to keep or acquire as much as possible. Precedents are only gradually becoming established, and they will make it easier to negotiate new rights. Watch for news of legal settlements, as they will establish new patterns of behaviour. Even agents and lawyers are having a difficult time over some of the negotiations for IMM rights, so if you are involved in IMM it is worth preparing very thoroughly for any negotiation.

Other writers and creative people will often share experiences and deal information if you don't have an agent or lawyer and if you are unsure about the norms for a deal.

Interactive multimedia, the brave new frontier that we are rushing into with little knowledge of what it will bring, is exactly the kind of arena in which collective strength will benefit writers.

1   *The Bookseller*, 25 February 1994.
2   *ALCS News*, July 1993, article by Geoffrey Adams, copyright consultant to ALCS.
3   Jane Dormer, editor of *The Electronic Author*, published by The Society of Authors, Winter 1994.
4   *Newsweek*, 31 May 1993.
5   Carol Robinson in *Publishers Weekly*, 6 Septmber 1993.
6   ibid.
7   *Variety*, 9-15 January 1995.
8   Carol Robinson, ibid.
9   ibid.
10 *InterActivity*, 411 Borel Avenue, San Mateo, CA 94402-3516, USA. The magazine is of particular interest to writers, publishers and producers concerned with the creative aspects of IMM.
11 Carol Robinson, ibid.
12 ibid.
13 *The Electronic Author*, Winter 1994.
14 Paul Gray, Atelier Pictures, 10420 San Marcos Road, Atascadero, CA 93422, USA, tel 805 466 4660, fax 805 466 4729.
15 Carol Robinson, ibid.
16 *Variety*, 9-15 January 1995.
17 Jan Green, *Variety*, 2-8 January 1995.
18 These organizations provide excellent information, a good reason for becoming a member. See Chapter 19 for more details on writers' associations.
19 *Authors in the Electronic Age*, June 1994.
20 ibid.
21 *ALCS News*, July 1993; Harvard University, under the auspices of the World Intellectual Property Organization, March-April 1993.

13 Agents

How to get, use, fire or do without one

Agents are sometimes perceived in a derogatory way. The people we sell to think that we charge too much, some clients believe that we don't find them enough work, and probably that we also charge them too much. Being in the middle has its inevitable downside. And the days are long because we can't read during office hours. Over eighty hours a week is quite a common working week for an agent. Yet most of the agents I know really enjoy their work. There are many uplifting moments and there is no other job I would rather do. We learn not to be personally affected by the rejections, even if they are for work about which we care passionately. We enjoy the successes, large and small. And most clients at most agencies seem satisfied much of the time.

Why have an agent

The most obvious answer is that a good agent, like a good lawyer or accountant, will save or earn you more money than they will cost you. So instead of worrying about all the commission you are paying, think about the extra earnings you will have at the end of each year. This is an idealized picture, but if you write well and handle your side of the relationship with your agent well, it is likely to come true.

Most writers know there is a lot of competition to get produced or published. A good agent should be able to cut through the competition to get the script or book into the hands of a buyer. And not just any buyer but the right buyer, who will then pay adequately before producing or publishing it well.

Good agents are regularly sought out by producers and publishers, who want to know what writers they represent and what new material is available. So an immediate network can be accessed by a writer who joins a good agency.

Given the number of scripts and manuscripts in circulation, there are advantages for a writer in having an agent. But whether a writer has an agent or not, it is important that they know how the job of an agent is done. Some writers have full-time jobs and do not have the time to act for themselves; many writers do not like the cut-and-thrust of negotiating, or the legalese of contracts. For them it can be a relief to have an agent.

Agents are not therapists, although some clients treat them like that. The good agent-client relationship can encompass everything from nanny, loans, marital advice, soul-searching, eating and drinking, holidays, as well as editorial and business advice.

Agents need to be realistic, to counter the healthy optimism of clients who sometimes think that what they have written is wonderful. They also need to be able to enthuse about the good work done by clients who have little confidence in themselves. So agents sometimes bring the cold light of reality to bear on a piece of writing. An agent who is good at his or her job will not let their clients 'die of encouragement'.

13. Agents

Some writers approach agents because production companies refuse to consider work submitted directly. The production companies do this partly to avoid the danger of plagiarism suits. It also means they don't have to plough through enormous quantities of totally unsuitable material. If you get a letter from a production company which says that they will only look at your material if it is submitted by an agent, it does not mean they want to look at it. There is a presumption, therefore, that if something is submitted by an agent it has at least been read, that the agent thinks it might be good enough and also that it could be suitable for the producer in question.

Just because your agent loves your work, it does not make it saleable. We do not always sell everything we like (or necessarily like everything we sell, although usually we like the writer). Don't make the elementary mistake of thinking, as so many writers do, that once they have an agent they can get on with the writing and all the business, legal, tax and other aspects of their career will be fine. If that were true, writers would never leave their agents and agents would never fire their clients. And both do it reasonably often. You cannot get the breadth of experience on contracts and deals, or the range and size of network, if you only sell your own material.

I may be biased, but I think that agents can make a significant difference to their clients' careers. Most British and American writers who are reasonably successful – book and script writers – choose to have agents. On the Continent, writers' agents are a relatively new phenomenon (except for the representation of stage plays).

Having an agent doesn't automatically bring success, and doesn't necessarily mean you write better. It can help you in those areas if you have a good agent. But it depends on your work and your attitude. The complaint that is often heard in writers' groups is that you can't get an agent when you most need one, when you are starting, when you don't know what to write, or who your audience is, or what you should get paid.

Apart from a number of short courses and some university degree courses, there are relatively few places to learn to be a scriptwriter in Britain. We don't have the industry-oriented higher-educational opportunities for creative writing that they do in the States. So writers can get some basic training from, amongst others, working with agents.

Agents are business people too!

It should be remembered, however, that agents run businesses. They have to make a profit from the 10-15% of the income earned by their clients. All their overheads have to come out of the commission before there can be a profit. Agents may take a long-term view, but their interest is in prospering as a business, which means investing time and money when they believe that they (through their clients) will make money.

One of the ways agents have of evaluating success is whether they make a sale. Agents usually look at scripts or manuscripts with that in mind. It may not matter whether the writing in question is highly original and complex, or a straightforward episode of a long-running series. Advancing the client's career, selling what they have written, collecting the money and deducting the commission due are the core of the agent's functions.

I don't know what our submission-to-sale ratio is, but the majority of script submissions made by all agents fail. Every agent has stories about selling a script or a book on the twentieth or even thirtieth submission. The average number of submissions per script or novel is probably far less than that. If it doesn't get sold reasonably quickly, it's put on the shelf, unless the agent really loves it.

Agents who make submissions which get negative reactions tend to grin and bear it and get on with the next submission. There is no point in letting it become personal, or taking each rejection badly. Even if you know you have offered the work to the right person but they can't see the merit in it, or they want to buy it but can't afford it at that time, you have to move on.

Something that hasn't found a buyer may, of course, still sell. Agents are usually in a better position than writers working on their own to identify potential new buyers. The problem arises when you have tried all the likely outlets but haven't found a buyer. Writers like to think that their agent will continue to go on submitting. The time comes, though, when an agent can't find any serious players who have not seen the script. How far down the list of minor players the agent goes depends on how keen the agent is on the piece of work and on the writer.

Sometimes, if a script is getting a poor reception, an agent may stop submitting it in order to preserve the writer's standing with other companies. Each submission costs an agency money. The real cost, taking into account the telephone calls, the dictation and typing of the submission letter, the time spent photocopying, packing and the cost of postage, as well as a portion of the overheads of the agency, can be £50 to £100 per submission. Remember, a lawyer may charge £150-250 per hour. An experienced agent's time may be calculated at a slightly lower figure, but twenty minutes checking material or a contract, dictating a letter, reading and signing it, could easily cost an agency £50-100.

Eventually, if a script or manuscript gets no bites at all – even if it gets close – an agent will stop submitting it. If the writer doesn't agree with this then the writer and agent should talk about it. If they fundamentally disagree, then perhaps the writer should find a new agent. However, it would usually be better for the two of them to work together to develop something else that may have a better chance and then later, if the circumstances change, try to sell the previous piece of work. All that needs to happen is for some of the writer's work to start selling.

Further advantages

One area in which an agent ought to be of immediate benefit to a client is through the agent's extensive network of contacts, both with potential buyers and with the industry in general. For example our agency is a member of:

- Association of Authors' Agents
- The Screenwriters' Workshop
- The New Producers' Alliance
- The Romantic Novelists' Association
- Royal Television Society
- Society of Authors
- Society of Bookmen
- Women in Publishing
- Writers' Guild

13. Agents

My partner, Carole Blake, is an ex-President of the Association of Authors' Agents. In addition, we sit or have sat on various book, film and television committees and juries in the UK and on the Continent and are therefore well placed to gain further information about the industry which can be used to the benefit of our clients. Writers should be active members of the relevant organisations and associations that exist for writers.

Apart from being able to find a buyer, and hopefully be able to improve on an offer for a script or novel, an agent should be able to help the client retain and exploit certain rights in the material. If it is a book deal, then translation rights, serial rights and film rights will seldom form part of the package sold or licenced to the domestic publisher.

If it is a script sale to a broadcaster, the agent might be better placed to limit their rights or licence, but retain publication or novelization rights. Any good agent should be in a position to exploit these 'retained rights' on behalf of the client. Merchandising rights are more commonly controlled jointly by the production company on behalf of the writer and themselves. Try to get at least 70% of the revenue, which is difficult; don't accept less than 50%. There is usually a commission deducted before the split because production companies often use specialised mechandising agents.

Sales made from rights retained in publishing deals can create new 'profit centres' for the client, which add to the cash flow, because these monies are not set against the advance payments made in the initial deal. Should the publisher have acquired all rights worldwide, then subsequent sales revenue will go to the publisher first to pay off the initial payment or advance, rather than flowing through direct to the writer.

Once the advance has been earned, then the writer's share will be due to the writer, but will not be paid until the accounting dates in the contract, which are usually once a year (but try to insist on twice a year for the first three years).

Agents can also establish the real 'market' price for a hot property by auctioning it. In the book world this is fairly common, and there are book auctions going on in London, New York, Germany and many other countries all the time. Auctions do not always result in the size of deal hoped for by the seller. But, if properly run, they can prove invaluable to writer and agent as a way of establishing the highest price the market will pay.

There are occasions when the advance paid is greater than the book is likely to earn. Usually the publisher is paying a premium to get that particular author into his or her stable, hoping that over several books the backlist sales will result in substantial profits. Even if an advance is not earned out, a book can be profitable for a publisher.

In the film and television world auctions are unusual. Shane Black and Joe Eszterhas have auctioned spec scripts. This is probably beginning of a trend in higher payments to the most bankable scriptwriters, who are willing to write spec scripts. It will not make much difference to the average writer, unless the spec script is obviously commercial and is in the hands of a good agent who can play buyers off against each other.

I believe that it is desirable and advantageous for a serious and professional writer to use an agent. As a team the sum is greater than the parts.

How to get an agent

Writers attract agents by what they have written not, usually, by who they are. Sometimes a well-known person will be taken on by an agent because their name alone means that producers or publishers will see potential. But it is the quality of the writing that is most important. Here are some basic points to bear in mind when getting or changing an agent:

1   How do you decide which agent to chose? If you cannot get a recommendation, try identifying the writers whose work you most like and contact their agents. This is, if nothing else, an indication of your investigative abilities and can also be a little flattering to the agent. But your work should be of a similar quality to the writers you admire.

    If you read a novel you like, ring the publisher, ask if the writer has an agent, then contact the agent. The writer may have no agent, in which case the publisher will probably control the rights on behalf of the writer. In the publisher's catalogue an indication is usually given as to who controls the rights. If it not the publisher then usually an agent's name will be given. You can also look at the acknowledgements – writers sometimes thank their agents. You may need to be able to recognise names, because the acknowledgements do not always specify that one of the thanked people is the agent.

    If the work is a TV play or episode then ring the broadcasting company or independent producer, who should be able to tell you.

    In the UK the *Writers' & Artists' Yearbook* or Cassells' *Directory of Publishing* list most of the agents. You can also see which agents are members of the Association of Authors' Agents. In the *Writers' & Artists' Yearbook*, for example, there is a brief paragraph on their areas of interest. Our entry reads:

    Blake Friedmann Literary, TV & Film Agency Ltd (1977), 122 Arlington Road, London NW1 7HP tel 0207 284 0408 fax 0207 284 0442

    e-mail julian@blakefriedmann.co.uk. Directors: Carole Blake, Julian Friedmann, Barbara Jones, Beverley Jones, Conrad Williams.

    Full-length MSS. Fiction: thrillers and contemporary and historical women's novels and literary fiction; non-fiction: investigative books, biography, travel; no poetry or plays (home 15%, overseas 20%). Specialise in film and television rights; place journalism and short stories for existing clients only. Represented world-wide. Preliminary letter, synopsis and first two chapters preferred. No reading fee.

From this you can also discover the commission rates and whether an agent charges a reading fee. Writers should *never* pay a reading fee to an agency. There are some editorial consultants who, for a fee, will provide an analysis of the project and recommendations for improving it, but an agency considering material for representation should not charge to read it.

    What a directory entry does not tell you is if that agency is looking for clients or whether their list is full. Even if it is full they may still take on a well-established writer or an inexperienced writer whom they think is brilliant. But most established agencies take on relatively few new clients in any one year.

2   It is advisable to get a recommendation to an agent. If you know any writers, ask what they think of their agents and whether their agents are taking on new clients. If you don't know any other writers then join a writers' group.

It does help if you can write to the agent and say X or Y recommended me to write to you about representation. But make sure that X or Y is really known to the agent!

3   Personally I think you should not start by trying to talk to the agent on the phone. 'Cold calls' are not the best opener, although some agents will take them. Phone calls are efficient under certain circumstances. This is not one of them. I will not talk to a prospective client unless I can read something first (the exception is if they already have an established writing career). From a phone call I suppose I might be able to tell the caller that the subject they have chosen didn't suit or interest me or wouldn't (in my opinion) work in the marketplace. A letter takes a minute to read, but a polite phone conversation can take ten or fifteen minutes. By talking to me they will not be taken more seriously. So send something in to be read even if it is just your CV and a writing sample. The same is probably true of approaching producers. It is writing, not telephone technique, that counts at this point in the relationship. Because we receive over a hundred applications from writers a week it is obvious that we could not take cold calls from all these people. Apart from anything else, we need to be free to take calls from producers or publishers who are looking for writers.

4   It is essential to be able to tell the agent or producer succinctly in your covering letter the type of story you are writing or have written. If it is not right for the agent, then you save both of you time and money. If you can summarize well, you've already provided the selling 'handle' and this may attract the agent.

There is a school of thought which recommends against sending in a script or treatment first. If your introductory letter is short and enticing, with a couple of good lines about the project, you should get a request from the agency asking to see the material.

This may create a sense of obligation in the agent to consider the material more carefully than if he or she had not requested it. I think that this is too tenuous. Life is too short. I don't think it is more courteous to ask if the agent wants to see the material. Just don't bury them in it. Agents usually try to read submissions as quickly as they can. Their first reading priority should be to their existing clients, especially with material that has been commissioned or purchased. Only then should they read material from prospective clients.

There have been occasions when we have loved the quality of the writing in the script or chapter, but not the idea or story. If all we had read was the treatment or synopsis we would have rejected the material. We usually read both, though if we don't like the writing in the chapter or the script we will not read to the end.

In the covering letter you can also explain why you have written what you are submitting, whether you have written and been produced or published before and what your career aspirations are. But don't oversell yourself or you will be judged more harshly when the agent comes to read your submission.

You should also tell the agent how long the script or manuscript is (for a script the length is usually only given in pages; for a manuscript pages and word count should both be given). State whether you have been produced or published before, and whether the material submitted to the agent has been submitted to other agents/producers/publishers. Some agents won't read material if it is with other agents at the same time.

5   Always send a stamped, addressed envelope. Our agency, along with many others, does not return unsolicited material unless there is a SAE. We receive over six thousand unsolicited submissions a year, which is why we think that it is reasonable to request return postage.

6   Do not send an entire novel, even if you have written it. If it is a script for a feature film or a 30- or 60-minute episode, then send the whole script. And always include a short synopsis or treatment. We receive badly presented material on a regular basis, so you should be aware of the following:
a) The material must be typed and on one side of the paper only.
b) Use double-line spacing with good margins on all four sides.
c) Type dialogue and directions correctly: this is particularly important for film and TV scripts (each has a different layout which can be checked in most books on screenwriting).
d) Be consistent in spelling, headings, paragraph indentation, capitals, etc.
e) Read through when finished for spelling and typing mistakes. Show that you care about your work. It really does create a better impression.
f) Don't bind, punch, staple or paperclip anything. But do number the pages. It's a recurring nightmare for some agents and editors that they will be reading a script or manuscript which will drop on the floor (or in the bath!). Then they discover that the pages aren't numbered. In the US it is obligatory to punch three holes and use stationery pins.
g) Make sure your name, address and telephone/fax number are featured prominently on the title page. Include an email address if you have one.
h) By all means put a copyright line, followed by your name and the year on the title page, but do not put it on every page.

7   Always include a short synopsis or treatment. This should be more than one paragraph but not more than, say, three pages. At this stage, a prospective agent needs to know a little about the subject, characters, period and locations, but do not bore the agent with unnecessary detail. In fact, showing that you can be to the point makes you more attractive. A full treatment can be too long at this stage.
     I prefer not to read a script or manuscript until I have read a short synopsis. This helps me assess the type or genre of the work and whether it is of interest to the agency. From it and from my reading of the opening scenes or chapters, I can also assess whether the writer has achieved what he or she set out to achieve.

8   Do not send random pages from the script or ms. (This does happen, really!) A submission of, for example, pages 1, 5, 27, 93, 176 and 206 does not show a writer in the best light, and do not send chapter one or scene one and then the final chapter or scene. The first consecutive 20-30 pages will give an experienced reader an idea of your writing style and ability.

9   Always include a short CV, giving the agent some idea of your background. This can influence the decision to see the script or novel. It might help if you have experience

which is relevant to either the subject of your writing or that you have professional writing experience, even if in a different field.

10 Assume that any good agent is busy. It can take from two weeks to two months for something to get read. In our agency we always read our existing clients' material first. We have about 160 clients, most of whom are working most of the time. This means that there is always material from them arriving to be read.

After that has been done we read the material from prospective clients. Usually this is read in the order in which it comes in. We try to be as quick as we can, but there are times when a succession of business trips (and even holidays) may mean that there is little time to read. We do not use outside readers, because we believe that no one else can tell us if we like the way someone writes.

Therefore, give your submission at least four weeks before sending a polite reminder. And if you must telephone, do not insist on speaking to the agent. If I get a call from someone chasing me for a response to unsolicited material, all I can do is point out that over the previous four weeks there were over five hundred submissions to the agency. Neither I nor my colleagues keep the details of these in our heads, so we have to get back to the caller. By all means leave a message, but write rather than ring. We are aware that it must be frustrating to have to wait.

11 You can create chance meetings with agents by networking. If you go to seminars and workshops, lectures and trade fairs, you will meet agents. Usually, they are reasonably happy to have a brief conversation about whether they are considering new clients.

Don't leap into a long pitch. Nothing puts an agent off like a writer who muscles in on a conversation the agent is having, in order to offer them a script or manuscript. It may be a masterpiece, but you are unlikely to endear yourself to this agent.

Remember also that if an agent is at a trade fair they are working for existing clients. Time you take up detracts from that. Have a one-page description of your project and career to hand over. Make sure your name and address/phone number are on the sheet of paper (you would be surprised how often they are not).

Once you have the interest of an agent, you should meet him or her. It is important to find out how well you get on with each other. Prepare for the meeting. Think through your career objectives, read a few books about the business, read the trade magazines. Make up an agenda so you don't forget anything. Usually an agent will be happy to talk through a career strategy with a new client. It is, after all, also in the agent's interests to do this.

Listen to the advice given. You presumably listen to advice from your accountant or dentist. If you do not agree with it, say so, but do not dismiss it out of hand: 'I'm not sure I agree, but I will think about it carefully'. Or 'That's interesting. I will think it over'.

If an agent suggests revisions, remember that they will have spent their own time and money reading your work. An agent will only suggest those revisions if they think the script or manuscript will benefit. The revisions will also have been suggested with knowledge of the industry and the marketplace, not simply with the intention of interfering with your work.

If you treat an initial meeting with an agent as an opportunity for gathering information, you will benefit, even if you don't end up by working with that agent. You might gain information on other areas you could try writing in, such as series and serials (do you watch enough of them?). Or whether you should try a novel as well as scripts.

In America all bona fide agents are registered with the Writers' Guild who can provide a list of them. The Guild in America has much greater negotiating power than the European guilds or associations, largely because American writers are far more politicized than those in Europe.

From the above you should be able to identify an appropriate agent, submit some material and hope that not only does your writing attract their interest but that they have room for a client like yourself. Don't be surprised if the successful agencies are full.

How to use an agent

It is important for writers to understand why an agent suggests certain courses of action rather than others. If the writer either doesn't understand, or disagrees with his or her agent, they should discuss it. Do not accept advice blindly.

Agents have certain fiduciary and legal obligations to clients. Some knowledge of this is helpful, particularly if there is cause for disagreement. I will look at this later in the chapter when dealing with how to fire your agent.

Sometimes writers have agendas that they haven't discussed with their agents. This may be because the writer does not really know why he or she is writing or what their priorities should be. If a client says, 'I need as much cash as fast as possible', then the agent can try to achieve that (even though it could lead to a lousy deal). In general, to maximize the financial return, you may need to be prepared for it to take longer. This is obviously also true if you are selling your own work.

The main functions of an agent are to find work and money for the clients, to sell what the clients have written speculatively or are in the process of writing, to do the best deal they can and to ensure that the producer or publisher (and the client) fulfils their obligations under the contract signed as a result of the sale. It does not matter whether the agent found the buyer, or the buyer found the writer or the piece of work. Agents do not get their commission only because they find the buyer. If a writer wants to pay less commission because he or she has found the buyer, then such a writer ought to be prepared to pay some of the costs incurred in the submissions that do not result in a sale.

What agents lose on the submissions that don't attract deals, they have to make up on the sales. Agents should represent 'writers' not scripts or manuscripts. The career of the client should be uppermost in the agent's mind, not just any quick deal to keep the client happy today. The work of an agent therefore encompasses far more than doing deals. In our agency we spend a great deal of time on creative editorial work. This is partly because we enjoy it, but mainly because we recognise that it makes money for our clients and therefore for ourselves. At the end of the day, whatever the writer's motivations are for writing (and agents may share some of the more personal and subjective ones) most agents run businesses in order to make money.

13. Agents

You should remember that to use your agent properly you need to keep him or her well-briefed. This means the agent should hear from the writer, not from the producer or publisher, when things are going wrong, or if deadlines will not be met.

You should not make the mistake of letting the producer or publisher get between you and your agent. The agent and writer should work as a team, and there is room for healthy disagreement on both creative and business matters between them. Disagreement can be constructive and your agent will be on your side far more often than on your producer's or publisher's side. When it is the latter, there is probably a good reason for it, and you should consider your agent's advice carefully. But you are the principal, so it is up to you whether or not to accept advice or a deal.

It is very helpful when pitching a writer to a producer for an agent to be able to say that a client is working on something that is going into production or that a client is writing a script for a producer of some stature. We might therefore sometimes encourage a client to take a deal that may not be as good as they or we would like, precisely because it will open up other avenues. This is always discussed.

That is the way the business actually works. Anyone who tells you differently is not telling the whole truth. Just pushing material around is a fairly thankless task. It helps when a writer gets a good reputation and producers ring up and ask to see his or her work. That is why I emphasise so strongly the importance of building your reputation, and developing your knowledge of the industry. It leads to what agents call 'repeat business', which is more profitable. It pays off and is often the way in which less talented writers get more work than talented writers. Strategy and tactics should always be discussed between agent and client. We never mind spending time explaining why we think the client should do something, or why we are following a particular route with their work.

They may disagree with us. If we think that their decision will be damaging to their career and reputation, we may choose not to go on working with them. After all, we also have careers and reputations to worry about. But if a good agent is discouraging about a particular storyline, or about the way it has been written, it may mean that it is not good enough yet (remember that your agent probably sees more material than you do).

Be wary of listening only to what you want to hear. Seek criticism; always try to improve on your work, and you will have the right frame of mind for attracting an agent, if you also write well enough...

When an agented writer is approached directly by a producer, script editor or publisher, the writer should report back to the agent, who may have background knowledge of that person of which the writer is unaware. And always tell the person that you are represented by an agent. Smaller and newer producers seldom have much money. They should know that if an agent draws up a contract it will cost the agent money. So why would an agent want to do a deal with little or no money involved? They don't. It is as simple as that. But agents do it because they and their clients mutually agree that it is a risk worth taking and an investment worth making.

Writers should be aware of the difference between writing original ideas and writing a script based on a producer's idea or treatment. The former is your copyright; the latter isn't. Your script itself will be your copyright (until sold), but if the underlying idea is not yours then you cannot exploit your script without either acquiring the underlying rights or getting permission from whoever holds those rights.

There is rarely any value in an idea. Real value comes with the execution of an idea. In general, writers and producers should pay more attention to and put a greater value on the development of the idea than they do.

In the working relationship with an agent, you should establish a price for your work and your time. If you don't value what you do, why should anyone else do so? If a producer asks you out of the blue what you will charge for writing something, you should either have a good idea or graciously ask the producer to talk to your agent about it. It is perfectly acceptable for a writer to say that he or she never discusses money.

However good your relationship with your agent is, be considerate of his or her time. If you need information from the agency, think about who else there is on the staff who can give it to you more easily. I don't appreciate authors who ring me to ask for a copy of their last royalty statement. The person to approach is the agency's finance director, who takes care of that side of the business. My job is to try to make money, if not for that writer, then for another one. A successful agency generally benefits all of its clients. We tell all new clients who is responsible for what in the agency. All members of staff are listed in the author/agency letter we sign with our clients.

Show an interest in your agency. It is like any other professional relationship. It needs nurturing, which means not being too egotistical. You should, of course, receive the same consideration in return from your agent, but the length of time it takes an agent to return a client's call does not indicate how seriously the agent takes the client.

One final thought about how to use agents: after deals are concluded and signed, some agents don't send signed copies of their clients' deal contracts to them. You should always keep a copy for your own files, in case anything happens to you. This may be the only way your accountant can sort out your taxes (as long as you also keep all royalty statements and other documentation). It is also the only way in which you will be able to brief your new agent, should you want to change agents, or enable your Estate to find out what your assets are if you drop dead.

Be your own agent

Writers are sometimes too anxious about getting agents. Many of the situations writers find themselves in can be dealt with without an agent, especially if the writer has made adequate preparations. For example, it is not uncommon for a producer to attempt to get a writer to do some work on a treatment or script for little or no upfront money. This happens particularly often when the idea originates with the producer.

Unless you know what the acceptable rates of pay are for treatments or scripts, or what sums of money would be appropriate for the advance on a novel, how will you be able to calculate your fee or advance? Many new writers are so grateful that someone is interested in them that they undercharge.

Other writers ask for unreasonable figures. Either way, if you handle it badly you may lose out. The writer needs to know something about the business, and should also be prepared to manipulate the producer. So if a producer shows interest in something you have written, don't fall over yourself with gratitude. Be cool. Otherwise there is a danger that you may 'give the script away'. You should quietly mention that you expect no less than the Writers' Guild minimums. If you have received the minimums before then try to 'up the ante', perhaps by 10% or even 20%, if you are not very experienced. If the producer says he or she can't afford to pay above the Guild minimums, then, as a favour to the producer, offer to do it at that rate, as long as you are paid a back-end bonus. This is usually paid on the first day of principal photography (this is a quasi-legal term, sometimes abbreviated as '1st dpp', describing the start of filming or taping).

Be prepared to walk away from a deal, or at least bluff. That often gets a few extra percentage points. If you hold out for a higher figure and the producer won't agree, then gracefully change your mind. It is easier than you might think. Perhaps not the first time, but having done it once or twice it doesn't seem so forbidding. Insisting on a higher figure than you have been offered may seem nerve-wracking at first. The other side may be just as intransigent. Use a bit of brinkmanship and some of the time you will win.

The problem for writers is that it is not easy for them to know what other writers get paid, or what particular producers tend to think it reasonable to pay. Agents have an advantage here. A producer who fights over every last penny and then pays late, is not the sort of producer to whom agents will wish to submit their hottest properties. Agents usually have better knowledge of likely producers than do writers working on their own. You need to do some research if you are going it alone. Use the PACT handbook for background on the independent companies, or if the companies are not members of PACT ask them for a company profile. Don't be shy. It's your career.

If the producer asks you to write something and you ask for more money, but they then withdraw their offer claiming your price is too high, tell them that the project really appeals to you but that you would like 24 hours to think about it in order to reschedule some other work, or whatever. The excuse doesn't have to be true, but must be credible.

The lack of an agent should not stop a good writer from selling his or her writing and being reasonably well paid for it. Whether the writer wants to do all the chasing up of late payments, VAT wrongly paid, overseas tax exemption forms and all the other bureaucratic paperwork that accompanies deals, as well as checking the contract, is another question. Some writers choose to have their lawyers negotiate deals and even collect the monies due. A one-off lawyer's fee can be significantly less than 10 or 15% of all money coming in from a contract that has a long life.

There are many cases where it is easy for an agent to make a significant difference. We sold a first novel in the UK in 1994. By the time it was published, one year later, we and our associate agents had sold it to twenty-four countries for a total of about £1 million. By 1998 it was up to 39 countries. The novel, *Free to Trade* by Michael Ridpath, would undoubtedly have sold without an agent. But it is unlikely that the various publishers would have paid as much if the author had submitted it directly. By auctioning the manuscript it was possible to get publishers to bid against each other, thus establishing the true market price for the work. Deals like this do not happen every week, because such promising manuscripts don't come along that often.

If you are going to represent yourself, you need to be imaginative about getting your work on to the right people's desks. Don't come across as too pushy, but you will not get far by being too retiring either. Preparation, research and networking will all help.

The author/agency agreement

Writers often ask about the importance of having contracts with their agents. The Association of Authors Agents (AAA) advises that the business relationship between writer and agent should be formalized in a contract. This is the simplest and most effective way for each party to know the other's obligations and responsibilities.

Below are some of the key points of which you should be aware in the author/agency agreement used by members of the AAA.

1 Should you wish to terminate the representation you should be able to do so at any time. The writer, as principal, must control his or her own career. It is normal however, to give thirty day's notice.
2 All approaches regarding your work should be referred to the agent.
3 The agent should not commit you to any agreement without your approval.
4 You should warrant that you are the author and sole owner of the work you ask the agent to represent and that the works are original and contain nothing unlawful in content, do not violate the rights of any third party, are not an infringement of any existing copyright, contain no blasphemous, indecent, defamatory, libellous, objectionable or otherwise unlawful matter, and that all statements in your work which you say are facts are true. You should also have to indemnify the agent against loss, injury or damage caused by any breach of your warranty.
5 The agent's commission should be clearly stated. In our author/agency agreement it is described as: A percentage of the income arising from all contracts for the exploitation of works you create entered into during the period we represent you (and after that only to the extent mentioned in point 8 below) at the following rates:

Books, serials and columns, UK	15%
Books, serials and columns, overseas	20%
Radio, television, film	15%
One-off journalism and short stories	25%
Audio, abridged and unabridged, British	15%
Audio, abridged and unabridged, overseas	20%

In the European Union VAT must be added to the commission charged.
6 The agreement should state clearly that if anything is contained in any such contract which you do not understand or do not wish to accept, it is your responsibility to make this clear before you sign the contract.
7 The agent shall be entitled to charge you for:
   i)   books and proofs bought by the agency for promotional purposes or for submission to publishers abroad
   ii)   photocopying of manuscripts and sales material (press cuttings etc.)
   iii) couriers
   iv)   other exceptional expenses which may be incurred with your prior approval
   No administrative, postage, telephone, telex, fax or other overhead costs should be charged to clients. Nor should there be reading fees.
8 The representation will continue until terminated by either party giving not less than thirty days written notice to the other whereupon, unless both agree otherwise, the agency will cease to represent the writer but shall continue to be entitled to

commission in respect of all income arising from contracts for the exploitation of the writer's works entered into while they were represented by the agent and from all extensions and renewals of such contracts. This last point is very important.

Firing your agent

How do you fire your agent? Easy. Look at the agreement you have signed. If there is a thirty-day notice period then write a letter giving the agent notice. If you do not have a written agreement with your agent, then write to him or her informing them that you are withdrawing from them the right to represent you. You can make this immediate but it will be better all round if you make it thirty days, allowing the agent to get in any answers and offers from submissions already made.

You then have the right to accept or reject such offers. If you accept an offer made in this period, then the agent becomes the 'agent of record' for that deal and he/she negotiates the contract and collects the money, remitting to you, less the agreed commission, for the duration of the life of that contract.

It is important that you keep clear the fact that you are the principal. You will sign the contract, not your agent. Unless you have inadvisedly signed a contract which commits you for a period longer than the thirty days' notice, you are free to fire your agent whenever you choose.

You may feel nervous about doing this. That is natural. Most people do not like firing others, especially if they still have a continuing relationship (which you will regarding revenues from previous contracts). It is your career and you must put yourself first, before your agent.

You should also remember that an agent has certain obligations to clients in common law. These can be summed up as follows (this is not an exhaustive list):

1. An agent has legal and fiduciary obligations to clients.
2. The rights and duties of Principal and Agent are to be determined in a contract between them. If there is no contract, then the fact that the relationship exists implies a contract.
3. The primary duty of an agent is to carry out the business the agent has undertaken with the Principal, and to notify the Principal if he/she is unable to do it.
4. The agent must always act in the best interests of a client.[1] The agent must either follow the client's instructions or, if it not possible to obtain instructions, the interests of the client must guide the agent's actions.
5. There is an obligation on the agent to keep proper accounts and to disclose them on reasonable demand to the client.
6. The agent is obliged to disclose a conflict of interests.[2]
7. The agent must disclose any information gathered by the agency which is relevant to the client's interests.
8. The agent must not receive any secret commission or bribe with regard to a client's contracts.
9. The agent should not bind the client unless the agent has general or specific authority to do so.[3]
10. An agent should exercise skill, care and diligence in what he or she may undertake to do on behalf of clients.

The most common misunderstanding in firing agents seems to be the question of whether the agent is entitled to continue to collect commission on monies coming in from earlier contracts. Unless there is something written and signed to the contrary the 'agent of record' (ie the agent who handled the contract) is entitled to commission on all revenues from that contract during its lifetime.

If, after an agent has been fired, the contract, say for a licence to publish a book or for the rights in a script, should terminate, then the owner of the rights – the writer – is free to relicense the rights with a new contract that is not associated with the former agent.

Whether or not your representation contract gives the agent the protection of thirty days in which to collect in offers from submissions already made, you can instruct the agent not to make any more submissions. You can also refuse to accept any offers that the agent brings in after he or she has been fired (ie during the thirty-day period).

However, if there are live contracts that the agent will be handling on your behalf, it makes sense to achieve an amicable separation. If this is not possible, you can instruct the producer or publisher to pay direct to you, rather than to your ex-agent, the monies due, less the agent's commission, which should be paid directly to the agent.

Should you get a new agent before you fire the old one? You can certainly start talking to new agents before you break the news to your existing one. In our experience, agents treat such conversations in confidence. If it makes you feel more secure, interview several other agents before making a decision. Tell them you are represented but that you want to move. They may ask for the reason for the move. Usually there is complete confidentiality. If an agency became known for not respecting their clients' confidentiality, they would find it hard to attract new clients.

You may decide to leave because you are approached by another agent. Sometimes the agent does so because he or she has read something you have written and liked it. The new agent may not necessarily know you already have an agent.

Sometimes they know you have an agent and hope to induce you to leave, perhaps by promising to get you better deals. Knowingly poaching clients from other agents does happen. It is against the code of practice of the Association of Authors' Agents, and a member agent can be expelled for doing it. So if an agent is a member of the AAA he or she cannot sign up a new client until that client has formally left the previous agency. (AAA members do tend to be more book-oriented than script-oriented, although some – such as ourselves - do both.)

It is worth asking if a prospective agent is a member of the AAA. You will then know that the professional behaviour of such an agent is governed by a code of practice and that they have a minimum of three years' experience at a certain level of turnover. Should you have a complaint, you can take it up with the AAA. If the agent is not a member of the AAA you have less scope for sorting it out. You can complain to these organisations or the Society of Authors or the Writers' Guild if you think your agent has behaved badly.

However, when approached by an agent under any circumstances, use the occasion to get information from the new agent about their perception of the market for your work. If your relationship with your current agent is good, mention to your agent the approach by the other agent, and the fact that you declined to join their agency. Pass on any information gleaned from the other agent. Your agent may tell you it is exaggerated; on the other hand you may stimulate more focus and energy from your agency.

If you begin to feel that your agent is doing nothing for your career, it will rapidly undermine the relationship. Whatever the cause – and it can originate from either party – if your relationship is not that good, this might be the right moment to leave. Make the leaving as businesslike and unacrimonious as possible They are still the agent of record for your past contracts; you need them to cooperate with your new agent. The new agent should request sight of all your contracts and should arrange to collect and copy them before returning them to your ex-agent. You may have copies of them yourself, which would speed up this process.

You will not be the first writer to fire an agent. Don't worry too much about it. Just do it sensibly and constructively. Both you and your agent will survive.

Other sorts of agents

Some writers in Los Angeles think it is better to have an agent who also represents the other elements in a film, such as stars and directors. This is known as a 'packaging agent'. A packaging agent can be an advantage at times, but unless an agency is big enough and has enough high-powered agents and clients, it may be better to be represented by an agent who is more specifically focused on your writing.

Whether your agent is a one-person company or whether you are represented by the very large agencies such as CAA, ICM or William Morris, the personal relationship is always very important. Although some of the big LA and New York agencies have branches in Europe, there is much less packaging in Europe and it is usually only writers with high-profile track records who can be used in packaging.

There are also agencies who only represent actors and actresses, and some who include directors amongst their clients. Personally I think that writing is sufficiently specialised, which is why we primarily represent writers (and a select few directors). You might be represented by a literary agency for books and a different scriptwriting agency for film and television work. But if an agency also represents top directors and stars they will sometimes know that a particular type of story or writer is being sought before that becomes common knowledge.

There are also 'personal managers', who can do the work of agents, although in the USA they more often work in tandem with agents, looking after the biggest stars (usually actors and actresses). Personal managers tend to handle the client's financial affairs, which can include much more than the fees they are paid. For example, a star could have a portfolio of investments, tax problems and so on, which the personal manager will take care of. Few literary agencies handle those matters.

Clients who earn substantial sums of money are sometimes advised to use specialised accountants in addition to agents.

Lawyers can be used at times instead of agents. It is generally accepted that audiovisual contracts, like many other types of legal agreement, are best dealt with by a specialist. So if you do not have or wish to use an agent, you might use a lawyer.

Each can handle the negotiation, but there are some relevant differences. Firstly, agents charge a commission only on money paid to clients from contracts signed while the agent represented the client. The commission is agreed beforehand and the agent's share remains fixed irrespective of how much or how little money comes in.

Secondly, agents have obligations to go out and sell their clients, which lawyers usually do not; so your agent should be working for you even when no deals are being done.

Thirdly, lawyers usually charge by their time. If you do not have an agent and are only going to do one deal which will, over time, bring in a great deal of money, it will almost certainly be cheaper for you to use a lawyer. They will charge a fee for the negotiation, and will then receive no further money from you unless there is more work to be done. You will have to take over the collecting of the money or the chasing up if it is paid late (something that agents spend extraordinary amounts of time in doing).

You don't get charged anything for telephoning your agent from time to time, even if it is only for a gossip. Try that on most lawyers and the clock starts ticking. So there can be a comfort factor in using an agent. If, however, the legal matter is litigation, then a good, recommended lawyer is the right person to have beside you.

Conclusion

Good agents look for long-term relationships with their clients. How much a client earns for an agent in a given period of time is not the only factor the agent takes into account, especially if the agents believes in a client's abilities and shares the determination to make a success of the client's work. There are many instances where agents have worked with writers for years before either made significant money out of the arrangement. Unfortunately, there are also cases where a suddenly successful author feels that he or she has become too big for the agency and, because of the success gained with the agency, they leave.

Obviously, the client/agent relationship is most effective if there is mutual respect. It should be a team effort, and when it works it is extremely rewarding. But never forget that your writing career is the only one you have. The agent has other clients.

Notes

1   It should be made clear that agents have more than one client and therefore any client should understand that while acting for one client the agent is also representing others. This would apply unless the Agent had led the client to believe that that client was the only client of the agency.

2   The mere fact that it has been disclosed does not avoid the problem for the Agent.

3   Third parties who become involved in negotiating a contract are entitled to look at the ostensible authority someone has when contracting with them. That is, your agent may have the ostensible authority to sign an agreement which binds you, the writer. Generally speaking, literary agents have the authority to negotiate, not to sign the agreements. Clients can give their agents a general power of attorney or a specific mandate to sign a particular contract. It is better if writers always sign their own agreements, preferably after reading them.

14 Handling Meetings

Most writers, even those who are only 'semi-professional', have had exposure to business meetings. But it is still worth outlining some ground-rules, as a meeting can make or break a project. The chapters on pitching and negotiating deal extensively with meetings in practice; here I will look briefly at the theory.

The theory of handling meetings, like the theory of pitching, needs modification in the light of the context in which it takes place. If you are the supplicant, the meeting will need to be handled very differently from the way in which you would behave if a producer were desperate to buy your script or novel before anyone else could.

In 'interview theory' one is advised that if you want to get someone you are interviewing to reveal more than they intended to or want to, leave lots of silences and they will fill them in. In other words, ask a question; they answer; you say nothing. They will usually start talking, and in a revealing way.

In most business meetings you are unlikely to need to be so overtly manipulative. Use initial meetings, especially over a meal, to get the measure of another person, particularly if you may be embarking on a close working relationship with a complete stranger. The clues and bits of incidental information one picks up in comfortable social situations can be valuable in advancing the objectives of both parties.

The more you talk the better they get to know you; the more you listen the better you get to know them. So don't fall into the ego trap of telling them your life story (which suggests that you are someone who wants to be admired and liked).

There are numerous books and courses on handling meetings. A basic knowledge will prove beneficial.

Before the meetings

A common failing in meetings is lack of preparation or planning. This is likely to cause you to lose the initiative. Preparations can include simply reading all the background papers and making up an agenda so that you have the salient points at your fingertips during the ebb-and-flow of the meeting or negotiation.

If the meeting is to discuss contractual points, familiarity with the contract is essential, although, if you are not well prepared, you can insist on going through it clause by clause. It is possible to hide the fact that one hasn't read a contract prior to the meeting, but it's less impressive than being able to demonstrate detailed knowledge of the document.

Prepare your own agenda. This is very useful and often impresses the other side. You can even take multiple copies to the meeting and hand them out. If they have also prepared an agenda it will be interesting to see who was the more thorough. Even if you keep your own agenda to yourself as a checklist, it can stop you forgetting matters you wish to bring up.

Thinking through the points on your agenda before you get there can help you feel that things are under control during the meeting. Before arriving, you should have worked out your ideal, realistic and fallback positions for all the key points you know will be discussed.

Inside the meetings

Once inside the meeting, it is preferable to take the initiative (unless it is inappropriate for you to do so). Simply handing out an agenda can achieve this.

Perseverance (especially if polite) is also desirable. For instance, you may be unhappy at the way a point has been resolved, but someone else has the initiative and moves on to the next point. You need to get in there quickly and ask for more discussion on the previous point. You may then be able to persuade them to see it your way. Don't be afraid of attempting to do this. It may seem difficult to impose yourself on a room full of people, but if done in a civil way it is usually respected.

On the other hand, once you have gained a point, you might want to move on quickly. If you control the flow of the meeting it is much easier to keep the momentum going when you are benefitting the most. The Chair has considerable power and, if you are faced with a Chair with whose decisions you do not agree, you need to ensure that you address yourself politely but pointedly to the Chair to make sure you do get heard.

Most film/TV meetings are much less formal, with no Chair, but some people more or less subtly manage to control these meetings. They tend to get what they want. So be prepared to act.

You also need to be creative in meetings. Most of the meetings we are talking about fall into three categories: a) pitching ideas, b) editorial feedback, and c) discussion and negotiating the deal. If you are 'selling', then being flexible and creative in response to the 'buyer's' views can be very effective.

To be creative, listening is essential. When the buyer makes a comment, you can, for example, redefine or rephrase what you are selling so that it appears closer to what the buyer wants. It must, of course, in reality be capable of meeting the requirements of the buyer, or it will subsequently be rejected however great your pitch (and you will get a reputation for making excessive claims).

To get the most from this tactic, you can ask the other person for their views in order to give you something to respond to, and you can then rephrase, in your own words, what you think they want to hear.

Asking questions

Asking questions is nearly as important as listening. There are many ways in which to ask questions, each way selected in order to get you a particular result. Marion Haynes puts this particularly well:

Questions are of four basic types:
- General which elicit a broad range of potential responses.
- Specific which focus on an idea, leaving a limited range of responses.
- Overhead which are asked of a group allowing volunteers to respond.
- Direct which are asked of a selected individual.

General and overhead questions are less threatening and therefore better to start a discussion. Direct and specific questions are best used after participants become comfortable with group discussion.[1]

Whether you are using questions to elicit discussion, to pre-empt it or to stop it, or to bring in someone whose views you want to be aired, using questions confers initiative and control.

Dealing with Intimidation

What happens when the other side takes control, when they have all the big guns and behave in an overbearing way? Staying cool under pressure may be even more important than being able to put the other side under pressure.

Here is a brief checklist suggested by Gavin Kennedy, for use when you are confronted with unpleasant, intimidating and aggressive behaviour in a meeting:

- speak more softly than they do;
- speak more slowly than they do;
- give way to their interruptions, but pause for a few seconds each time they finish;
- do not respond in kind if they swear;
- do not argue with their attacks on you and their apportioning of blame;
- do not defend yourself against ascribed motives;
- ignore all threats.[2]

Control is the key to the successful management of meetings. You may not enjoy meetings, but why waste them? Handling meetings will provide many direct benefits for your work.

Notes

1   *Effective Meeting Skills*, Marion E. Haynes, Kogan Page, 1988.
2   *Pocket Negotiator*, Gavin Kennedy, Economist Books/Hamish Hamilton, 1993.

15 Negotiating

In *The Oxford Companion to the Mind* negotiation is described as:

> ...the use of communication between parties to reach agreement....both a highly specialized
> social skill and a part of everyday dealings between people. It is a highly complex
> proceeding, involving the full range of human motives, attributes and behavioural skills.[1]

A great deal of advice is available on negotiating in books and courses. The problem is
that most of us don't think we need the advice. As a result of this we lose money and
points in almost every negotiation in which we take part.

Specialists like lawyers get training in negotiation. A book on negotiation for lawyers
makes the point that it is now recognised 'that a body of knowledge exists which can
assist lawyers in becoming more effective negotiators'. The book goes on to describe
three main styles of negotiation, and advises on how to use and counteract them:

> An analysis of the literature indicates that at least three main styles of negotiation are
> commonly utilized, each style in turn giving rise to the use of appropriate strategies. These
> strategies are not necessarily unique to specific styles, being capable of being used
> interchangeably. The three main styles, however, are clearly distinguishable, each having
> distinct objectives...the 'competitive', the 'co-operative' and the 'problem-solving' styles.[2]

If lawyers take it this seriously, it is probably prudent for producers, writers and agents
to take it a little seriously! You already spend a great deal of time in your personal and
professional life negotiating, whether you are aware of it or not. If you are good at
negotiating in your private life, you will probably be good at doing so when it relates to
your work.

Most writers (and some producers) do little or no preparation for a negotiation. It is
rather like a writer sitting down at the word processor and keying in the first line, only
to assume that the next will come without any real planning.

There are very simple steps you can take to improve your negotiating technique. If
you are going to spend three months writing a script, it makes no sense to give it away.
Yet negotiating is generally thought of as an arcane activity in which agents, lawyers and
producers engage, but writers don't.

This may actually be true, but to some extent agents get to do so much of it partly
because writers and producers don't seem to like it, are not always particularly good at it
and don't get that much practice at it. There is a danger that once you have an agent (or
lawyer) you will hide behind them and not involve yourself in the negotiation process,
which is about your career to a much greater extent than it is about theirs.

In addition, however skilled a negotiator, the stance adopted by your agent or lawyer
will to some extent reflect your position in the negotiation. Inform yourself of the details

even if you are not present. It can be easier to negotiate on someone else's behalf when they are not present.

I find it extraordinary that negotiation doesn't form a major part of producer training courses. At the EU MEDIA programme for the training of producers, EAVE, a lack of negotiating skills was found amongst young producers from all EU countries.

So, where do writers go to learn to negotiate? The books and courses on negotiating usually have nothing to do with the film or television business. But they do provide confidence and insight.

The basics

This chapter contains a number of basic guidelines, but these are not hard and fast rules. However, the points will provide a structure that can be used in dealing with any negotiation. With these guidelines you should be able to make better-informed decisions before and during negotiations. It's rather like structure in storytelling – it helps you choose the next step.

The guidelines are in no particular order, so let's start with an important one:

1. Know yourself

To get the best out of yourself as a writer you need to know yourself. You need to know, for example, whether you have a tendency to be cowardly when faced with aggression or confrontation. Are you the sort of person who really likes to be liked and will do almost anything to avoid being rejected? In your writing, this may also influence your choice of characters and how you make them behave, as well as the way you negotiate.

Everyone has personal weaknesses and strengths. By being aware of your own, you are less likely to let yourself down when faced with pressure from the other side.

If you hate haggling, or are desperate for money, or realise that you are out of your league, the chances are that it will show that you are negotiating from a position of weakness. You can overcome this if you know what you are doing and you prepare for it.

When there is much at stake and they think that they are in a weak position (or indeed, even in the wrong), some people become aggressive and hostile; whereas others, although being reasonable and 'in the right', might concede the point because they are not good at confronting aggression in a negotiation. Try to become assertive, not aggressive.

Negotiating about something really important to you might make you feel nervous about failing. You want the deal. You don't want to get screwed. You want people to like you. You don't like the idea of being thought greedy. You are a nice person.

As a result you are probably at a disadvantage if the negotiation is with someone more experienced than you (who may also be a nice person but is perhaps a tough, successful negotiator), and that person behaves more professionally than you do during the negotiation.

If a producer is keen to buy rights, he or she will not like it when their offer is rejected. No-one likes to be rejected. Yet rejection is an inevitable experience in the business. You need to build up your confidence so that it doesn't put you off your stride.

If you built chairs and someone didn't want to buy one, that would not be such a personal rejection. But when you have put your innermost and most intimate thoughts on paper, to have someone say 'I don't like it' is not pleasant.

To help you deal with rejection, here is a famous rejection letter. It apparently comes from a Chinese economics journal:

> We have read your manuscript with boundless delight. If we were to publish your paper it would be impossible for us to publish any work of a lower standard. As it is unthinkable that, in the next thousand years, we shall see its equal, we are, to our regret, compelled to return your divine composition, and to beg you a thousand times to overlook our short sight and timidity.[3]

Faced with the usual blander rejection letters, or with deadlock in negotiations, you need to move forward. So what personal characteristics will help you overcome the fear of failure in a negotiation or the depression that follows rejection?

They include confidence, determination, a willingness to take risks and a belief in yourself. If you don't have some or all of these – or if you can't simulate them for negotiation purposes – you will be at a disadvantage. You may need to take someone into the meeting with you, or delegate the whole process to an agent or lawyer. Avoid too much delegating if possible, as you will gain many insights into the industry and your career potential by engaging in the interpersonal and professional process that takes place during negotiations for your work.

2. Know the enemy

Much of the time, negotiations take place between people who know each other well. It is a small industry and if you are a regular player you tend to get to know other players. If you have been around for a while, you grow up with other players. You come to realise that people you have known for years are now running everything. That's when you realise you are getting old.

This familiarity can usefully short-cut negotiations. You know X is devious, or Y is tough, so you gear yourself up for the confrontation. Despite the fact that confrontation is at the heart of the negotiation, there are many ways of permitting face-saving for both sides and avoiding ultimately damaging conflict between the parties by trading and by making concessions. In other words, you may be on opposite sides for the duration of the negotiation, but afterwards you will both be working for the success of the project that is the subject of the negotiation.

Usually the deal is closed once each party believes they have enough of the points they need. A considerable amount of face-saving may be involved. Sometimes you must give the opposite side enough to go back to their bosses (or clients), or they will dig their heels in and you end up by losing something you want to win.

Knowing with whom you are negotiating is helpful to your cause. It is, of course, possible to negotiate with a complete stranger, but I would suggest that you spend some of the opening time of the meeting getting to know them. For example, if you know you will be having a heavy negotiation with a total stranger, invite him or her to lunch.

Ordering and eating helps create a pseudo-social environment in which you begin to get to know the adversary.

Remember, the industry we work in is very gregarious and sociable. There is a great deal of eating and drinking with the people we do business with. We may have arguments over deals but we usually want to be able to work together again. So in the end there is a tacit agreement to negotiate hard at the time, but remain civil and friendly the rest of the time.

Don't let yourself be upset by an apparent difference in power, experience and status. You should know if they are playing games. These include keeping you waiting unnecessarily, trying to position themselves in a higher chair, so that you have to look up at them, issuing unreasonable ultimatums, talking expansively of their many successes and their wealth before making a measly offer. Don't be impressed or intimidated. This is acting on their part. The bottom line is hopefully they want what you've got to sell.

Confirm the meeting on the morning it is due to take place, emphasise the time agreed so there can be no confusion and they will be reminded. Check the chairs when you go into a room and try to choose where you will be sitting if you can. If you are in an uncomfortable position, change it. This is not a politeness competition.

3. Preparing for the negotiation

Here is a quick, non-exhaustive checklist of preparations:

1 What result do you want to achieve?
2 What do you know about the other side?
3 What do they usually pay for this sort of project?
4 What is your bottom line, the least you will accept?
5 Do you have a range of bargaining points you might be prepared to make or points you might concede?
6 Prioritize your goals: decide on aspects of the deal like fee, schedule of payments, residuals, profit-sharing, reversion, credit and so on. In other words, have you given the negotiation enough thought? That is really the basis of strategy – it helps you win.
7 Whether you are a writer, producer or agent, have you made a checklist? The following should be thought through before you start talking (even on the phone) to the other side about the deal:
  a) what are you selling/buying?
  • is it a licence (a permission to an individual)?
  • is it an assignment (usually of rights, an intellectual property transaction)?
  • what limitations are there (eg does it exclude radio, stage and publishing rights)?
  In other words, if buying, attempt to acquire broadly; if selling, license or sell narrowly.
  b) for how long will you sell/buy the rights? Work out three positions: ideal (what you would most like); realistic (what you think you might get); and bottom line (the minimum you can accept).
8 Know your own arguments and anticipate their responses. Hold something in reserve to counter them.

With this brief list you should be able to go into a negotiation reasonably prepared. But note the points in the rest of this chapter – there is much more that will stand you in good stead.

4. Strategies

Many general strategies are involved in conducting negotiations. Most of these common-sense attitudes will be beneficial. For example:

1   Have an open mind.

2   Let the other side have their say and do not interrupt, or you will appear to be rejecting their proposals out of hand (ie let them think you have thought about it).

3   Make only viable counter-proposals.

4   Use a colleague to buy you time if you think the negotiation is going too fast or is out of your control. Making a phone call to get (or to pretend to get) advice can be effective.

5   If they want to force the closure of a deal, you may need to be manipulative. For example, if you are faced with a stalemate, say you need to discuss it with your boss, client, wife, partner. The next day, go back with a very clear and fair compromise: 'We will agree to X if you agree to Y'. If you have read them correctly you can offer to trade X, which you don't feel strongly about, for Y, which you do. You can also state that your boss etc. won't budge beyond a certain point, which implies 'take it or leave it'. But be careful of brinkmanship; it is possible to lose a deal you want if you misjudge.

6   Do not lie (or if you do, don't get caught!). It weakens your credibility, which is important the next time you need to negotiate with these people.

7   Don't be afraid to recapitulate, while in the meeting, and later on paper. Misunderstandings can creep in easily; recapitulation will help to avoid them. After every significant round of negotiations you should follow up on paper with a faxed or e-mailed summary of your understanding as to what has been agreed, what has still to be agreed, and what each party has undertaken to do. Confirm the next steps in the negotiation, especially the dates by which actions are required. This is particularly important if time is a factor.

8   Don't be afraid of imposing deadlines (also known as 'a guillotine'), especially if you are prepared to walk away from the deal. Being willing to say no to an unsatisfactory deal puts you immediately in a stronger negotiating position.

Agents can often use their clients as a fallback in a negotiation: 'I don't think I can get my client to accept that point. But if you give me this one I will try.' If you are out there negotiating on your own, it might help to have a fictitious partner if necessary.

It also helps if you empathise or can appear to empathise with your opposite number. It helps the interpersonal relationship. If you both want to get the deal done, doing it on a friendly basis will probably benefit both of you. And it may even hasten your next deal.

Knowing your priorities, being able to keep the ball in play (ie keep the negotiation going when it looks bad), judging when to close the deal, all require a combination of analytical and interpersonal skills. It helps if you have experience, because there are some things, like knowing when to go to the market, that you can only learn by doing them and seeing the results.

5. Know when to go to the market

This is really about getting that extra bit of leverage. If you try to sell something before it is ready, you will probably not get the optimum deal. If the market isn't ready, you will need to prepare it. Alternatively, if you wait too long someone else might beat you to it.

This is why agents rarely send material out cold. I usually start by talking up the writer, the script or the book to potential buyers. I then consider their initial reactions and gauge how enthusiastic they are for that particular property or person, and how enthusiastic I am about them as the prospective buyer.

I attempt to relate how much the buyer wants to purchase with what resources they have and how well I think they will do with it. All this is part of knowing when to go to the market.

The fact that a writer has finished a script does not mean that this is the optimum time to sell it. Ideally, I like to sell scripts or manuscripts before they are completed, which means talking them up early. It can give our side the benefit of input from the buyer, in the form of comments on the script or manuscript that we can respond positively to, depending on whether we want to encourage the offer or not.

Because most producers will insist on the right of cutoff (being able to fire the writer if certain stages are not achieved, in the producer's opinion), I like to know what changes they are likely to make in the script or to the story before I sell it (there are sometimes occasions when I do not think that they are asking the writer for enough changes).

The timing of the invitation to purchase can affect the deal and the working relationship that the deal will bring about.

Firstly, going to the market is something that you should have done before you committed to writing the script. Do some preliminary research, get an idea of the storyline, but then check the market out before you dive in. If the feedback is negative, consider it carefully, analyse it and act accordingly. If it is good then press on.

Secondly, if you can work closely with the producer who is buying your script, you have a better chance of retaining your integrity in the script. Don't assume that in a disagreement over a script the writer is always right. The producer or script editor is just as often right. But you increase your opportunity to persuade if you get in there early and get to know the other side. Even better, get them to like you.

Thirdly, if you get on with the producer and major changes have to be made to the script, you have a greater chance of being paid to make those changes, rather than having another writer brought in. Many producers don't like the process of telling a writer that there have to be sweeping changes to the script, so they find it easier to bring in another writer. Help them keep the faith with you by showing that you have a collaborative, not a combative, attitude.

For all these reasons, I prefer selling a piece of writing before it has been completed. Without an agent you may not have as much access to the marketplace, but you can still do a lot to improve your position from one of relative passivity.

6. If possible, do not name your price

You may be surprised to discover that their opening offer is higher than you would have asked for. But be prepared to wring additional concessions out of them despite their good offer. If they offer a higher price than you expected, say that you were hoping for more than that. You can be gracious in accepting their offer, in not demanding a bit more (which you would probably get), but get in quick with a polite demand for something else that you really want.

That assumes you know what else you want, which you won't unless you are prepared for the negotiation. It is also worth remembering that in negotiating, you should be trading. If you make a concession, they give you something in return, and vice versa.

If you do have to name a price first, it is clearly sensible to suggest one which is on the high side. If you want a reputation for being fair and reasonable you will not go too high. But you may nevertheless find that they are shocked at your suggestion (however reasonable it may be). Their reaction may be a ploy or it may be genuine.

You must leave room to be able to climb down, assuming you want the deal. So you need to have a 'fallback position'. This is usually the minimum figure acceptable to you. But don't state it unless you have some demands you want to make as part of the compromise, such as a much shorter option period, or whatever.

7. Know the going rate

If you don't know the going rate, it is difficult to bluff about not naming your price. If pushed, you need to be able to either give a price, refer them to your agent or elegantly get round it and induce the other side into proposing a figure.

For example, there is a rule of thumb about writers' deals in the film business (less common in TV deals) that says the script writer should get about 2% of the budget. If a writer is pushed into quoting a price, the answer can be just that: '2.5% of the budget!'

This leaves open the stages of payment, the definition of the budget and dozens of other clauses in the contract. But I am assuming here that you are not actually negotiating the whole, detailed contract, but are concentrating on the 'heads of agreement', which is how most film/TV writers' deals start by being negotiated.

This refers to the main points in the agreement. Much of the detailed negotiation is usually done after the broad strokes of the deal have been agreed. Quite often, the deal-making producers agree the key points, then leave the lengthy negotiations to lawyers or 'Business Affairs'.

8. Shoot high

I have mentioned a couple of times the importance of not short-changing yourself. So much can stem from the price you get paid for a script or a book, including what you get paid for the next one (and the level of residuals, which are pegged to the initial figure), that it is worth looking at this a little more closely.

If you do not ask for more than you expect to get, or at least more than the minimum you are willing to take, you will never find out what the market rate is. Market rates are set in bazaars. I am not talking about Writers' Guild minimum rates, although sometimes that is all one can get, but a negotiation is capable of establishing the price for a script or manuscript.

Taking the initiative can affect your income very directly. That is one reason we, as an agency, like auctioning books (it's very rare to auction a script). The auction establishes what two or more producers or publishers think a particular script or book is worth to them.

9. Be prepared to say no!

You must be prepared to say 'No' when it is appropriate. It is wonderfully empowering. As mentioned above, if you can walk away from a deal, you are in a position of negotiating strength. If you can't turn down an offer, however bad it is, you may still be able to bluff. If your bluff does not work and you have to accept their terms, do it gracefully and reluctantly (if that's not a contradiction in terms).

If you lose out on the negotiation, don't feel it is the end of the world. Make it appear as if everything is OK, it was a fair fight, and express your great pleasure at the prospect of working together as a team. And start thinking about your next project.

Remember that in this business you can be at each other's throats over a deal one minute; the next you are on the same side, taking on the rest of the world.

10. Body language

One of the most important aspects of negotiating, apart from knowing what you are going to say, is listening and watching. Be aware of every nuance in their voices, watch their eyes and be aware of your own. We are sometimes asked for advice about a negotiation which someone else is conducting. It is like walking blindfolded. You can't get the information you would normally obtain by watching and listening to the way in which they make their offer. You know what irritability looks like. For those of you who are writers this should be easy. Finger-tapping, looking into the distance, arms folded tightly around the chest. People can simulate body language just as easily as they can lie about anything else, but not looking for it means you might be missing valuable information which you could use in your counter-moves.

You can also deliberately use body language to signal your own feelings. Sometimes you will be giving away too much to an experienced negotiator. So be aware of what signals you want to give away. You can and should use gestures (and words) to defuse a situation that is getting out of hand. For example, if you try something on, and elicit a sharp negative reaction, 'Well, if that's how you feel there is no point in going on!!', move quickly. Assuage the ruffled feelings. Smile, hold your hands out in front of you, palms up, be conciliatory.

There are additional comments about body language in Chapter 7.

11. Know the parameters

If you are batting deal points to and fro, how sure are you about the relative values of the points? Is it worth conceding point A if you get point B? This is where experience makes it easier, but you can teach yourself many of the tricks that normally come with experience.

There is a dynamic relationship between how much you receive (or pay) and what you sell/license (or get). The more you receive (or pay) the more you usually concede (acquire). As a general rule I believe that it is always worth looking at particular concessions in relation to how much money the other side thinks they are worth. There are sometimes points in a deal which are regarded as 'deal-breakers'. If someone bluffs and says a particular point is a deal-breaker, it is difficult to retract immediately without seriously losing face (and negotiating power).

A straightforward negotiation might go as follows: you set up the sale of audio-visual rights in a script or book, by inviting an offer for 'a one-picture licence' (ie excluding the assigning of copyright, sequel and remake rights. It is what it says – a one-picture licence). The prospective buyer makes an offer of X but says that he or she must have all the usual rights, including copyright, sequel and remake etc.

If you decide that this is not a deal-breaker, that you are willing to consider their demands, you make a counter-proposal of, say, 2X. They may counter that with an offer 1.5X, and so on until you reach agreement. In other words, the additional rights they wanted have a price. It is just a question of arriving at mutual agreement as to that price.

You control some of the parameters of the negotiation, and your initiative before the negotiation starts can influence not only the other side's expectations but also the outcome. So consider what limitation you want to impose on the negotiation from the start. Be flexible if the terms are acceptable. Being too anxious to make any deal is more likely to let the other side win.

Calmness and perseverance are the mark of a tough negotiator. Agitation and loudness indicate an aggressive (and probably weak) negotiator. The former is undoubtedly better, although there are occasions when it can be appropriate to signal great displeasure and hopefully rapidly push the other side to the brink by losing one's temper. But be careful, one seldom thinks clearly under those circumstances. Don't assume that because you have a lawyer or an agent, you need not bother about your deals and your contracts. You should ask your adviser for a full briefing on the strategy to be employed, the kinds of choices and compromises to be made.

Unless you have briefed your adviser very well, he or she will not be able to read your mind. If your relationship with the adviser is new it is even more important to be thorough. If the adviser is impatient about explaining things, remember, it is your career. This is one time when you are paying for a job to be done and you are entitled to know what is being done in your name. After all you are the principal. You will sign the contract, not your agent.[4] Despite this, few writers read every line of their contracts.

You must always be prepared to take the initiative. This means judging when to do so, and how. If there is a stalemate you might benefit if you suggest a solution. We sometimes find producers will agree to the overall purchase price for a script or a book, then ask for unacceptable things, such as very long option periods, or large repayments if the rights are to revert after the agreed period.

When we sense that they are digging their heels in on these points, we suggest that we would be willing to agree if they increased the purchase price by so many thousand pounds. Faced with a reasonable but unpalatable compromise, they will sometimes concede.

If you don't know the parameters, then read contracts as avidly as you read scripts. Find out from your writer or producer pals what deals they are doing. Don't be isolated. You only hurt your career by allowing yourself to be isolated.

Read about negotiating skills, go to one of the many courses available. The fact that this has nothing directly to do with film and television is irrelevant. You are training yourself to use skills which you can apply in all sorts of professional and interpersonal situations.

This is perhaps a good moment to mention the long term/short term compromise. In many negotiations, one needs to obtain a short-term gain, but has to sacrifice a long-term benefit. Or vice versa. If you need cash quickly, sell outright if it will get you the maximum upfront cash. An agent can't tell you if it is advisable to do this. If you need the cash, only you know how badly you need it.

Better planning may include writing some scripts for episodes of long-running series, which produces faster income but may not be what you really want to write. It may take several months to land a commission from a soap, but once you are writing for it, if you deliver good scripts, there is a chance that the producers will want more, and it can provide a regular income for a time. This might even enable you to take a hard line in negotiating a deal on your magnum opus.

There is something to be said for paying as much attention to this aspect of your career as you might pay to your scripts. Many months of dedicated writing, seldom enjoyable in its own right, deserve the best chance in the marketplace.

Negotiation may appear daunting (a 36-page contract filled with legal jargon isn't fun) but do not seek avoidance solutions or displacement activities. Instead, see the challenge in the same light as that presented by a plot problem or character motivation problem. Negotiation gets easier the more you do of it, it is financially rewarding and, for writers, it can also be a microcosm of the sort of conflict that scripts should be filled with.

As the *Oxford Companion* notes, 'The nature of the pressures is unlikely to be the same for both parties...tacit collusion is common between opposing negotiators cognisant of the pressures to which each other is subject...(and) as the pressure to settle increases, the parties concentrate on tractable issues, with (in the case of successful negotiations) a trade-off on the remainder in a final decision-making crisis.'

That could be the basis for a screenplay.

Negotiating with Producers

Most negotiations writers have are with producers. There are specific situations which differ from, for example, their negotiations with agents (see the previous chapter).

Let's start with a few thoughts about the problems that sometimes arise in the relationship between producers and writers. I should perhaps say here that some of my best friends are producers...

1 Producers often think that because they are paying, they know best about the writer and the script.

2 Producers usually do not invest enough money or time in the development, rewriting or packaging of their projects.

3 Producers often select the wrong writer. For instance, they may commission an

adaptation from a writer who is good at original scripts or an original script from a writer who is best at adaptations.

4   Producers are seldom trained to write script analyses and are often not good at talking to writers.

5   Producers too often, if they can afford it, rely on big-name writers who are inappropriate (perhaps on the basis that if a script is lousy the producer cannot be blamed since the writer was so experienced...).

6   Producers are often more interested in the deal than the script. Too many producers behave as if the definition of a producer is someone who produces only money.

Fortunately, there are some very good producers. But writers have little control over the production of their scripts and are seldom encouraged by producers to get involved in any way other than just as a writer for hire.

Writers can be as problematic as producers. For a start, writers, too, often think that because they thought of an idea it's worth writing about. They don't always research the market adequately. They seldom understand enough about the problems faced by a producer who is trying to raise the money for the film written by the writer.

For this reason, producers and writers often fail to benefit from the real contribution the other might have been able to make.

Looking at the relationship (rather than the negotiation) from the producer's or script editor's point of view:

1   Be sure you know what you want from the writer. The writer must be sure he or she knows what is wanted.

2   Be sure you are clear in briefing the writer. Always follow up with written confirmation; ask the writer to do the same. You will be depressed to see how often the writer has not understood what you think is clear, and it may be your fault.

3   If the writer fails to deliver an acceptable rewrite after you have clearly explained what is wrong with the current draft, cut your losses and get another writer. Be sure your contract with the writer takes this possibility into account. If the idea is an original idea from the writer, this may be less easy, but it can be done.

A good script, a good story, is the most important element in the package. A great director, a great actor or actress, cannot rescue a bad script. Unfortunately, a common definition of a good script is one that raises money. However, as you must realise, money does not guarantee a good film.

Getting the script right is one of the least expensive items in the budget. Yet producers, who often find raising development money very difficult, can seldom allocate sufficient money to development, as a result of which the script doesn't have a chance and the film fails. That is why so many bad scripts are filmed.

Too many producers, under pressure as a result of lack of time and lack of development finance, go into production prematurely. One can't fault them for the tremendous effort they put into raising the finance and putting the deals together. But if the result means paying too little attention to the script once the money has been found, then the fault is theirs. Writers, directors and agents who do the same are also to blame.

15. Negotiating

In order to handle the negotiation over deals well, writers need to know something about what producers do. And this includes 'packaging'. Packaging involves bringing together various the elements such as casting, director, cofinanciers or coproducers in order to get the film financed. Large Hollywood movies can be financed entirely, simply by getting the right stars and director attached to the project.

Anybody can package. A producer can be a packager or vice-versa. Writers can and should learn to package. It may be just a form of fantasy, a wish-list. But it shows you were thinking through the implications of your script for the film.

All it involves is persuasion, selling, convincing and negotiating. Remember, the purpose is to get money from someone. The key questions are: what do you think you're giving them for the money and what do they think they're getting for it?

Writers don't usually get too involved in packaging, but it is important to know something about it and great ideas about casting can help raise the stakes for your script.

Key points to remember

In the close and often very rewarding relationship that develops between writers and producers, there are always moments, as in any negotiation, where you are on different sides. Good producers usually respect writers who can take care of themselves. Apart from arguments over the deal, conflict occurs over the script (these are often channeled through the script editor). Such conflicts also involve negotiation, but there are a number of other areas in the producer/writer relationship that are worth remembering:

1 Cashflow is too often forgotten in the detailed negotiation over the dozens of other clauses. You can get the cash to flow quicker, particularly if you can't get quite as much as you would have liked. So when the other side won't budge over the sum they are offering for a particular stage of the work, agree to what they want on condition that they pay the money faster. A small amount of money paid earlier to a writer can make a lot of difference; to a production company it may be marginal.

2 Always take copious notes. It buys you time to think and enables you to follow up verbal negotiation with written confirmation. The note-taking starts while you are on the phone, even prior to talking about the deal, but while in meetings do it obviously, or have a colleague do it while you concentrate on the verbal interchange. It sends a clear message about your seriousness.

3 If your summary of the negotiation appears to be acceptable, but at a later stage the other side tries to dispute something, you can (righteously) point to the letter or fax you sent which they didn't challenge at the time.

4 You can attempt to use 'acceptable' tricks. Stall for time; get the other side to clarify statements which in the cold light of day sound extreme, then rephrase the point more in your favour; find ways to avoid agreeing to something you don't want to concede, perhaps by stalling or suggesting moving on, and then come back to it later when they don't want to concede something and do a trade ('I'll drop my demand here if you drop yours there'). It is not uncommon to include specific demands in a negotiation with the sole intention of letting the other side take them out again by trading concessions.

5 If you will be handing over the negotiations to a lawyer or agent, it is better to say so

at the outset. People don't always react kindly to surprises, even if they are reasonable surprises.

6   When the two sides have whittled the discussion down to the final contended points, take stock. If you think that you will not get them to give in, ask for concessions that do not affect their cash flow or finances in the short-term, such as a profit share (or a higher one if you already have a small one). You could also ask for bonuses on production or once certain sales targets have been reached. If it far enough away it will probably not be the problem of the person you are negotiating with, and they may be more likely to concede.

7   When the final contract arrives it should be marked 'DRAFT'. Until you have had a chance to look at it, it remains 'subject to approval'. It is usual for agents to say (and it is always accepted) that even when one has agreed the main points in a contract, the actual wording is subject to the client's approval.

   You should check the contract carefully against your notes and copies of the confirming faxes or letters you have sent or received after each round of negotiations. Whole clauses are sometimes left out, not deliberately, but through sloppy drafting or typing. You might find an error in your favour. Point it out, have integrity. Seizing the moral high ground is also a negotiating ploy.

8   Producers usually negotiate a writer's deal with some idea of a rough budget and therefore what they are allocating to the writer (and everyone else, including themselves) is or should be predetermined (though not written in stone). Whether the producer can or should pay more than was budgeted for in order to get a writer may be dependent on whether a cut can be made elsewhere in the budget, or whether the budget can be increased because the writer is sufficiently bankable for the producer to be sure of raising the extra money.

9   Finally, there is the vexed situation in which writers are asked to do work for nothing. This is dealt with below in more detail.

Writing without pay

The first thing to remember is that if you originate something, then you own it until you license or assign it (unless you are a full-time employee, in which case it might belong to your employer, depending on the wording of your contract of employment). If you are writing something original, do not assign the copyright in it unless you get fully paid. There should be a clause in the contract which specifically states that copyright is not transferred until the agreed payment has been received.

When producers ask for 'free options' or free extensions to options, there are a number of things to think about when trying to make a decision as to whether to go ahead. If it is an extension of the option, then they've obviously shopped the material around already and will have received some rejections. But they may still have people interested if they can improve the material. Since they have invested money (and pride) in the project, they still have a vested interest in selling it or producing it. You may therefore be asked to do some writing for nothing to help improve the material.

If you take it away from them and option it to somebody else, that party will need to know exactly where it's been before. If they acquire an option without knowing and then find out, it will cause some disillusionment with you and with the project. Unless the new producer has some angle on financing the film which the previous one didn't have, there may be a case for staying with the first producer.

It's important to make sure that they are doing the right thing to raise the money. You can only do this if they have they kept you in touch with their submissions, not only to whom they have sent the material, but what the reactions have been. Have you been sent copies of the rejection letters? There is much that can be learned from these, including not taking rejection too personally, but you are entitled to know how they are presenting your work. If it is a novel that they have turned into a treatment or script, is the treatment or script good? Are the rejections due to their poor presentation? Is the producer loading too much on financially so that the budget is unrealistic? Is he or she taking too much out for himself or herself? Potential financiers might be put off if the budget is not realistic.

Is the producer sufficiently bankable to be an asset? Or could it be that the very enthusiastic and wonderfully supportive producer who is running around with your project is in fact perceived by potential financiers as a liability? Sometimes broadcasters or bigger producers who like the project won't get involved in it because they don't want to have another producer on board who brings in nothing except the underlying rights.

If a producer asks you for a free extension of an option, and you feel you should agree, negotiate an additional payment on to the back end (ie after the film is shot or released). At that point it probably won't be their money and they are more likely to agree simply because it is in the distant future. If they tell you that it makes the overall deal too rich and this will put off an investor, the chances are they are wrong unless you are asking for too much.

If the option was £200 and the purchase price for the book or script is £25,000 and you are asked to grant a free extension for, say, a further year, ask for £5,000 on the purchase price. Even if you only get £3,000 it is better than nothing. Don't settle for less than £3,000, as an option of £2,500 (i.e. 10% of the purchase price) would have been industry practice and you are in effect deferring that. Hold out for £5,000! I don't believe that sort of money is going to put off a serious investor, although the producer is not being unrealistic in saying that the package will look a little less interesting if the costs loaded on the back end are too heavy.

If someone says they want a free option, another response is to say, 'This obviously cannot be a very high priority for you'. In other words, remember when you are negotiating (and ordinary conversations are negotiations in this context) that you need to manoeuvre and manipulate. You may need to put the other person on the defensive because you are trying to gain an advantage.

While it is unquestionably correct to be very professional in all your dealings, there is nothing which says you have got to be nice when being ripped off. Whether you're a writer in a confrontation with a producer or a producer in confrontation with a broadcaster (or a writer), being burdened by a need to be liked invariably leads to making bad deals.

A producer who might respect you more because you wouldn't ask for what is rightfully yours, is not the sort of person whose respect you want. Is there any difference between trying to get a free extension to an option they've already paid for and trying to get a free option in the first place? Not a lot.

Going into partnership

There are occasions when a producer has no cash but is prepared to put in a great deal of legwork to raise the money. You need to make a calculated decision as to whether this producer is reliable, imaginative and as conscientious as you would like him or her to be. If your script or idea is sitting on the shelf gathering dust or if, indeed, the idea comes from the producer, but you have to work on a treatment, then try to think of yourself as being in partnership with the producer.

Suggest that your agreement should be in the form of such a partnership. In other words, it should be a more advantageous agreement than just a writer for hire who isn't being paid. Think of the producer as being out there hustling on your behalf, not just of yourself slaving away, unpaid, on the producer's behalf. Make sure the producer keeps you informed about what he or she is doing, but make sure that you do have a contract and that it is fair. You should always get a bonus or premium for having done the work for nothing. So add something on to the payment due on the first day of principal photography (1st dpp). If the producer respects you then the producer should be more than willing to accept this. Try to avoid bonus payments at dates later than the 1st dpp, such as first theatrical release. The film may never be released.

Don't agree to write something for nothing so that the producer can attempt to set it up, and only after it is set up will the producer talk to you about a contract. Always remember to put your name on the document as the copyright-holder. If the idea came from the producer the copyright in your treatment or script should still be yours, but add the words 'based on an idea by [the producer]'. This makes it perfectly clear that the producer cannot deal in the treatment or script without involving you. You can't deal in it either, without involving the producer, since the idea belongs to the producer. This is fair.

Always ask to see a copy of the final presentation document that the producer is using, especially if he or she has had it retyped. Check the text and check the copyright line and credit. If the producer has made changes then these changes should be justified.

Most producers are hard-working and fair, but they are often forced to work under great pressure in a very competitive arena where lack of development finance is a real problem. Teamwork is more effective than dissension in the ranks. Both sides have more to gain from pulling together than from scoring off each other.

Appendix 1 contains several genuine examples of negotiating letters. These demonstrate some of the approaches to resolving conflict in the context of deals between scriptwriters and producers.

Conclusion

Negotiating with producers is a large part of any successful scriptwriter's business dealings. It can be complex, but it can be rewarding. Knowledge is supposed to be power. In this instance, it can also be money. Writers who are able to talk the producer's language have an advantage over those who can't. Writers who can negotiate confidently do too. These writers sometimes end up as very good producers. Don't avoid negotiations or close examination of contracts. Both are a sign of a healthy career.

Negotiating with Directors

There are occasions when writers have to deal with directors as well as producers. The power balance is not usually in the writer's favour, which is why having the producer as an ally can help in a dispute with a director who wants to rewrite some of your material.

James Park, in analysing the relative failure of the British film industry in terms of the lack of great writers, points out that the imbalance between the power of the writer and the director is part of the problem.[5] 'Critical ideology,' he says, 'gives the crown to the director, leaving many writers uncertain about their role in the process. Directors not only tend to have the stronger, more assertive personalities, but they also have the power to wreck the script once shooting starts. Directors can and do sometimes refuse to involve the original writer in making changes to the script. As a result changes made for correct reasons can produce an even worse result.'

Of course there are many directors whose ability to take a weak script – or a script with weak elements – and visualize what will work for an audience, is a great asset for the writer. However, few writers ever have any say in the choice of director.

Notes

1   Edited by RL Gregory, 1987.
2   *Negotiation*, Diana Tribe, Cavendish Publishing, 1993.
3   Reprinted in *The Times*, 9 July 1982.
4   Actually, some agents do sign contracts on behalf of clients, although I prefer not to, unless it is a series episode contract, similar to one that the client has signed before. If I have to sign, I prefer to have a Power of Attorney authorizing me to do it.
5   James Park, *Sight & Sound*, Summer 1990.

16 A Basic Agreement

The importance of legal awareness

Important Note

Most areas of the law require specialist advice. But writers should be aware of aspects of law that particularly affect them. Certain decisions about what to write or how to write it may be possible only with some understanding of the law. How do you write about potentially litigious matters without infringing anyone's rights ? How do you avoid libelling anyone if you don't understand something about the law? And does your contract cover you on these points?

A detailed catalogue of all the possible clauses in the most common contracts involving writers and producers working with writers, would fill a book longer than this one. Legal or contractual negotiating advice that is both basic and brief is likely to be misleading. The caveat therefore is that these chapters are for guidance only and are necessarily general. Before acting on the information here you must be aware that there are risks in not seeking professional advice over legal matters. I am only an agent, not a lawyer.

Should there be a potential infringement of copyright either by or against you, or should there be a potential libel action either by or against you, you should get professional help sooner rather than later. Not only are these complex areas of the law, but they have potentially severe penalties. Having a good lawyer can be a valuable insurance policy. If you can't afford a lawyer, find out from the Citizens Advice Bureau what your legal rights are. If you are a member of PACT or the New Producers' Alliance, you can book a free session with a lawyer. The Writers' Guild, the Society of Authors and the Authors' Licensing & Collecting Society can also provide legal advice.

Negotiating realism

When you sell something you have written, or when you are commissioned to write a treatment or script, you will usually be asked to sign an agreement. The terms of this agreement should always be negotiated to improve on whatever was first offered. In other words, don't just accept what you are offered. Always try to improve the proposed deal. Producers or broadcasters generally make offers close to what they are prepared to pay, but rarely do they make their best offer at first. Negotiating can make a significant difference to the initial offer. But counter-proposals must be realistic to be effective.

Without any knowledge of the terms and conditions in typical writers' agreements, or a basic understanding of the agreements or contracts that determine the obligations and remuneration, writers cannot know whether it is worth their while committing the necessary time to a project. If a producer or publisher tells yuo that you do not need to take professional advice they could risk invalidating the agreement they are asking you to sign.

In addition to this, many writers fear that they are in danger of being ripped off. This is often because they don't understand their contracts. Some writers have been ripped off, but most producers are honest and honourable. To prevent suspicions creeping in to spoil the relationship, it is important that both sides are open with each other about deal points and contractual matters. It pays to make sure that all the details are clearly understood by both parties; this is one of the most time-consuming but useful aspects of an agent's work.

In this chapter we will look in general at the commissioning process and at options, by going through some of the main clauses found in 'standard' contracts. First we will look at the legal requirements for a contract to exist.

What is a Contract?

Certain things have to happen for a contract or an agreement to exist. There has to be:

a) an offer, which contains the principal terms of the deal unconditionally and absolutely: ie if you reject one term of it it is not absolute;

b) it must be accepted unconditionally;

c) there must be an intention on the part of the parties to be legally bound by the agreement;

d) there must be some consideration; in other words, there must be a payment of some sort, not necessarily in cash, which must relate to the present or the future not to the past.

The basic agreement

Two of the most common kinds of basic transactions for writers working in film and television are determined by whether the writer is being commissioned, ie, hired to write something (sells his or her services), or sells an option to something that he or she has already written. The latter may be an idea, a treatment, a script, short story, novel or whatever. There are, of course, many other types of deal, such as those involving the licencing of books, articles or doing rewrites. But these two transactions are the most common involving script writers:

1   Writers can be commissioned by another party to write a treatment or script. There will be payment for the service of writing. The contract will probably be governed by union agreements, and will usually involve the assignment to the commissioning party of copyright in the products and services of the writer.

2   A writer may have written a spec script (or a novel) which another party wishes to acquire rights in to make and exploit as a film or TV programme. This usually starts with an option to acquire the rights at a later date on pre-agreed terms. (Although this may be a sale of rights or a licence, for convenience I will refer to it in this chapter as the 'assignment'.)

When there is more in development than can be absorbed either by the broadcasters or by producers with development finance looking for feature films (as has been the case in the UK since the early 1990s), producers and broadcasters option less, and attempt to pay less for what they do option. Deals therefore become tighter.

Against this background of difficult market conditions, writers have to negotiate the sale of their services or of their already-written work. In the first category of basic transactions the producer is most likely to commission a treatment before commissioning the script.

The deal is usually in stages, and until the writer has delivered stage one (usually the treatment) and it is accepted, the commission of stage two would not proceed. Some contracts stipulate payment on delivery, others on acceptance of the work delivered. It is preferable for the writer to be paid on delivery, although this is not always possible.

The Writers' Guild/PACT agreement for film script commissions by independent producers has seven stages for delivery/payment:

1 commission of treatment/payment of about 10% of total fee
2 delivery and acceptance of treatment/payment about 10%
3 commission of first draft script/payment about 20%
4 delivery of first draft script/payment about 20%
5 commission of second draft/payment about 10%
6 acceptance of second draft/payment about 10%
7 principal photography payment the remaining 20%

For television there are four equal stage payments (see WG/PACT agreements in Appendix 4).

Variations in negotiations (apart from the payment sums) include whether the second payment is due when the treatment is delivered or only when it is accepted, and whether the fourth and sixth payments are due on delivery or acceptance. I do not have strong objections to payment on acceptance for the treatment, as it is very rare for the first or even second draft of a treatment to get it right. So a couple of rewrites of a treatment without additional payment, as long as the goal-posts are not moved by the producer, may not be unreasonable, especially if the payment on commission is an adequate one.

As long as the brief from the producer has not changed, the writer should be willing to do a certain amount of rewriting without additional pay before acceptance, as long as the producer is providing constructive and prompt feedback. Should the writer be a very experienced one, and should the brief be consistent (ie not have radically new story or character elements introduced by the producer), then limiting the number of rewrites to one or two and a polish is sensible. Should the writer be inexperienced then more protection for the producer is not unreasonable.

What is clearly unreasonable is the established industry practice whereby film treatments attract only 20% of the basic fee. This has a direct and detrimental effect on the development of scripts, as it effectively reduces the amount of time spent on the treatment. Underdeveloped treatments usually lead to inadequate scripts. This practice is a significant contributory factor to the relatively poor level of development in scripts in Britain and the rest of Europe. In television the BBC may pay only 10%; under the WG/PACT agreement for television it is 25%. Neither is satisfactory.

Typical Clauses from a Script Commission Agreement

To save you having to read through the sometimes arcane legalese in which most agreements are written, I will list some of the typical clauses in a script commission agreement, together with a brief description and some comments. This is not an exhaustive list, but should provide the basis for more detailed discussion, either with your agent, your lawyer, the staff of writers' associations or with other writers. Try to find ways of improving not only deal points (money, periods of time etc) but also the protection afforded to you in the agreement.

There are of course many types of writers' agreement, including those for the commission of a pilot episode, for the option of a spec script, for the option of a book, for a television movie (as opposed to a feature film), or for the development of a treatment or series 'bible'. This chapter will cover some typical clauses common to these. It will not cover every possible clause.

You can also compare these clauses and the topics in Appendix 3 with contracts you have or are offered. Appendix 3 is an A-Z on contracts and law. It has a wide range of topics of a legal and contractual nature that affect writers. For convenience these will be listed in alphabetical order, and many of the terms used in the clauses discussed in this chapter are described in Appendix 3.

Preamble

There can be clauses at the beginning of a contract that set out the date, the parties to the agreement, and provides the agreed addresses for the parties to which correspondence about the contract must be sent.

Recitals

This clause tells us what the set up is prior to the clauses which make up the agreement. In other words, the Recital is not an operative clause and neither party is bound by the contents of this clause.

It usually begins with the word WHERAS, and has phrases such as 'WHERAS the Writer has written...' It ends with the phrase NOW IT IS AGREED, and everything after that phrase is what the parties have agreed and are bound by once they sign the document.

Definitions

Numerous definitions are listed at the beginning of a contract to make sure that it is unambiguous. A number of words and expressions may be defined. 'Writer' is usually the description given to one of the parties. When later used in the contract, the meaning given in the Definitions Clause is the meaning specifically and expressly agreed in the contract. The word in question is always spelled with a capital letter, eg Writer, Producer, Work etc.

Other definitions might be of the Treatment, the First and Second Draft Scripts and the Principal Photography Script, Television Series and Serials, and any other relevant form that the Work can take.

Engagement

This clause states that the producer engages the writer and the writer agrees to render his/her services to the best of his/her ability and skill in writing the Work which is the subject of the contract. The clause can contain details of the delivery schedule for the various drafts of the treatment and script(s).

If the contract is for a series originated by the writer, the writer, as a negotiating tactic, should try to get a guaranteed number of scripts in the series. One formulation of this could be that, subject to the writer's availability, the writer will be guaranteed at least half the scripts in the series (if it not a 13 or 26 part series) on condition that the scripts delivered by the writer are acceptable and that the writer can deliver within the reasonable schedule required by the producer. The longer the series, the fewer the guaranteed scripts.

In other words, if your scripts are not acceptable you get no more to write. Or, if you cannot meet the delivery dates required by the producer, you will not be further commissioned. But if it was your original idea/treatment you could argue in respect of the scripts that you don't write, that you should receive a format fee of at least 10% of what you received for your script or of what the best paid writer receives (whichever is the higher) on all the scripts you do not write. You should also try to get a 'created by' credit on all the episodes you didn't write.

Assignment of Copyright/Grant of Rights

The writer will have to assign or license some or all of the copyright in the work to the producer. This clause can also cover reversion in the event that the producer has not commenced production within an agreed period of time.

It can include details of what specific ancillary rights, like merchandising rights, are included in the grant of rights, and whether the writer has to waive his/her moral rights. (See Appendix 3 on moral rights.)

Reserved Rights

Where a script or treatment is commissioned it is usual for all rights to be assigned or licensed to the commissioning party. If rights are acquired in an existing work it is more common for the rights' owner to be able to withold some of the rights.

In order to permit the making and exploiting of a film, some of the copyright rights need to be assigned or licensed to the producer. But it is not necessary for all the rights making up copyright to be licenced or assigned. Where successful in witholding certain rights, these commonly include publishing, radio and stage rights. There is usually a period of time, called a 'hold-back' (perhaps between three and five years), after the grant of rights before the reserved rights can be exploited by the holder of those rights. Merchandising rights are not usually held back, because their main value stems from the 'screen time' created by the film or television programme(s).

It is important to reserve as much as possible, without jeopardizing the deal as a whole. However, if you do not have an agent or are unable to exploit reserved rights, it may be better to let the producer control them as long as you receive an appropriate share of the revenue. For example, if you reserve the publishing rights, you might be able to get 100% of the royalties if you write the book. If the producer controls the rights, you might get 50–75% if you write the book. But if you do not write the novelization, and another writer is brought in, you might only receive 25% of the royalties, with the rest going to the novelizer (perhaps 50%) and to the producer (25%).

Warranties

The writer will have to provide certain warranties, which can include the following:
- that the writer is free to enter into the agreement and shall not enter into any agreement that might conflict with it;
- that the material written by the writer is original (this will be modified if the material is based on a novel or is otherwise supplied by the producer);
- that the writer has not previously assigned granted or licenced the rights in the material that are the subject of the agreement;
- that the material will not infringe anyone else's copyright;
- that the material will not defame anyone;
- that the material is not obscene.

The writer will have to indemnify the producer against any breach of any of the warranties given by the writer. This will usually mean covering all costs and damages arising out of or resulting from legal actions against the producer arising from a breach of the warranties made by the writer. Should there be claims regarding a breach, which fail to prove that a breach actually took place, then I do not think the writer should have any obligations. For example, the writer should not be liable to pay if a crank chooses to sue and fails to win. If no breach is proven, the producer should cover the costs. If a breach has taken place then, depending on the wording of the indemnity, the writer may be liable under it.

The writer should always try to ensure that there is a reverse warranty, so that if legal action results from information or material provided by the producer to the writer, the producer agrees to indemnify the writer.

Warranties must be taken seriously. Whenever possible, writers should attempt to insert the qualification 'to the best of my knowledge and belief'.

Suspension/Termination

In a commission agreement the writer can usually be fired or the agreement terminated if he or she fails to deliver an acceptable treatment or script, delivers very late, fails to fulfil their obligations because of illness, for example, or fails or refuses to perform or observe services undertaken in the contract. The clause usually deals with what payments the writer is still entitled to after suspension or termination.

It is important for writers to notify producers as soon as they know delivery will be late. This may not stop them from being fired, but it decreases the chances. Writers should also insist on being given the right to do at least one rewrite before termination. In other words, if the first draft delivered is not acceptable, the producer should provide notes detailing what changes they require, and the writer should be given the chance to revise the script accordingly.

Even if it is an original idea or treatment, if a writer fails to deliver an acceptable treatment or script after being given a chance to rewrite, or if the writer is in default of the contract, the producer must have the opportunity of getting another writer. The original writer should still be entitled to certain payments (depending on the details of the agreement and what proportion of the film is based on the original writer's script).

Assignment to Third Party

This clause allows the producer to transfer or assign their rights to the material written by the writer to a third party (the assignee or licencee). The clause should provide if possible that assignment is only permitted '...provided the Assignee or Licensee enters into an agreement directly with the Writer to observe and perform the Producer's obligations.'

It should be made clear that any assignment will not relieve the producer of his or her obligations to the writer, except perhaps to the extent that the assignee complies with its direct obligations to the writer. It is an important protection to have this 'direct covenant' and producers should have no objection to its inclusion.

Compensation/Payment

This describes the payments that the writer will receive 'subject to the performances of the Writer's obligations and warranties'. The payment stages are usually clearly laid down, and these tend to be contingent upon delivery by the writer of the appropriate drafts of the treatment or script. The most frequent complaint from writers is late payment by producers. You can try to insert a clause requiring interest at, say, 2% over base rate on monies paid late. This won't guarantee the payment on time but in my experience it does help speed it up and the interest is a small consolation too. Or put in a clause which states that delivery by the writer of the next stage shall be extended by however long overdue the producer has been in payment for the previous stage. In other words, writing time only starts being counted once appropriate payment has been received for the previous stage.

Non-payment does not usually constitute a breach of the agreement. In other words, the contract may not necessarily become cancellable if the writer does not get paid. The usual legal recourse for non-payment is to sue for the money in a court of law[1].

It is usual commercial practice if you enter into a contract with a film company that they will require your agreement that the rights granted to them under the agreement you are signing cannot be rescinded because of non-payment. The agreement will usually state that if you have any grounds for an action against them then you must sue for damages. The reason this is industry practice and is not worth fighting is because you may be selling the rights to your script or your book for say £10,000, but the film may cost say £10 million.

Financiers are not prepared to risk the underlying rights on which the film is based being removed from them because someone has not been paid every penny that should have been paid. Financiers are generally very concerned that people do get paid but they cannot afford to let there be high risks attendant upon large sums of money due to perhaps some inadvertent failure to pay a very small sum of money. So non-payment is usually specifically agreed not to be a breach of the agreement.

It's important also to distinguish between a licence and an assignment. A licence is a permission (not a property transaction like an assignment) and if there is no payment the writer (or licensor) is entitled to state that non-payment is a fundamental breach, since it demonstrates that the producer does not intend to be bound by the contract and therefore the contract can be terminated.

Because an assignment of copyright is a property transaction (of so-called 'intellectual property'), the general rule, which is frequently spelled out in detail in an assignment contract, is that non-payment (except possibly for total failure to pay) will not cause the contract to be revoked or rescinded. So you would probably have to sue for damages, ie for money that is owing.

When you are offered a contract, look at the wording with regard to the question of consideration. If it has the words 'in consideration of £X' that is better than if it says 'in consideration of the purchaser's agreement to pay £X'. The former makes it absolutely clear that you should be paid £X (for whatever was agreed that you would do, assuming that you fulfilled your obligation).

Credits

There should always be a clause which determines what credit the writer will be given on screen. It might state where the credit will appear, how large it will be, and usually also states that if there is an 'inadvertent failure by the Producer to credit the Writer that shall not be deemed a breach of the contract'. This latter point is standard industry practice and is not worth arguing about.

The exact form of the credits is often left until after the film goes into production. If the writer is a member of the Writers' Guild, the clause usually states that the writer '...shall be accorded such credit as he/she is entitled to under the terms of the Screen Credits Agreement made in 1974 between the Writers' Guild and the then BFPA (or as subsequently amended)'.

Disputes Procedure

Credit disputes are usually arbitrated by the Writers' Guild, if the writer is a member. Other disputes can be taken to court or the agreement may provide for an arbitrator.

Expenses/Travel/Subsistence

If the writer is expected to travel more than, say, 30 miles from home or place of work (whichever is agreed in the document) the producer agrees to provide expenses for travel, and should 'overnights' be involved, for accommodation.

If flying abroad some producers agree business class travel and *per diems*, a small sum to cover incidentals. If the producer is covering all meals then the per diem may be no more than £10 or £20 per day. However, if meals are not included it should be considerably more.

Collecting Societies

The producer should agree that any money payable to the writer from collecting societies[3] whether in the domestic market or from abroad, is for the writer not the producer. Writers should register with the ALCS, to make sure that they receive any monies that can be collected on their behalf.

There is an anomalous situation as to whether agents should receive commission on money collected like this, or from PLR (Public Lending Right: money paid to authors by the government on books borrowed from public libraries). Personally I believe that if the contracts for the scripts or books bringing in this revenue were signed while the writer was represented, then the agent should receive their commission in the usual way, as they would for any subsidiary deal under that contract.

However, the collecting agencies collect on behalf of the authors and prefer to remit directly to them. It has become industry practice for some reason among most agents not to seek commission from these monies, which may explain why agents do not seem to work as closely with the ALCS as I think they should.

Pension Scheme

If the writer is a member of the Writers' Guild pension scheme, and the producer is a member of PACT, then both the producer and the writer can pay small sums of money into the pension scheme on behalf of the writer. It is not obligatory to enter the pension scheme.

Law

There should be a clause towards the end of a contract stating that the agreement 'shall be subject to the laws of England and the exclusive jurisdiction of the English courts' (assuming it is a contract drawn up in England).[3]

Finally...

There are usually also clauses covering a number of other points. Among these are:

- permission for the producer to use the approved likenesses, biography and name of the writer;
- when commissioned to write something, agreement for the producer to make the writer's services available to third parties;
- agreement for the producer to 'adapt change revise delete from add to and or rearrange...the script'.

Option Contracts

In the second basic type of deal writers are offered, the producer is likely to want to take an option on what the writer has already written (eg a book or script), entitling the producer to exclusivity for an agreed period of time, during which no one else can acquire the rights in the material for the purpose of making and exploiting a film or programme(s). The option usually states how much the producer pays for the exclusivity to acquire the rights, what rights are being optioned, how long the producer has the option for and how the option can be renewed or extended. Usually, attached to an option agreement is the second part of the contract, called the 'Assignment', which states the purchase price, the grant of rights and all the other details necessary to transfer the rights to the producer so that he or she can make and exploit the film to be based on the rights acquired.

If, before the expiry of the option, the producer 'exercises' the option in the way prescribed in the option agreement, then the rights granted by the Assignment will pass to the ownership of the producer, subject to the producer paying the exercise price. This payment is known in contracts as 'consideration' and some consideration is required for a contract to be legally binding. It is usually but not necessarily money. Make sure the rights don't pass unless you have been paid.

During the option period it must be made clear what the producer is entitled to do in relation to the Work. Raising money in order to be able to make the film is perhaps the most important activity which the producer must have the right to do; actually starting production of the film, however, should not be possible under an option agreement. Only once the option is exercised, can the production begin.

It is worth noting again here the difference between commissioning a Work and optioning a Work, because when a producer commissions a writer, the producer will usually own the Work to be written and all the accompanying rights, such as sequel and remake rights. There will therefore not be anything in the contract about these as all rights in the Work are owned by the commissioning producer. But where the Work existed prior to the producer's offer to acquire an option, some of the ancilliary rights may have already been sold, such as publishing rights, stage or radio rights.

So where there is a commissioning, and the producer requires the Writer to assign the copyright, the producer will usually want the right to make 'films in general', not just one film (as they might acquire in a one-picture licence). But this raises the issue of what payments should be made to the writer if more than one film is made, or if a spin-off television series is made, and so on.

There are therefore commonly provisions for such additional productions as sequels and remakes or television series, in addition to the feature film rights being bought under the agreement in question. For sequel and remakes it is usual for producers to offer 50% of what the Writer received for the first film. For a television series there will usually be a fee per episode (depending on the running time of the episodes). The fees for television spin-offs do not always carry residuals, though you can try to obtain them. All these additional fees or percentages are dealt with in the Assignment at the time that you sell the Work.

The amount paid for the rights to make the first film will be an agreed sum paid on exercise of the option (at which point the rights usually pass to the producer) plus an additional top-up payment on the first day of principal photography. This is usually measured by reference to the size of the budget. In other words a fee of £50,000 may have been agreed or say 2% of the budget, whichever is the higher. So on the first day of principal photography the difference between £50,000 and 2% of the budget will be paid if the latter is greater than £50,000.

The Writer will usually receive what is known as 'profit participation', commonly between 0.5-5% of 100% of the film's profits.[4] Writer's profits should be assessed on the same basis as the financiers' definition. The reason for this is that the Writer won't be able to know how the financiers are defining profits, so having Writer's profits defined by reference to financiers' profits ensures that the Writer does not receive a less-favourable calculation of profits. In the commissioning situation, because the producer is 'at risk' the writer therefore tends to have to sell all rights, but gets top-up or residual payments depending upon the performance of the production(s). When dealing with an existing novel union agreements do not apply (although agents try to mirror them, obtaining for example residuals when selling a novel to a broadcaster), but it is usually possible to reserve some of the rights, negotiate provisions for remakes and sequels, determine who will write the novelisation, and so on.

Residuals are usually seen as a way of topping up a basic fee. With an option the producer buys time because he/she cannot or does not want to pay the purchase price at the beginning of the relationship, or anyway not until they have established that they can raise the money for the production of the film. So the option is often thought of as time for the producer to go out and raise the money.

It is not easy to generalize about what sums of money should be paid for commissions or options, except by reference to the WG minimums (see Appendix 4). Detailed information on deals can often be acquired by the sharing of experiences between writers.

Notes

1   If the sum is not large the Small Claims Court is a relatively easy solution.
2   See chapter 19 for more details.
3   In the UK, Scotland has certain laws that differ from England and Wales. For the purposes of this book no differentiation is made.
4. The writer's share of profits is often stated as a percentage of the producer's profits (commonly 5–10%)

17 Protecting Your Work

Writers are concerned that by talking about what they're doing, or by showing outlines, treatments or scripts, they might have their ideas stolen. There is a small possibility of this, but it's one you should be aware of. However, don't get paranoid because it'll drive you nuts. In my experience, theft like this is extremely rare and even when there are suspicions there is seldom proof.

At any one time there are literally thousands of writers working on scripts and the likelihood is that more than one of them is writing something very similar to what you are doing now. There is very little evidence to suggest that the theft of ideas by producers – never mind fully worked-out storylines – is common in the film or television business. The cost of a movie is so great that the producers, whether Hollywood studios or not, are unlikely to try to avoid the relatively modest payments to acquire the rights to the material, particularly in view of the risk to the production from a legal action. Anyway, can you always be totally certain that your ideas have never been 'stimulated' by something said or written by someone else?

There is little you can do to prevent producers to whom you have shown an idea or script from 'shopping it around'. They sometimes talk to studios or broadcasters to ascertain if it is the sort of project that has a chance of getting financed. Unless they have purchased the option they should not shop it around. It devalues the property and is not fair to the writer or to a producer who subsequently acquires the property.

This also happens with potential best-selling novels. If New York publishers fight to acquire the rights to publish a book, Hollywood majors have ways of getting sight of the manuscript even before the book is sold. They seem to pay retainers to people in publishing houses to photocopy such manuscripts and courier them to LA. It can prove embarrassing when a bona fide submission to a studio by a producer who has optioned a novel is met with the response that the studio read the manuscript months ago and decided to pass. They did not, of course, tell anyone about the rejection as the manuscript had not been officially submitted. Scripts can circulate unofficially too, although it may be a good thing for the script to be widely seen. If the writing is excellent there is a chance that the writer will get employment or find a buyer for that particular script.

What reasonable precautions can you take to ensure that you're not going to have your ideas stolen? Writers probably do have more to fear from other writers (rather than producers) stealing their ideas, although, again, this is not something of which I have been aware as a significant problem in thirty years of working with writers. If you are in a writers' group, in which discussions take place, then by all means agree to regard everything you hear about each other's work as being in confidence. Sign a piece of paper if it makes you feel better.

Breach of Confidentiality
Ideas cannot be protected by copyright unless the idea is in a material form (eg written

down, drawn, painted etc.), in which case the material form will be protected by copyright (but not the idea in it). If it is not in a material form, or if it is only a phrase or couple of lines, that phrase, for instance, will be protected but not the idea in it. The issue, therefore, is that ideas themselves aren't protected but there are certain circumstances in which the law will protect the confidential communication of an idea to another person.

If you communicate an idea verbally or in writing to someone, the law (in the UK) may imply a duty on the part of the recipient of that information (which may include ideas) to treat it as confidential even though there has been no express agreement or contract to do so. This is an easier way of defending the possible theft of an idea than attempting to sue under the copyright laws. But, as with most aspects of the law, it is not quite as simple as this.

The law regarding confidentiality differs depending on the country. In the UK it applies if the idea is sufficiently original, and has been communicated to somebody in circumstances which impose this duty of confidence. There have been cases establishing that such circumstances would include submissions by writers to professionals such as agents, producers, broadcasters or publishers. In addition the idea must be capable of commercial realisation. But if an idea becomes publicly known, it may no longer be possible to claim the protection of the law of confidentiality. So if you tell everyone in the pub your idea for a new soap, you will not be able to take legal action under confidentiality if someone in the pub uses your idea.

There are a number of actions you can take to increase the protection for your ideas:

1   Put them into material form. Once you turn your ideas into a material form you'll begin to get increased protection. The more specific the material form, and therefore the longer and more detailed the document, the greater will be your protection in copyright.
2   If possible get your idea produced. Many writers keep their 'best' ideas to themselves in case anyone should steal them. If the idea is really good, the longer you wait the more chance there is that someone will independently come up with the same idea.
3   When you do communicate your ideas you should say that you are talking about them in confidence. If you are writing to anyone about an idea you can put the words 'In confidence' at the top of the page. Even if it suggests that you might not trust the recipient, at least it puts that person on notice that this is a special circumstance.

The key legal case which changed the law in the UK was that concerning three actresses who went to Thames Television with an idea for a TV series about three women who had formed a rock group. After many discussions and meetings it appeared that one of the actresses was unavailable because of other professional committments. Thames nevertheless went ahead and made a series about three women who had a rock group, without involving the original actresses. It was called *Rock Follies*.

The women and their manager/composer sued and won, partly because they could provide a record of meetings and telephone conversations with Thames. The judge ruled that they had taken the idea to Thames, and that Thames had used it in breach of the duty or obligation of confidentiality which Thames owed to them.

17. Protecting Your Work

The case was called *Fraser and others vs Thames Television and others*. It laid down certain tests which would make it easier to protect ideas, than using the laws of copyright. Prior to this case it was thought that you could only use an injunction if there was an imminent breach of confidentiality. The case established that you could sue for breach of confidentiality and obtain damages after the breach had taken place.

The essential elements of the case were that an obligation of confidentiality may exist even if there is no contract between the parties. This therefore applies to those occasions when writers, for example, pitch ideas to producers (or agents or any executives in the industry).

In order to sue for breach of confidentiality a plaintiff needs to establish three things:
a) that the information was of a confidential nature;
b) that it was communicated in circumstances which implied a duty or obligation of confidentiality;
c) that there has been unauthorized use of the information to the detriment of the plaintiff.

It is possible for an idea communicated orally to receive protection under the confidentiality law, as long as the relevant conditions exist, namely the idea must have been communicated in such a way that the other party knew it was confidential, the idea must be sufficiently developed, it must not be in the public domain and it should have some originality about it.

In other words, if you talk about an original idea of yours to someone in the film or television business, and you do so in private (ie not in public), they are probably legally obliged to treat it in confidence. I would therefore suggest that you do what our lawyers told us to do when we opened our agency: keep a telephone notebook. This should be a bound book, in which you make notes every time you have a meeting or telephone conversation and out of which you never tear the pages. When the book is full, just store it on a shelf.

In our agency we've had clients win several copyright infringement cases because we could prove that certain conversations had taken place. Or rather we could prove that we had a record of them. The court places weight on contemporaneous records. It might take the view that someone who keeps detailed and careful records in a methodical way is likely to be telling the truth. I suppose it could be argued that the lawyers for the other side can ring up everybody you claim you spoke to on a particular day to get verification. Keeping methodical records also ensures that you have a record of all the conversations for your own purposes.

In essence, the law of confidentiality may mean that when you pitch an idea to a professional they are not permitted by law to use that idea without involving you, or paying you. But if you hear the chilling words, as you're in mid-pitch, 'Oh, we've got something very like that in development', there's not a lot you can do. If you are paranoid you can ask for information about it and who's writing it. If they're telling the truth they'll probably give you the details. But there's always that horrible moment when you think that they've just recognised how brilliant your idea is, and they are not going to do it with you. I imagine that in at least 99% of cases they are telling the truth.

Copyright

Protection under the law of copyright is automatic for a work that is sufficiently original. The law gives the copyright owner the right to prevent the copying, adapting or translating of the work, and enables the copyright owner to obtain damages if his or her rights are infringed.

Copyright law is complex and if you are in any doubt about your rights, or whether you may be infringing someone else's rights, consult a lawyer. There are a number of general points that can be made about copyright, but it is difficult to be too specific in a book like this.

Copyright pitfalls are easy to stumble into. For example, when a producer has or acquires an idea for a film, a number of writers may be considered until one is chosen. The idea is given to the writer who then comes up with a treatment or script. If the writer has not been contracted, and the producer doesn't like the treatment or script, the writer is unlikely to get paid anything at all. The producer should not show that writer's treatment to any other writer however, unless the treatment has been paid for. If another writer copies or adapts it, it could be a breach of copyright.

Unless the producer has acquired the necessary rights in what the first writer wrote, the producer and the second writer could be infringing the first writer's copyright. Obviously the producer can communicate the idea to the second writer because the idea originally came from the producer. A sensible producer would agree a fee for the first writer, even if it is nominal, so that what the first writer has written can be used by the producer and any writers that the producer wishes to hire. Or the producer might agree to pay the first writer a proportion of the script monies allocated to the project, depending on how much of that writer's work was used.

If you are worried about someone rather casually stealing your work, then you may make them less likely to do so by putting notification on the front cover that it is 'registered' with the Writers' Guild. It's a mild deterrent, but it doesn't actually prove that the material is your copyright. Don't confuse registration with the Writers' Guild (as above) and registration with the Copyright Office in America. You no longer need the latter to obtain copyright protection, although you do need it to obtain certain rights of action.

Various copyright treaties or conventions exist between countries for mutual recognition of copyright by each member country. If a copyright first comes into being under the law of one country then it may be recognised in another country (which is a signatory to the convention) as a valid copyright, without further formality.

In effect the legislation, in any country which is a signatory to the Universal Copyright Convention, is intended to provide protection of the rights of authors (or owners of copyright) in literary, artistic and scientific works. These include writing, music, scripts or cinematographic works, drawings, paintings, sculpture and so on.

Copyright legislation restricts other people from doing certain acts with the material that is the copyright of someone else. For example, only the copyright owner has the right to copy the work, issue copies to the public, perform, show or play the work in public, broadcast the work (including transmission by cable) or adapt the work (into any form or medium), which also includes translations. Only the copyright owner can licence (give permission) someone else to exploit some or all of the copyrights in a work, or can assign those rights to another person.

Copyright laws protect ideas in their material form. The general rule is that the idea behind a story or plot for a script would not be protected under copyright laws, but the script itself, and the written description of the dramatic incidents in the script, would be protected. There is also a doctrine known as 'the sweat of the brow doctrine', which takes the view that you don't have to be particularly original for copyright protection to exist. There is, for example, copyright in a compilation, a programme listing, even a football coupon. So the work that goes into creating a document can be relevant.

The notion of copying includes the notion of adapting. Because a copyright work can be an adaptation, it does not have to be a straight copy in order to infringe. A translation into another language counts as a copy, as does an adaptation into another medium.

Copyright legislation treats copyright as a property right, which can be bought or sold, similar to buying or selling, say, land. Copyright in the UK is not a personal right, such as a permission or a licence. Copyright, unlike personal rights, consists of a bundle of rights which can be transferred – some or all – to somebody else to whom they then belong.

What the copyright owner essentially therefore has is the right to restrict the copying of the work – using 'copying' in the widest sense. This does not mean that the author or owner can necessarily place restrictions on someone else publishing a work which is the same or similar, as long as that work has not been copied or adapted from the work in question. For example, if by coincidence another account was independently written without any knowledge of the former work and happened, by chance, to be very similar, then copyright laws would not enable the author of the original work to restrict the publication of the second. There must be an act of copying for an infringement to take place.

Writers sometimes post a copy of their script or manuscript to themselves or their agents in a sealed envelope which is not opened. This is because if there were to be a dispute as to whether the writer had copied from some other work (or something had been copied from theirs), they might be able to establish priority in time as regards the writing of their work. If they can establish priority, then it would have been impossible for them to have copied the other work because theirs came first. It is therefore more likely (although not necessarily the case) that the other work could be considered to have been copied from theirs, if it were to be shown to be substantially similar, because it had been created at a later date.

Protection afforded by copyright laws is also limited in time. Different rules in apply in different countries as regards the period of protection accorded to a work. It is possible, while negotiating your deal, to grant copyright for a limited time, say ten or fifteen years. But producers usually want (and need) the widest definition, otherwise they are less likely to be able to raise the finance for the film based on your work.

As a result of European Union laws taking effect, there will eventually be harmonization of copyright throughout the European Union. In 1995, the period of copyright protection for almost all literary or dramatic work in the EU was increased from fifty to seventy years from the end of the year in which the author died.

There will be complex transitional provisions, as some works which are in the public domain will come back into copyright. If you think that this might affect something you are working on, check with the Writers' Guild, the Society of Authors, ALCS or your lawyer.

Normally, a grant of copyright in a contract in the UK will say: '...for the full period of copyright and all extensions and renewals thereof'. That provides for the notion that there may be renewal periods of copyright in subsequent laws passed in the UK or elsewhere.

You do not need to sell the whole of your copyright in order for someone to make a film based on your script or book. You can sell parts of it by dividing up the bundle of rights or restricted acts, and you can sell some of those rights but not others.

For example, you could make a partial assignment of copyright to a producer wanting to make a film, retaining for yourself those parts of the copyright necessary to authorize printing and publication of copies of the work in book form, or sale of merchandising rights for example. The list of rights making up the bundle is sometimes known as the 'grant of rights'.

The so-called film and allied rights usually include the right to adapt a book, write scripts (or get them written) or alter an existing script. They include making a film(s) based on the script(s), and exploiting that film or those films by all means and in all media (eg video, TV, cable). In addition there are other grantable rights such as the right to trail the film on radio or promote it by issuing publicity which may contain synopses of the story, or to make sequels and/or remakes.

The purchaser will also have to have the right to use the title, content and characters for the purposes of promotion. This would include the right to use the writer's name and 'likeness' (photo) for promotion.

In return for all of that there will be negotiation about price and restrictions. In other words, the deal will involve:

1   Duration (for how long).
2   Extent (ie territory or country).
3   Partial or complete copyright (ie which bits are being parted with).
4   The price to be paid.

Normally for a legal sale of copyright to take place there must be what is called a 'consideration' or payment. This is either in the form of money or a promise of some sort, such as according you a credit, script or casting approval. It must be a two-way transaction.

The person selling the copyright needs to be clear about exactly what rights are being sold, what territory or territories are involved, what rights are being retained, and what price is being paid. The purchaser will want to know what rights are being acquired, for what period of time, for which territories, and what the price will be.

The purchaser and seller will need to know what if anything happens if the film does not start production (the first day of principal photography) within an agreed time. Usually there will be a clause referring to reversion of rights or termination of permission to make and exploit the film.

Breach of Contract

There are two kinds of breach of contract. The first is a repudiatory breach. This runs to the very heart of the contract because the party who is in breach is effectively tearing up the contract and does not intend to be bound by it. This is called a repudiatory breach.

The other party must decide whether to accept the repudiation, in which case the contract is treated as at an end and they can sue the first party, though not under the contract (which has come to an end), but for loss and damage suffered by the fact that the contract is now terminated.

Alternatively, the other party may argue that they do not accept the tearing up of the contract. The other party therefore treats the contract as continuing with the intention of making the first party observe all of the terms therein. The other party must however remain willing to perform their part of the contract. In this case, the other party would sue under the contract, usually for remedy of specific performance, ie a court order compelling the party in breach to honour the contract.

There is a second type of breach of contract, which is a non-fundamental breach or non-material breach. It is less serious and cannot be construed as repudiating the contract. Usually there will be remedies stated in the contract to deal with minor breaches.

For example, producers are reluctant to allow any circumstances to arise in which, having invested money in a film, they could lose their rights because some small sum of money hadn't been paid. So non-payment is usually resolved by going to court, but the contract remains in force. It is important for writers to be aware that non-payment is usually considered to be a non-repudiatory breach of contract.

Other aspects of Copyright
Copyright in Titles

There is no copyright in titles unless they are very long; two or three words are too insubstantial to count as a copyright infringement. It is therefore unlikely that there will be a copyright infringement if you use the same title as someone else, but be careful that you are not open to be accused of 'passing off'. This means trying to sell your goods by confusing third parties as to whether they might be the goods of another party. There may also be trademark protection which can stop you using titles.

When the author does not have copyright

In the case of certain works, copyright does not begin with the author. Works brought into existence by an employee can be the copyright of a company employing that person. The author of a 'film' under UK law can therefore be the person or company who made the arrangements necessary for the making of the film. It is important to make the distinction between the copyright in a film from the quite separate copyright in a script or book. It is also interesting to note that the finished film involves a large bundle of different copyrights, ranging from the script to the soundtrack.

The Copyright Line

The copyright line is important for protecting the copyright in a work. It is set out in the

Universal Copyright Convention so that owners of copyright can gain the protection of the Convention in other countries, but need to have the copyright line on the document for it to be protected.To assert your ownership of copyright, put the year of first publication and your name after the copyright symbol: 'Copyright © 2000 Julian Friedmann'. This is valid even if you only circulate copies to a small number of people. It is not a good idea to put the copyright notation and your name at the top or bottom of every single page. It's unnecessary, irritating to have to read, and also suggests that you are paranoid. By all means state on the front page that it is a copyright document.

Assignment or Licence?

A further distinction to be made is that between an assignment and a licence. An assignment of copyright is a property transaction, which a licence is not. A licence is a permission given by the copyright owner to another party to use an agreed bundle of rights in a certain way. The other party at no time owns those rights. The assignment or licence document is commonly annexed as an exhibit or schedule to the option document, which deals with the acquisition of a right to buy the other rights later.

Copyright of unpublished or posthumous works

An unpublished work is usually the copyright of the person who wrote it unless it is work for hire. And in the event of posthumous publication, copyright runs for the legal duration from first publication. There are certain circumstances in which the term of copyright can be extended. If a war has taken place, for example, regulations may permit the duration of copyright to be extended. But the general rule is that copyright is fixed for a limited number of years, which can vary in different territories, and once a work is no longer in copyright it is in the public domain. This means that it can be used or exploited without payment or permission.

Exceptions to copyright infringment

There are several exceptions to copyright infringement. Most jurisdictions provide some kind of fair-dealing provision. 'Fair dealing' enables the copying – within reason – of copyright work for research, educational or private study, for current affairs comment or review or criticism purposes. It is, in effect, a form of defence against copyright infringement, and it is necessary for there to be sufficient acknowledgment.

Droit Moral

Droit moral is that part of copyright law which deals with what are known as moral rights. (See for further details in Appendix 3 under MORAL RIGHTS.)

Release forms (see also Appendix 3)

Release forms are becoming much more common and many large companies and studios now ask writers submitting scripts to sign these before the script has been read. The release form is a waiver of rights in case some form of plagiarism or infringement of copyright subsequently emerges. I don't think there is much you can do about release forms. If you have to get your script read you will need to submit it. It's unlikely that a bona fide company with a reputation will rip you off. Or if it does, it's unlikely that it would be done intentionally. They've got too much at stake. Having to sign the form may leave you feeling suspicious, but it's just one of the realities of a business in which there is a premium on ideas.

Some of you may have had the experience of sending a script to a producer, particularly to a Hollywood studio, and getting it back with a letter saying it needs to come through a recognised agent. The letter is usually signed by a lawyer and may state explicitly that your script has not been read. This is because of the risk of a plagiarism suit. The truth is they don't want this risk, nor do they want to waste time reading the script in case it is unusable. If a script comes from an agent it is more likely to be a viable one and the company is less likely to be sued.

If you are really worried that your script might be 'stolen', you can always ask the person to whom you are sending it to sign a confidentiality letter. That suggests, unfortunately, that you don't trust them. As the vast majority of successful writers don't insist on confidentiality letters, you will come across as someone who will not be easy and pragmatic to work with. The companies who ask you to sign a release form are unlikely to be willing to sign a confidentiality letter. They are probably more concerned about receiving nuisance claims than you are about having your idea stolen.

Registering scripts

Copyright can't exist until something has been written down. You don't have to do anything (except in the USA) for copyright to exist, other than write the script. 'Registering' it doesn't make any difference to the validity of the copyright.

There are various organizations which for a fee allow you to send them a script and they'll register it. You can also send it to yourself in a sealed envelope, to prove that it existed at a certain date. It's a modest protection but it doesn't stop somebody else coming up with a similar idea. It just shows that at a certain time you had that idea as well.

Originality

For a script to be copyrightable it must usually be in some way original, although 'the sweat of the brow doctrine' allows the extent of originality to be minimal under certain circumstances. This doesn't mean that if it's an adaptation it's not original. But to adapt something you've got to acquire the rights in the underlying material, or you will be infringing someone else's rights, unless the underlying material is out of copyright.

If someone else comes out with a script or book that has similarities to yours, you need to establish that they did or could have seen your work. Someone who lives in another country, who has no known contacts with you or your milieu, is probably telling the truth if he or she claims not to have seen your script, unless you establish that there are too many similarities between your work and theirs for it to be coincidental.

It is possible, for example, for someone else to have described your story or script, without saying that the story was in a script. You need to prove some connection between the other person and your script in order to establish plagiarism.

Concluding Dos and Don'ts

When it comes to complex matters of copyright and defamation, there are a number of simple dos and don'ts which are worth repeating:

Dos

1 Do check your facts.
2 Do keep evidential records. If you have negotiations over the phone or face to face, make notes and keep them.
3 Do confirm in writing what has been verbally agreed. It can save you unnecessary work, time and money.
4 Do alert those you talk or write to about your ideas that you are doing so 'in confidence', if that is appropriate.
5 Do put ideas into a substantial material form so they will be protected by copyright.
6 Do always put your name, address and phone/fax number or e-mail address and the copyright line on the title page of every copy of a script, treatment or manuscript. If you have an agent put your name and the copyright line, and the agent's name and address rather than your address.

Dont's

1 Don't send out your only copy of your work.
2 Don't worry about getting people to sign release forms before you send them your work, unless you believe it is really necessary. It does suggest paranoia.
3 Don't steal or make use of original ideas communicated to you without permission. This is particularly important if the ideas were communicated in confidence, implied or stated.
4 Don't copy other people's work unless it is out of copyright. And always try to give full acknowledgement. Remember, a work may be in the public domain (ie out of copyright) in some countries but not in others. So be careful.
5 Don't worry too much about having ideas stolen. It is better to worry about how you can write better than the next person.

Conclusion

It is easy to fall prey to fears of losing ideas, but plagiarism can rarely be proved. If you find out that an idea on which you were working has been written by someone else, often the best thing to do is get on with something new and console yourself with the thought that your idea was viable. Next time, you will need to get it into production first.

The most important protection of your ideas is to put them into written ('material') form. Then do everything you can to get them produced. Always keep notes and send confirming letters. Learn the basics of copyright. After all, as a writer or producer, 'copyrights' are what you're dealing in. Being aware of the elementary protections offered you in law is an important part of being able to protect your work.

18 Financial Survival

Apart from the obvious full- or part-time jobs, what can writers do to earn extra money if their chosen field is not producing enough income? In my view, other areas of writing are worth looking at to provide additional finance.

Below is a selective list of alternative sources of income and entry points for a writer to break in too. Without several really good calling-card scripts you will not give those in the industry who are there to 'discover' you a chance. Don't rush in with unfinished or unpolished work. It is harder to go back a second time.

Series and Serials

Writers who are dedicated to a particular aspect of scriptwriting, such as feature films, can often be found moonlighting on a wide range of other forms of writing, from corporate videos to novelizations. However, the most common source of alternative income, and arguably the best training, is writing for long-running series and serials. Even if it is not your preferred format, it is scriptwriting, it keeps your hand in, it is demanding (and that should be satisfying if you are a pro) and it can produce a regular income.

Amongst the reasons for this being an important alternative source of finance are the following:

1 The stories and characters are often provided.
2 A bible and previous episodes are usually available for research purposes. You should beg and borrow as many scripts as possible to read.
3 There is a script-editing support-system built in.
4 If the first script you write for a long-running series is accepted and produced, there is a strong likelihood – unless there were personal problems between you and the other members of the team – that they will commission another from you. This enables writers to earn reasonably regular money.
5 It provides writers with intensive writing experience, as the deadlines are almost always short. Proof of being able to handle writing as part of a team (ie working with script editors) and working under pressure, makes others in the industry feel confident about commissioning new ideas or episodes of other series or serials.
6 Budgets for single drama, shot on location, have risen wildly compared to studio production, which is used for most sit-coms and soaps. Some high-rating part location, part studio-based, series are seen as an encouraging alternative to the more static traditional studio-based drama. The higher the budget, the less likely newcomers are to get a chance.

Alan Plater, one of Britain's leading scriptwriters and ex-President of the Writers' Guild, has estimated that when there were only two channels, BBC and ITV jointly screened more than 200 plays a year. This figure, he believes has dropped to about 50.[1]

Even taking into account the films shown on Channel 4 and the BBC's Screen One series, some of which are written by newcomers, it seems that despite the increase in channels there is now less scope for new writers creating original drama. Radio remains an avenue for them, but the soaps and series are still the easiest to get into and the closest to a real apprenticeship in the craft of script writing.

Apart from the enormous body of work that exists in the form of scripts, there are also numerous books on soaps, and writing courses are increasingly providing access for the study of long-running series.

Many well-established writers regularly work for series and soaps. It is not particularly easy and shouldn't be regarded as a soft touch, especially by new writers. Apart from the fact that there is competition for commissions and high standards are required, there is also the need to be very disciplined and fast.

Soap episodes are often written in a week or two, after the briefing and storyline has been provided. You may have to perform numerous rewrites to accommodate the needs of the cast, the producer and the script editors, all of whom are working on a number of episodes at once.

For some series, like *The Bill*, you have to prove yourself both with existing scripts and by creating storylines before the script editors will take you on to do an episode. There is no room for egos, on the part of the writers anyway. In other series, you also get taken on on the strength of your scripts, but they provide the storylines.

Once you have half-a-dozen broadcast series or serial episodes under your belt, you will find it considerably easier to be taken seriously by agents and producers. I would recommend that you continue to work on series television even when you start concentrating on original work. It keeps your hand in, keeps you in touch with people in the industry and is much more likely to lead to openings than if you closet yourself at home with your word processor.

Radio

Radio is also thought to be a good place for beginners to start. Radio encourages new writers in the way that Channel 4's Film on Four did when it started. However, writing for radio is no easier than writing for film or television and requires much the same application of research and technique. You need to listen to a lot of radio plays and you need to read radio scripts (quite a few have been published). You can also read books about writing for radio. But most of all you need to listen.

Radio has a certain flexibility that film and television lack. You can have armies of thousands of people, you can set the scenes in any time period you wish, and the special effects department will do the rest. Remember that people listen to radio drama for much the same reason they go to the cinema and watch television. They want involvement with the characters, and the best way to do this is, as ever, through dramatic situations. It is by providing accessible dramatic situations that you enable a listener to invest their emotions.

BBC Radio Drama tends to be swamped with submissions, so be patient, but it's a very good place to start. However, don't send a rejected television script or a film script, saying you think this would make a good radio play. You've got to rethink and rewrite it as a radio play. Similarly, don't send a radio play script to television and suggest that they consider it for a TV play. It suggests that you are lazy and the chances are they'll reject it unread.

BBC Radio and some of the commercial radio stations will provide guidelines to the sort of material they are looking for.

Adaptations

Adaptations from books have always been popular on screen, and are sometimes thought to be safer and therefore easier for relative beginners. This is not necessarily true.

Films and television programmes are enormously expensive to make and involve huge risks. How does anyone know if a script will make a successful film? They don't, but if the film is based on a book which is a bestseller, and it fails, then it's not the fault of the producer who selected it, or so he or she hopes!

The difficulty in reading a treatment is compounded if it is an original storyline. Not only does the reader have to judge the way the story will work when extended into a script, he or she also has to decide whether the storyline will appeal to a big enough audience. If it is an adaptation of a successful book the audience can be taken for granted.

The same could be said of sequels. It lessens the risk if there is already a precedent to go on. You also have the fact that the market for the adaptation or sequel has already been softened up by the success of the original. Scripts which are adaptations often fail. Some novels may do well as books but be inappropriate as the basis of a film without massive alterations and not all writers or producers will make the changes necessary to an already very successful book.

Best-selling authors are also not easily persuadable that their *magnum opus* needs a hatchet job. There was a delightful cartoon some years ago by Honeysett in *The Listener*.[2] It shows the Script Department room at the BBC with a few people sitting round a table and one man standing throwing a book out of the window. He is saying, 'This is the first thing we do with a novel when adapting it!'

There is another way of approaching adaptations with a view to increasing the earnings from a book. If a scriptwriter writes a novel he or she can retain film and television rights and sell them on condition that they get to write the script. A novel adapted for a mini-series, for example, can sell three or four times as many copies as one that has no tie-in.

Novel Writing

It is generally thought to be easier for a scriptwriter to write novels than for a novelist to write scripts. The latter requires technical knowledge that the former does not. Well, perhaps it requires more technical knowledge, but novels are like long-distance running, they require great stamina.

As with scripts, novelists should encourage criticism from editors, agents and publishers. It helps make them want to work harder for the writer, apart from the fact that the books will probably sell better. Novelists at the top of the earning tree can earn far greater sums of money than script writers. And there are many more novels published in a year than there are films produced.

The schedule for writing novels is also gentler. Usually, a publisher will want to publish a second novel about one year after the first. If you also have some script writing to do it is not difficult to fit the book in around the script deadlines.

If you do succeed in getting a novel published, think about writing the next one with cinema or television in mind. Your research and development work will largely have been done when you come to write the script.

Shorts

Short films are a traditional route into scriptwriting and directing. They are favoured by film schools because money for production is so scarce. Many would-be directors write their own short scripts. I think that this is a mistake unless they are really good writers, in which case they should find a better director.

There are established writers who might enjoy providing a short script for a young director, and the finished product has a much better chance of success if based on a good script.[3]

The Collecting Societies

Apart from creating works that earn you money, you should also make sure you collect all monies due from your existing scripts and books that have been produced or published. Books borrowed from public libraries earn Public Lending Right for their authors. For scriptwriters there is potential income to come from satellite broadcasting and cable transmission, particularly on the Continent.

The Authors' Licensing and Collecting Society (ALCS) [4]

Part of this organisation is the CLA (the Copyright Licensing Agency) which arranges for educational institutions to be licensed so that they can make photocopies in return for paying a fee. The monies go to the publishers who pass half of it on to the writers.

The ALCS collects over £3 million a year for film, television and radio writers. This money comes from sources outside those with whom the writers are contracted. For example, ALCS was able to claim significant sums of money for videos now in German video catalogues. Fees came from television programmes shown on domestic channels in Germany, and fees are also paid by broadcasters for the public reception of broadcasts to television sets in bars, hotels and public places.

In Holland, which is almost completely cabled, there is a retransmission fee payable for programmes broadcast on the Dutch domestic channel and ALCS collects the fees for those programmes written by British writers. (BBC1 and 2 are received in Holland, and Belgium and some other countries, though contracts with the BBC now take this into account.) Payments are also made to radio writers from retransmission in Belgium, Holland and Ireland, together with the monies from educational recording. ALCS is also working on claims for private copying fees from Austria and France, and from the retransmission of programmes broadcast on the Belgian domestic channels.

In order for you to receive any income due, ALCS must know who you are and what you've sold to the broadcasters. If you are a member of the Writers' Guild or the Society of Authors they will have your name on record, but it is advisable to join ALCS separately and to let them know whenever you sell a script. You won't normally know when one of the programmes, based on a script of yours, is retransmitted on a cable network in Europe, and therefore you won't know that you are due to get some money. Your original fee from the UK does not usually cover these uses of the work and even if you sold the script on a buy-out contract you may still be entitled to receive these fees.

ALCS is also involved in other activities relevant to writers and it publishes regular newsletters and reports.

Other sources of finance in the UK include:

1   British Screen Finance Tel: 0171 323 9080

2   BFI Production Board Tel: 0171 636 5587

The British Film Institute has always been very supportive of writer/directors. But it has cut back on its production fund.

British Screen Finance and the BFI Production Board now come under a new umbrella organisation called The Film Council (temporary tel 0207 436 1357).

3   The European Media Development Agency Tel: 0171 226 9903

This is one of the EU MEDIA Progammes and the most important new development fund in Europe this decade. It has been indirectly responsible for putting up overall investments in development in Europe. The largest loans go to bigger independent companies and broadcasters who are working with independent companies. For more extensive and up-to-date information on the EU MEDIA PROGRAMME contact the MEDIA Assistant for England tel 0870 0100 791, or the MEDIA Antenna Scotland tel 0141 302 1776/7, fax 0141 357 2345; or the Media Antenna Wales, tel 01222 333304, fax 01222 333320. It is possible that EMDA will close or change significantly in 2000.

Amongst the MEDIA supported training programmes for writers are:
*   SOURCES tel +49.30.886.0211, fax +49.30.886.0213,
    e-mail sources@compuserve.com
*   PILOTS tel +34.93.487.3773, fax +34.93.487.3952, e-mail pilots@intercom.es
*   ARISTA tel 0171.323.1775, fax 0171 323.1772, e-mail aristotle@lyceum.co.uk
*   North by Northwest tel 0171.323.2240, fax 0171.323.2241,
    e-mail northwest@firstfilm.demon.co.uk
*   EQUINOX tel+33.1.5353.4488, fax +33.1.5353.4489, e-mail equinox%siam@cal.fr
*   Euroscript tel 0171.387.6900, fax 0171 387.5880,
    website http://www.euroscript.co.uk
*   Moonstone tel 0131.220.2080, fax 0131.220.2081, e-mail screenlabs@aol.com
*   Sagas (interactive multimedia) tel+49.89.69.708145, fax +49.89.680.708190,
    e-mail sagas@extern.lrz-muenchen.de

4   Carlton Television Tel: 0171 240 4000

Some of the ITV companies have special development schemes for new writers, and Carlton has done a couple, but call the others and check the trades.

5   First Film Foundation Tel: 0181 969 5195

It provides valuable financial and editorial support for writers and producers.

6   Channel Four Tel: 0171 396 4444

Drama on Channel Four is divided into singles, series and the serials *Hollyoaks* and *Brookside*. Channel Four has run series of short films in the past and are always looking for individual voices and contemporary UK fiction. They receive considerable numbers of short scripts, probably because it's one of the best ways to break features. Worth cultivating for non-formula drama.

7   The BBC Drama Group Tel: 0181 743 8000

The BBC has various schemes for new writers as well. Speak to the Drama Group for details, preferably to a commissioning editor whose name you have researched. BBC-TV is the largest drama producer in Europe and it is important to be aware of its initiatives. There are frequent changes within BBC-TV drama personnel. The trade press is the best way of keeping up with the moves.

The above is a selective list of alternative sources of income and places for writers to break in. Without several really good calling-card scripts you will not give those in the industry who are there to 'discover' you a chance to do so. Make sure you offer them a properly finished, well-presented work. You are competing with all the other writers for money put up by producers or broadcasters, so try to stack the odds in your favour. It is difficult to go back a second time with the same project.

Grants, Awards, Bursaries, Subsidies and Scholarships

Other sources of finance are available to writers in the form of grants, subsidies and scholarships. Announcements can be found in the various trade magazines like *Broadcast*, *Screen International, The Bookseller* and *Writers News*. The *Writers' & Artists' Yearbook* has a section on prizes and awards. Other reference books also contain information about grants and prizes.

Tax

Writers need to know something about tax. This is easy to research superficially: the *Writers' & Artists' Yearbook* has a section on tax and social security contributions and benefits. For more detailed information get the very useful Ernst & Young UK *Tax Guide for Authors*[5]. Or ask the Writer's Guild or Society of Authors.

Cashflow for Writers

Cash almost always seems to flow more slowly than expected. There are exceptions, but for scriptwriters there are usually so many separate stages of payment, that the fee, which may have sounded comforting when the deal was proposed, usually takes far longer to come in than expected, and some of it may never come in at all.

Not much can be done about this. You can try to insist on delivery rather than acceptance payments; you can put in penalties for late payment (such as interest); you can insert a clause into the contract so that copyright does not pass over until you have received the principal photography payment, for instance. And you can put a clause into your contract prolonging your next delivery date by the length of time the producer paid late. Even if you deliver on time, independent producers do not always get paid promptly by broadcasters.

Always make sure that you invoice well ahead of time. Refer specifically in the invoice to the relevant payment. You can't invoice for a delivery payment before you deliver, but attach the invoice to the draft of the script that you are delivering. Have you agreed whether the producer has thirty or fourteen or only seven days to pay? This can help improve your cash flow.

If the producer is in another country have the money paid by direct bank transfer. It is faster than receiving cheques drawn on foreign banks in foreign currencies. And on your invoice put the words 'Bank charges to be paid by sender', so that whatever bank charges there are get paid by the producer not by you.

As mentioned above there are two kinds of basic deals, the optioning of a piece of work, and the commissioning of a treatment and/or script. Be aware of the cash-flow implications for each of these, so that you do not get any nasty surprises. Below are two hypothetical (but realistic) cash-flow projections.

The Option Deal

An option of £1000 for the first year against a purchase (exercise) price of £20,000. The option may be renewed for a second year for £1500 and for a third year for £2000. The first- and second-year options are set against the purchase price. The third year's option fee is not.

Period	Commencement	Expiry	Payment	Total paid
1st year	1/1/2000	31/12/2000	£1000	£1000
2nd year	1/1/2001	31/12/2001	£1500	£2500
3rd year	1/1/2002	31/12/2002	£2000	£4500

On exercise, the full fee is paid less the first two option fees (if appropriate). So if the option is exercised after just one year, a further sum of £19,000 is payable, making a total of £20,000. If the option had been extended for a second year, a further £17,500 is payable also making a total of £20,000. If the option is extended for the third year, then a further £17,500 is still due (because you would have received £2,500 for the first two options already), in addition to the £2000 paid for the third year option, making a total of £22,000. For cash flow purposes you would have received £4500 over the three years, with the £17,500 coming in during the third year.

The Commission Deal

If a treatment or script for a feature film is commissioned, along the lines of the Writers' Guild/PACT agreement, with a basic fee of £25,000 and a 100% buyout on the first day of principal photography (1st dpp), the cash flow will look something like this (the delivery and other dates are approximately what tends to happen):

Commission/Delivery	Percentage	Fee	Date	Period	Total
Commission of treatment	10%	£2500	1/1/2001		£2,500
Acceptance of treatment	10%	£2500	31/3/2001	3 months	£5,000
Commission of 1st draft	20%	£5000	1/5/2001	4 months	£10,000
Delivery of 1st draft	20%	£5000	30/6/2001	6 months	£15,000
Commission of 2nd draft	10%	£2500	1/8/2001	7 months	£17,500
Acceptance of 2nd draft	10%	£2500	1/9/2001	8 months	£20,000
1st day of princ. photo	20%	£5000	1/6/2002	18 months	£25,000

Total basic fee = £25,000
Plus buyout on 1st dpp = £25,000
TOTAL BUYOUT = **£50,000**

The first £20,000 comes in over eight months (ie at the rate of £2500 a month). The remaining £30,000 will not be paid at all unless the film starts principal photography. This can easily take more than a year; several years is not uncommon.

Notes

1   Article by Steve Clarke, *Daily Telegraph*, 18 February 1995.

2   Date unknown.

3   Contact the Short Film Agency at Canalot Studios, 222 Kensal Road, London W10 5BN tel 0181 968 1320 for free information.

4   More details on p 163.

5   Copies can be obtained from Laurence Bard at Ernst & Young in London, Becket House, 1 Lambeth Palace Road, London SE1 7EU, tel 0171 931 4866.

19 Research

Research can be divided into three basic areas: what you are writing about, where to sell it, and how to improve your writing. Information gleaned from careful reading of the trade papers can apply to first two. If you have an idea for a film and see that a similar one has already been announced, you should probably think again, but an announcement about an uninspiring television series may give you an idea for a new approach to a tired theme.

Once you have chosen your subject or theme, information is available everywhere. I am amazed at how much information overload there is and how little most writers do about it. Numerous books have been written specifically for writers. *Research for Writers* by Anne Hoffmann (A&C Black), *Writer's Handbook* by Cottam and Pelton (Barnes & Noble), *How to Research Your Novel* by Jean Saunders (Allison & Busby), *Researching Public Records* by Vincent Parco (Citadel Press) are four examples I see on my shelves.

Specialized bookshops are treasure troves for writers.
The Screenwriter's Store 10-11 Moor St London W1V 5LJ
(tel 0171 287 9009, fax 0171 287 6009, e-mail info@screenwriterstore.co.uk) is not really a bookshop, has a great catalogue of books and scriptwriting software as well as scripts and magazines about scriptwriting and are very helpful. Their website is at www.screenwriterstore.co.uk. They will get you any book or software programme you need. In London shops like the Cinema Bookshop at 13 Great Russell St, London WC1B 3NH (tel: 0171 637 0206), the bookshop at The Museum of the Moving Image (in the National Film Theatre on the South Bank in London), most large branches of shops like Dillons and Waterstones, and Offstage in Chalk Farm (0171 485 4996), will be worth visiting.

Assiduous reading of bibliographies can also pay dividends, and many of the books on writing have bibliographies. You can also cruise through *Books in Print*, which can be consulted in libraries and some bookshops, or on Compuserve which has both *British Books in Print* and *US Books in Print*.

The Internet is rapidly becoming an accessible research database for those who are plugged in. Nexis is a brilliant database, but is more expensive. It consists of magazines, newspapers and wire service articles from hundreds of titles, going back over ten years. Like the Internet you need a modem and PC to connect to it. You can call up articles using key words, or combinations of words. A quick search using the words 'sex' and 'Internet' threw up over 1000 articles. You can scroll through these on your screen and select what you wish to print or you can print everything (UK tel: 0800 895 107). Try also www.screentalk.org for further information.

For more specialized research, the number of sources is even greater. If you are writing thrillers or crime stories, for example, series of books are available, such as those published by Writer's Digest Books. The Howdunit Series, for example, has titles like *Police Procedural: A Writer's Guide to the Police and How They Work*. There are also other guides to private investigators, poisons, crime-scene investigations, death, murder and forensic medicine, weapons and so on.

The trade papers (*Broadcast, Screen International, C21, TV World, Variety, TBI, Moving Pictures, Writers News* to name a few) are essential. Select the one that most suits your needs, or try a second one for six months, then another, so that you get a broader picture. This is the best way to find out who has moved to which job. Usually when a commissioning editor or producer moves, they will want to find new material. That's the time to make submissions.

The other invaluable information to be gleaned from the trade press are ratings and box office figures. If you are interested in publishing then *The Bookseller* or *Publishing News* are valuable; for American publishing information read *Publishers Weekly*. These have weekly bestseller lists. Knowing who watches what and who buys which books is usually information that is underrated by writers. There is valuable information in Carole Blake's book *From Pitch to Publication*.

The *Writers' & Artists' Yearbook*: Published annually by A & C Black, an indispensable companion for every writer's desk-top. Information on writing markets such as articles, reports, short stories, books, poetry, scripts for theatre, radio, television and film. It also provides information on illustration, design, photography, picture research and music. For all of these there are names and addresses. It lists literary, film, TV and merchandising agents.

There are clear but brief chapters on merchandising, research, word processing, writing courses, ALCS, copyright law, libel, finance, income tax and social security contributions, the Society of Authors and the Writers' Guild. Worth buying every year.

The *Writer's Handbook* and *The BFI Yearbook* are also good general reference books. *Contacts* is also useful for UK addresses in the film and television and allied industries (tel: 0171 437 7631).

For Continental European information there are also good sources. *European Film File* publishes lists of European feature films planned or in production (tel: 0171 454 1185). The Media Desk of the European Union's MEDIA PROGRAMME is an invaluable source of information. It is based in Scotland and Wales (see above for contact details). *Screen International*, amongst others, publishes a yearbook which lists production companies and trade magazines from all over the world. There is a new French scriptwriting magazine *Synopsis* contactable at e-mail synopsis@altavista.net and a new British scriptwriting magazine, *Scriptwriter*, due in 2000 (contact the Screenwriter's Store).

Reading scripts also counts as research. Scripts are quite expensive to buy in Europe but can be obtained from the Screenwriter's Store. Faber & Faber also publish scripts and books on film and television. You can obtain catalogues of forthcoming publications from these and other publishers if you write in.

American magazines for writers include *scr(i)pt* (tel +1.410.592.3466; fax +1.410.592.8062); *Written By* (the journal of the WGA West); e-mail writtenby@wga.org; tel +1.323.782.4522 fax +1.323.782.4802; *Creative Screenwriting* (e-mail erikPSC@aol.com; tel +1.202.543.3438). There are also websites like www.scriptmag.com, and The Screenwriters Workshop website also has links to others (www.lsw.org).

Writing Courses

Apart from reading about writing, going to courses can be extremely useful (if sometimes rather expensive). The dynamics of good teaching can have a significant effect and enable you to extend your talent and research and develop your own ideas and stories.

The courses I have attended or have been involved with, which I value most highly, are listed below. There are many others which are also of great benefit.

1. MediaXchange

Based in London and Los Angeles this organisation arranges many of the best workshops, including exchanges to the USA in which European participants get to meet and see the American film and television creative community at work. They also organise Robert McKee's STORY lectures (see below). MediaXchange is at 10-11 Moor Street, London W1V 5LJ (tel 0171 734 2310, fax 0171 287 0096). Check their web site: WWW.mediaxchange.com. In LA the numbers are tel 001 323 650 7818, fax 001 323 650 4791.

2. Robert McKee

Probably the best-known lecturer in Europe (and the USA too). His story structure class (three days) is a tour de force, partly because he used to be an actor, so his delivery is enviable. But the heart of the course is a classic analysis of why structure works. I have known writers' careers take off once the mysteries of script structure were laid bare.

There are doubters, however, who fear that McKee provides unintelligent executives in the business with a shorthand that they probably do not understand, but use nevertheless. The phrase 'the inciting incident' is bandied about in the Groucho Club by people unsure of its real meaning. I do not think we should be too worried about executives who can't think for themselves; they are perfectly capable of messing up, with or without help. I believe that the sort of analysis that McKee provides is invaluable if you are able to think for yourself. His lecture on Chinatown is a must, or buy his book, *Story*.
CONTACT: MediaXchange (above). Get on their mailing list.

3. Jürgen Wolff

Wolff is Europe's leading comedy lecturer. Apart from being the author of several books and numerous screenplays, his thoughtful courses provide insight into sitcom, comedy, and other forms of dramatic writing. he also shows writers how to develop their minds using visualisation, and how to 'write from the heart'.
CONTACT: tel 0207 323 3037. Fax 0207 323 3037, or Screenwriter's Store 0207 287 9009.

4. John Sherlock

Vastly experienced English writer who was at the top in Hollywood for over 30 years, writing novels, film and television scripts. Runs regular Master Classes in Dublin (lives in Ireland). Workshops cover script writing and novel writing. Very practical, down-to-earth and inspiring.
CONTACT: tel 00353 283 3260

5. Julian Friedmann

Lectures on the business of scriptwriting and runs pitching workshops.

CONTACT: Screenwriters Store or tel 0207 284 0408, fax 0207 284 0442, e-mail julian@blakefriedmann.co.uk

6. Linda Seger

Perhaps the best teacher of script editing around and author of excellent books on scriptwriting. Based in LA but comes to Europe regularly. Contact Screenwriter's Store.

Longer Courses

There are some excellent degree courses in scriptwriting at institutions such as The National Film and Television School, Bournemouth University (a BA degree) and several MA degree courses. These include De Montfort University in Leicester(the only degree course specialising in television scriptwriting),the London Institute, the Northern Film School in Leeds and John Moores University in Liverpool (where the is one scriptwriting and one scriptediting MA). The master's degrees are usually two-year part-time courses, so that people with jobs can attend. For further information on the MA in Television Scriptwriting at De Montfort call Dr John Cook at DMU tel 01162 551551 (extension 8683) or e-mail jrcook@dmu.ac.uk

For further information on media training courses throughout Europe, contact the European Audiovisual Observatory, tel: 33 8814 4407; talk to Lone Andersen. Also the BFI publishes a book annually on media courses in higher education.

Writers' Associations

Writers should become members of one or more of the national associations and organisations like the Writers' Guild (WG), the Society of Authors (SOA), or the Authors Licensing & Collecting Society (ALCS). There are also numerous other organizations like the Screenwriters' Workshop, or the New Producers' Alliance (NPA), which accepts script writers as affiliates. You may be a member of all of them, in which case you will receive their valuable newsletters and be able to avail yourself of the meetings they organise and the advice they dispense.

They are there for their members' benefit, though I have the impression that many writers who belong barely utilize the expertise or support from both staff and other members.

Most associations publish newsletters, which are invaluable sources of up-to-date information; they have staff able to help with individual enquiries; they run surgeries for members, many of which are free, at which experienced lawyers, producers, writers and agents will have private meetings (usually lasting half an hour) with the member to discuss a problem. The surgery alone can be worth more than the annual membership. The SOA also publishes a useful series of 'Quick Guides' on a number of subjects, particularly legal issues. The WG, SOA and ALCS will sometimes help members with legal problems, and the WG and SOA can also under certain circumstances help with legal costs. For that alone it is worth joining!

These associations also organise seminars and even parties from time to time. For writers who feel isolated, even if they do not have easy access to London, the various associations can offer a great deal. ALCS collects money on behalf of writers from cable transmissions outside Britain. Unless you are a member, which is not expensive, you may miss out.

Addresses:

Authors Licensing and Collecting Society

Marlborough Court, 14–18 Holborn London EC1N 2LE, tel 0207 395 0600, email alcs@alcs.demon.co.uk, website www.alcs.co.uk

Membership details: Membership is open to any author or successor to an author's estate, regardless of residency or nationality. The annual subscription is very modest. Members of the Society of Authors and the Writers' Guild of Great Britain have free membership of ALCS. Only members can receive German public lending right. Members receive ALCS News and Clarion free of charge, an invitation to the AGM and can call on the expertise of the ALCS office for copyright queries. Members' names are also registered on the CAE list, an international database of authors and composers. This list is used by CISAC societies to identify and contact writers to request permission for use of their work, or, in countries where the copyright law does not demand prior permission, to make appropriate remuneration via the relevant collecting society. Even if you are not currently a WG or SOA member, I think you should join if only to support the ALCS.

British Film Institute

21 Stephen Street, London W1P 2LN, tel: 0171 255 1444 fax: 0171 436 7950

Apart from the valuable library and reading room, the BFI publishes widely on film and television and produces a monthly magazine *Sight & Sound*. It has a library of television programmes that can be used for research. Among its valuable publications are *Media Courses* and *The BFI Film & Television Handbook*, both of which are published every year. The latter is an excellent source of film and television contacts and it also has a useful overview of the industry. Worth joining.

The Screenwriters' Workshop

Suffolk House, 1–8 Whitfield Place, London W1P 5SF, tel 0207 387 5551 or email: screenoffice@cwcom.net   website: www.lsw.org.uk

Membership details: previously called the London Screenwriters' Workshop, this is a voluntary organisation. Annual membership is very inexpensive. Apart from the magazine, numerous courses are run by and for members on different aspects of scriptwriting. Great camaraderie, helpful to new writers in particular.

New Producers Alliance

8 Bourlet Close, London W1P 7JP, tel 0207 580 2480, website www.newproducers.co.uk

A vibrant, fast-growing lobby and support group with close to 1,000 members.

Organises good meetings, workshops and seminars. Strongly recommended for writers to join. Not expensive.

Society of Authors

84 Drayton Gardens, London SW10 9SB, tel: 0171 373 6642 fax: 0171 373 5768.

Membership details: The basic subscription rate is £60 a year (payable by direct debit) with a concessionary rate for authors under 35 or over 65 who are not earning a significant income from writing. For historical reasons, the SOA is more popular with book writers than script writers. The latter tend to belong more to the WG. Personally, I think it is well worth belonging to both.

The Writers Guild of Great Britain

430 Edgware Road, London W2 1EH, tel: 0171 723 8074 fax: 0171 706 2413

Membership details: You can become either a temporary member or a full member. Temporary members are writers who have sold or licensed original written work to any individual, company or organisation. The work does not have to be published or produced, but you must supply evidence of the sale. Temporary members pay £70 a year.

Full members are those whose work has been produced or published. There is a points system: one feature = 12 points (which is enough for full membership); a short is 6, a TV movie of over 50 minutes is 12, under 50 minutes is 6, and so on, covering all aspects of television, radio and books. Full members pay £70 annually plus 1% 'of that part of their gross income from writing in the immediate previous calendar year which exceeds £7000. The maximum supplementary subscription is £850 making a total of £920.'

Affiliate members can be agents, research consultants, legal or financial advisers. The annual subscription is £150.

All Guild subscriptions are tax free. The Guild also has a pension scheme for freelance writers, and publishes a bi-monthly journal *The Writers' Newsletter*.

Additional information may be obtained from a new site www.produxion.com

Conclusion

Research pays off. Don't weaken your presentation, your treatment, your script or manuscript because your research was inadequate. And most importantly, don't let yourself down in meetings with people who are considering investing in you. You never know how much you really need to know about a subject to impress. Use the widespread facilities that are available to make yourself better informed. Attend meetings of your peers and support writers' associations. Unless writers become more politicized in Europe they will not be able to strengthen their negotiating position. This translates very directly into what writers get paid.

Appendix 1. Some Examples of Negotiations with Producers

A wide range of examples can be used to illustrate the negotiating process with producers. The following three examples of real negotiations illustrate something of the give-and-take and the tone used by both sides, as well as the positive attempts by each side to close the deal without conceding too much.

The names of the parties have been deleted, though a brief note identifies the stature of the parties.

Example 1

A talented but not very experienced British writer is being engaged by a medium-sized, successful Continental independent producer to write a script based on a book. The deal was negotiated over the phone and by fax; the whole negotiation took just over a week. The Agent drew up and faxed a draft agreement, to which the Producer replied two days later.

From Production Company to Agent

Dear Agent,

Re: Title of Film by X (writer)

I thought I would comment on your agreement so we can advance as much as we can while I get the underlying rights tied up.

2 a-h   I need two drafts and one set of revisions from Writer for the agreed price of US$24,000. I propose the second revision be optional, but in any event payment would not exceed US$2,000.

2 i Principal photography payment. I agree to 2% of the approved budget but the floors[1] and ceilings[2] are way too high given Writer's stature as a writer. We could agree to no more than a minimum floor of US$50,000 and ceiling of $90,000. I also need to request some exclusions from the budget total: specifically producer's fees, contingency and completion bond cost.

2 j We could agree to a maximum of 1% of the producer's share of net profits.

3 a I must insist we include language to the effect that shared credit and therefore shared

monies will occur automatically if and when Production Company on its own accord deems necessary to bring on another writer(s) to the project. ie shared credit/money would not be subject to a ruling from third party arbitrators.

I think these are all my comments. I reserve the right to amend this, as these comments are being sent to you prior to my discussing them with my partners. But in any event, I anticipate no further comments. I regret the firmness of my position, but as I mentioned last time, I need to have this deal reflect the Writer's limited experience.

Best,

Producer
cc. Coproducer and Lawyer

On the following day the Agent faxed back:

Dear Producer,

Re: Title

Thanks for your fax of…

You are driving a hard deal. I am happy to reflect my client's limited experience, but the deal must be fair.

2 a) to h): in your fax of 8 July you offered $15,000 for the first draft, $7,500 for the second and $4,000 for each of the revisions. We then agreed $17,500 for the first draft on the phone. That produces a total for two drafts and one revision of $29,000. So where you get the $24,000 from I don't know.

I am happy to make the second revision $2,000, but I'd rather not change what we've already agreed!

By the way, you are not obliged to commission more than the first draft anyway. Perhaps that makes a difference.

2 i): I can accept your minimum floor. The ceiling is very stingy. What if the film attracts major talent and the budget goes way up? That would be the Writer's doing. How about $140,000 as a ceiling, ie 2% of $7 million? If the budget is that high, a few extra dollars to the writer shouldn't hurt your cut.

We'll accept the specified exclusions.

3 a): this is grossly unfair. Are you suggesting that my client should get shared credit and

shared money if you brought in another writer to do a polish? Are you suggesting that a 20% rewrite should reduce the Writer's cut by 50%? Are you suggesting that where several successive writers work on a script, and then the director goes back to the first script (this happened to a client of ours) the Writer would get a shared credit and a fraction of his production payment? I sincerely hope not.

If you are unhappy about using an unfamiliar credit agreement to compute the credit in the first place, why don't we say that you will use your discretion to accord a reasonable credit, but that in the event of dispute the Writer can seek credit determination under the UK Screen Credits Agreement. The onus is then on you to see the writer is fairly treated.

Look forward to your response.

Yours,

Agent

Three days and a telephone conversation later a deal was agreed and the Agent drew up a revised contract. Using the Writer's agent to draw up the contract (rather than the Producer's lawyers) not only saved the Producer money but speeded up the deal.
     The following is the document that became the signed agreement between the parties:

To Producer

Dear Producer,

Re: Title/Writer

This letter sets out the terms of agreement between our client (Writer) and Production Company (you) relating to the development of the above titled project.

It is hereby agreed:

1. You hereby commission the Writer to write a first draft feature film script entitled [TITLE] based on material provided by you to him which he undertakes to deliver as soon as possible but in any event not later than [DATE].
     You shall be entitled at any time after delivery of the first draft script to commission a second draft script and thereafter two revisions to the second draft script subject to delivery dates to be agreed with the writer at the time.

2. As consideration for his services you undertake to pay the Writer the following sums:
     a) $8,750 on signature hereof.
     b) $8,750 on delivery of the first draft script. Until this payment has been received,

copyright in the Writer's script shall remain his. Upon payment, copyright in the script will pass to you.

   c) $3,750 on commencement of the second draft script.

   d) $3,750 on delivery of the second draft script.

   e) $1,000 on commencement of the revision to the second draft.

   f) $1,000 on delivery of the revision to the second draft.

   g) on principal photography of the film, a sum equal to 2% of the final approved budget of the film, less sums already paid to the Writer hereunder, with an aggregate minimum floor of $50,000 and an aggregate ceiling of $115,000. For the purposes of this agreement, 'final approved budget' shall not include budget items representing producer fees, contingency and completion bond costs.

   h) sums from time to time equal to 1% of 100% of the producer's share of net profits of the film as the same is defined in the main financing and producing agreement for the film, provided that no participant shall receive a more favourable definition, and in that event the Writer's participation shall be defined on the same favoured basis.

3. a) In the event that the Writer is accorded a shared main credit on the film, the sums payable on principal photography shall be divided accordingly: ie if there are two writers sharing the credit the Writer will receive half of the payments otherwise due on principal photography; if three writers share the credit he will receive a third of the sums otherwise due to him on principal photography, and so on. If the Writer is not credited, either as sole or joint writer, no sums shall be due to him on principal photography of the film pursuant to clause 2 g) and 2 h) above.

   b) You undertake to accord the Writer a reasonable credit in a prominent place and on front-end titles if appropriate and in major paid advertising where he is the sole or shared credited writer. In the event of any dispute between the parties relating to credits you agree to abide by a credit arbitration awarded by the UK Writers Guild based on the terms of the 1974 BFPA Screen Credits agreement (as amended).

4. The Writer as beneficial owner hereby assigns to you absolutely all copyright and other rights in the products of his services hereunder in all media for the duration of copyright as extended upon receipt of the payment in 2 b).

5. a) The Writer warrants that save insofar as the products of his services hereunder contain material provided to him by you, they shall be original to the Writer and shall to his best knowledge and belief contain no defamatory material.

   b) You warrant to the Writer that you own all the rights necessary to enter this agreement and you undertake to indemnify the writer against any loss, damage, cost or expense resulting from any breach of such a warranty.

6. In the event the Writer has not received sums contractually due to him pursuant to the terms hereof at any stage, then without prejudice to his right to sue you for payment, he shall be entitled to discontinue his services hereunder until such sums are duly paid, and

any applicable delivery date shall be extended for a period equal to the interval between the date payment became due and the date of actual payment.

7. You undertake to reimburse all travel, board and lodging expenses incurred by the Writer at your request and you undertake to pay him when he is required to travel a per diem. {NOTE: A per diem is the equivalent of 'pocket money' for incidentals. Per diems are usually in addition to meals provided and paid for the by the producer.}

8. All sums becoming due under this agreement shall be made payable to the Agency by direct bank transfer into Bank, account number, receipt by whom shall be good and sufficient discharge.

9. The terms of this agreement shall be governed by English law and subject to the exclusive jurisdiction of the English courts.

If you are in agreement with the above, please sign in the space provided below:

_____   For and on behalf of Writer

_____   For and on behalf of Production Company

Conclusion
In the end the deal reflected a compromise both parties could feel good about. The writer kept copyright until the first draft payment was made; late payments occasioned extensions to the delivery dates (something that encourages producers not to pay late) and an initially unreasonable credit and principal photography payment proposal was finalised in a much more equitable way.

Example 2
Some deals get changed during the writing/rewriting process, or even later. In other words renegotiating with producers is not uncommon. There are times when one compromises to get the deal signed so that the writing can start, but there remains an expectation that the agreement has not catered for all eventualities. So one has to be prepared to renegotiate at a later stage.

It is useful for writers to be aware of this. One should not sign a deal knowing that one wants to immediately start renegotiating. But deals are not always set in concrete, usually because the financiers or broadcasters or producers move the goal posts after the game has started, and request changes. Sometimes it is the writer who requests the changes.

Here are two examples of renegotiations to give you some idea of what actually does go on in negotiations. The first is with the lawyers for a large independent production company, also on the Continent. There are several projects being discussed at once. The main part of the fax deals with the fact that one of the writers has done more work than the agreement envisaged, as a result of script-editing feedback from producer and broadcaster. The writer is very experienced and her previous script for the same Producer/Broadcaster was very well received.

Whether the additional work had to be done because the early drafts were not good enough, ie the writer's 'fault', or because the producer/broadcaster changed their mind is sometimes difficult to say.

It is also not usually productive to apportion blame. One should rather concentrate on getting the next draft to work. Usually, if one analyses carefully who was responsible for a draft going wrong, there is blame on both sides. Producers are not always clear enough in their briefings and writers do not always listen carefully enough. Agents are capable of being equally culpable.

From Agent to Production Company Lawyer

Dear Lawyer,

Re: TITLE by Writer

Recapping on our telephone conversation this morning:

1. I would be very grateful if we could receive copies of Writer A's movie contract.

2. Please find enclosed a signed copy of Writer B's movie contract, together with an invoice for sums due on commencement. I would be most grateful if the invoice could be processed as quickly as possible.

3. On the question of Writer C's movie treatment, I don't want to be tiresome about this, but just let me make the following points so you see our point of view:

In the 18 February letter agreement, Writer C was commissioned to write a revised version of the original treatment you supplied. She has now written three versions and is about to write a fourth and the document (14 pages) is no longer an outline. It's very definitely become a treatment. The fact of the matter is that the Broadcaster won't make their mind up to commission a script until they have an elaborate document which is a treatment. In our original contract we provided for this stage to be costed at £12,000. What I am getting at is the discrepancy between the original payment and the amount of work actually involved. This process has not been made easier in Writer C's case by the fact that many of the ingredients of the original treatment that she was asked to base her draft on were thrown out by the Broadcaster who in effect asked for the treatment to be turned into a different kind of movie. Similarly, although the Producer (your client) claims that the writer has not written entirely according to brief, the writer says the notes she receives are not always precise.

However, the important point is that the project is progressing and improving and the

Production Company simply cannot blame the writer for all the difficulties entailed in that. Accordingly, I think it's exceedingly fair that the Production Company and the writer should split the risk: ie if the true value of the work she's doing at this stage will be £12,000 you should pay her no less than £6,000, ie another £3,000 now (in addition to the £3,000 on commencement). The important thing to remember is that the writer did indeed deliver satisfactorily on the previous script she wrote for your client and the result then was much approved by the Broadcaster.

Yours,

Agent

Conclusion

This was resolved with the proposed compromise. Sometimes it is necessary to lay out in pedantic detail the reasonableness of your claims, before the other side realise they are being unreasonable. But full marks to them for trying.

Example 3

This is a damage-limitation negotiation which occurred because the Producer, after three drafts of the script, and under pressure of time, decided to have the next draft written 'in-house', rather than by the original writer. The Producer then wanted to use money in the Writer's agreement to pay for the in-house rewrite.

From Agent to Producer

Dear Producer,

Thanks for your letter of 12 December regarding TITLE.

To be frank, I think this is a rather unusual situation and it hasn't been possible until now to analyse absolutely fairly the arguments on either side. However, may I make the following points:

1. It is clear that such problems as there were with the first draft script were not of the Writer's making. He was adhering to a brief expressly provided by you.

2. The second draft script went well and, in spite of difficulties with the third draft, it was far from inevitable that the writer would not be able to make good the final changes. He worked speedily on the second draft and got it 90% right by the end of draft three.

3. So all in all, the writer has showed good faith, worked diligently and delivered in accordance with a tight time schedule and a varying brief. He held himself available and by any normal standards was making satisfactory progress. If he was not able to complete a fully satisfactory final draft this was because he wasn't given the chance.

4. The fact that you made an executive decision to have the script internally rewritten by a script consultant was, therefore, a purely pragmatic measure. You were free to do so; but that does not automatically mean the cost of exercising that right should be borne by the writer. The writer wasn't the source of your problem. The problem was time, compounded by initial editorial misdirection.

5. Internal rewrites are common in the business, but in nearly all situations where this occurs writers still receive their acceptance payment. Indeed, it is usually customary to accept the writer's work if, given the circumstances, he has done his best. The writer is an experienced and acclaimed writer and it is an extremely reasonable inference to make that in this situation he did his best. Certainly we have never had this situation before.

6. Finally, striking a contractual note, the acceptance money in question is payable on acceptance of the second draft script. See clause 5 c) of the agreement. In effect, the writer's second draft was accepted (as second draft), because you then requested rewrites to the second draft script which, pursuant to clause 3 d) of the agreement, you were only entitled to do if the second draft had been accepted. In other words, the writer's full entitlement to the sums in question was dependent not on his writing a finally acceptable script but on his completing the second draft stage in such a way that you proceeded to further revisions, rather than cutting him off at that point.

In summary, I think that the writer's entitlement to the full acceptance payment is not only fair according to common sense and good faith and general industry practice, but under the specific terms of the contract.

I look forward to hearing from you shortly.

Yours,

Agent

Conclusion

The renegotiation was concluded satisfactorily for the original writer. The in-house writer also got paid. Lack of clarity in the briefing from the producer, or the producer realising that once the script was written the original brief was shown to be incorrect, is a frequent cause of development problems.

Notes

1   'floor' is the minimum guaranteed amount; 'ceiling' the maximum. So if 2% of the approved budget was below $50,000 the writer would still get $50,000; and if 2% was above $90,000 the writer would only get $90,000. The completion bond is an insurance policy in the event that the film runs into certain types of difficulty or goes over budget, in which case the financiers take over the movie or the completion bond makes available the necessary finance to complete the film.

Appendix 2. Deal Memo Examples

Like all sample contracts these were negotiated for a specific situation. It is risky to assume that they will apply to any other situation. They are for information only.

Producer Seeks to Commission Writer for a Feature Script – Sample Deal Memo from Producer

To: Agent
From: Production Company

Dear Agent,

<u>Title</u>

I propose that we structure a deal for Writer X to write a treatment and a first and second draft of the script along the following lines:

1. A writer's fee of £35,000:
     £2,500 for the treatment
          £1,000 on commencement, £1,000 on delivery, £500 for revisions
     £10,000 for first draft
          £4,000 on commencement, £4,000 on delivery, £2,000 for revisions
     £5,000 for second draft
          £2,000 on commencement, £2,000 on delivery, £1,000 for revisions
     £17,500 on first day of principal photography
   There will be a cut-off provision at each stage.

2. Writing and reading periods:
Treatment:	3 weeks
Reading period :	3 weeks
Revisions:	1 week
First draft:	10 weeks
Reading period :	4 weeks
Revisions:	3 weeks
Second draft:	8 weeks
Reading period :	3 weeks
Revisions:	2 weeks

3. Expenses

If Producer requires Writer X to render services hereunder more than thirty miles outside London, Writer X will be provided with business class round trip air transportation and a *per diem* to be agreed to cover out of pocket expenses.

4. Credit

The Producer will give the Writer credit in accordance with the provisions of the Screenwriting Credits Agreement operating between PACT and the Writers Guild of Great Britain.

All other terms in the contract, such as approvals, will follow the usual terms found in screenwriting agreements of this nature.

Yours sincerely,

Producer

Sample TV Movie Commission deal Memo

From Agent to Producer

Dear Producer,

Re: Title/TV film project

This letter sets out the agreement between Writer X and Producer (you) relating to the development of the above titled film.

It is hereby agreed:

1.   You hereby commission Writer X to write an outline for a 90-minute TV movie based on the subject of Y which he undertakes to write and deliver as soon as possible but not later than [date].

The outline shall be of not less than six pages in length.

2.   In the event that you wish to commission an extended treatment and/or a first draft script based on the outline written by Writer X, you undertake to offer Writer X first refusal to be commissioned to write the same subject to *bona fide* negotiations of the appropriate fees and residuals and other terms (depending on the broadcaster) at the time.

3.   As consideration for his services you hereby undertake to pay Writer X the following payments, as applicable:
   a) On signature hereof: £1,000.
   b) On delivery of the outline: £1,000.

4. On receipt of the delivery payment, Writer X as beneficial owner hereby assigns to you all copyright and other rights in the products of his services worldwide in all languages and media for the duration of copyright as the same may be extended.

5. Writer hereby warrants that, save insofar as the material commissioned hereunder contains material incorporated at your request, it shall be original to him and shall not to his best knowledge and belief contain any defamatory material.

6. At the time the further stages are commissioned, you and the Writer shall agree a reasonable delivery date, having regard to his existing professional commitments.

7. You undertake to reimburse all expenses incurred by Writer at your request, including but not limited to travel, board and lodging expenses, on production of receipts.

8. In the event the sums contractually due to Writer have not been paid, he shall be entitled to extend the delivery date due for any work in progress by a period equal to the number of days between the date the payment became contractually due and the date it is actually received.

9. All sums (excluding expenses) becoming payable hereunder shall be made out and paid to Z Literary Agency Ltd, receipt by whom shall be good and sufficient discharge.

If you are in agreement with the above, please sign in the space provided below:

_____   _____

For and on behalf of Producer   Writer X

Draft TV Series Bible Commission Deal Memo

From: Agent
To: Producer

Dear Producer,

Re: new TV series proposal A (working title) by Writer B

This letter sets out the agreement between Writer B and Producer (you) relating to the development of the above titled project.

It is hereby agreed:

1. a) You hereby commission Writer B to write a 15-page bible for a 60-minute episodic TV series. The bible shall comprise six short storylines, a treatment of one of the six storylines, character biographies and an introductory blurb setting out the

concept/rationale for the series. Writer B undertakes to write and deliver the same as soon as possible but not later than five weeks from the date of signature hereof.

b) Provided that within thirty days of the date of delivery of the bible you request revisions to the same, Writer B undertakes to write and deliver the revisions within twenty-one days of the date of notice.

2. As consideration for the assignment of all rights in the Work commissioned hereunder, you hereby undertake to pay Writer B the following sums:

a) £1,000 on signature hereof

b) £1,500 on delivery of the first draft of the bible

c) £2,000 on signature of a deal between you and a broadcaster or any other third party to further develop the series.

3. a) In the event a series is developed further, you undertake to offer Writer B first refusal to accept a commission to write at least three episodes in the first series and you undertake to use your best endeavours to procure that he is offered first refusal to accept a commission to write a further three episodes in the first series.

b) The script fee and terms of agreement for each episode shall be subject to *bona fide* negotiations at the time, but you will not in any event offer a fee of less than £8,000 per one hour episode. For the avoidance of doubt, no portion of payments received for the bible should be set against the script fee payment.

4. In the event that the first series is based on the bible you undertake to pay Writer a format royalty of 10% of the script fee paid to another writer or writers for each episode in any series commissioned from another writer or writers, the said format royalty to be payable in total on production of the relevant series.

5. Subject to full payment of the sums becoming due hereunder, Writer as beneficial owner hereby assigns to you exclusively and absolutely the worldwide copyright and all other rights in the products of his services hereunder in all media and in perpetuity.

6. You undertake to procure that Writer is paid a sum equal to 3% of the gross box office receipts generated during any run of any stage adaptation or musical based on the series, payment to be made at the end of each 4-week period of any run, and at the end of the run.

7. Writer undertakes that insofar as the products of his services contain material provided by you to him or incorporated at your request, they shall be original to him and shall not infringe the copyright of any third party and shall not contain, to his best knowledge and belief, any defamatory material. Writer indemnifies you and holds you harmless from all claims, damages, liabilities and expenses arising from any breach of any of his representations and warranties hereunder.

8. You undertake to credit Writer as originator of the series on copies of the film of each

and every episode based on the bible, such credit to be in a prominent place in the front end credits.

9. Time shall be of the essence, both in respect of payment of sums due under this agreement and of delivery of the material.

10. All sums becoming payable hereunder shall be made out and paid to Z Literary Agency Ltd, receipt by whom shall be good and sufficient discharge.

11. This agreement shall be construed in accordance with English law and subject to the exclusive jurisdiction of the English courts.

If you are in agreement with the above, please sign in the space provided below:

_____   _____

For and on behalf of Producer   Writer

Draft Deal Letter for TV Series Pilot Commission

From: Agent
To: TV Broadcast Company

Dear

Re: Title X by Writer Y

I met Director Z yesterday and he recommended that I fax you my proposal for Writer Y's fees on this project. I'm anxious to close the deal quickly, if possible.

The pilot script, a three to four page general outline and character notes: £4,500. Five one-page outlines: £2,000.

Writer to have first refusal to be commissioned to write all the remaining episodes in the first series at £4,000 per ep and not less than 50% of the episodes in any subsequent series.

Writer to receive a format royalty for every episode written by another writer equal to 10% of his going rate or that of the other writers', whichever is the greater.

The above terms on whichever Writers Guild agreement you prefer.

Thus, if the development budget is £6,500 we would expect half of the script fee and half of the outline fee to be payable on signature, a quarter of both on delivery and a quarter of both on acceptance.

Look forward to hearing from you shortly.

Yours sincerely,

Agent

Example of Negotiating Letter Re: Acquisition of Rights to a Novel by a Producer.
Negotiated by the Producer's Lawyers

To: Producer's Lawyer
From: Agent

Dear,

<u>Re: Title D by Novelist E</u>

SUBJECT TO CONTRACT

Thanks for your fax.
4 b): we can agree to a ceiling of £45,000 for a mini-series. I can accept that the rate per broadcast hour should be £10,000 for the first four hours and £7,500 for every hour thereafter.
  c): we can agree to a sequel rate of 100% for an author-originated sequel and 70% for a producer-originated sequel.

Re reversions: we can agree to a seven year reversion period for the original film but I absolutely cannot concede interest or production costs other than money actually received by Novelist for the rights on reversion. Payment to him is not a loan. It is part payment for the rights which are assigned conditional on their being exploited by the producer within the reversion period.

I can also compromise to seven years on sequel rights, although I feel this is far in excess of what you would practically need. The sequel period must run from production because there is the very remote possibility of production without subsequent transmission or release and because the previous reversion periods are linked into production not transmission or release.

Yours sincerely,

Agent

Appendix 3. A Brief A-Z of Contracts and Law for Writers

Disclaimer

This appendix (as well as the chapters, especially Chapter 17, dealing with legal matters) comprise my opinions about the matters dealt with in the chapters. But I am not a lawyer. However, in a book like this it is necessary to highlight areas of the law that affect writers. Simplifying some very complex areas of law is risky - the simplification tends to distort. But I hope that from these chapters writers and those who work with them will become more aware of the pitfalls and risks that writers face.

Creating wonderful scripts may seem a world away from knowledge about defamation, passing-off, copyright, or the other legal and contractual problems facing writers and producers. But it really is important to be aware that there are areas of law that will impinge on your life as a writer. A little knowledge may be dangerous. No knowledge is even more dangerous. If in any doubt consult a lawyer. Too many people think that they can save money by not using lawyers. Think of it as insurance. It is almost always well worth it. Hopefully after reading the relevant sections of this book you will at least know what questions to ask a lawyer.

This chapter is an easy-to-refer to guide. It cannot cover everything, but should provide some familiarity with many of the most common terms and clauses in contracts, and with some of the legal danger-spots for writers. Check the index of the book for other references to legal terms.

Above and below the line

Above-the-line costs are usually the script, director, cast and producer; below-the-line costs are everything else. The producer's fee, financing costs, insurance and the cost of the completion bond are sometimes separated out as a third category.

Agency Clause

If you have an agent, then there should be an agency clause which states that your agent will receive the monies from the producer, and the agent's receipt will confirm that the producer has paid. It is important, therefore, for you to have a separate agreement with your agent in which the agent's commission is spelled out, as he or she will deduct the commission before remitting the rest to you. (See also the chapter on agents.)

Agreements

An agreement can be binding whether it's oral or written, or part oral and part written. The question is: what is an agreement? An agreement consists of the following:

1   An offer which contains all the principal terms of the deal.

2   An acceptance of the offer which is unconditional and absolute. If, say, the offer lists ten points and you say you agree to all of them, that constitutes an absolute and unconditional acceptance. If one point isn't acceptable and you make an alternative proposal, that's a counter-offer and the agreement is not binding until such time as all points are agreed.

3   There must be some consideration between the parties and it must be present or future. It is not acceptable for the consideration, whether financial or otherwise, to have been given in the past. A court will not be concerned about whether the actual consideration is adequate or not (ie whether it is good value). So you could say that in consideration of your payment to me of £10 now (or next week) I promise to give you my car. But you can't have a legally binding agreement in which you say that in consideration of the £10 you gave me last week I promise to give you my car.

4   There must be intent on the part of both parties to be legally bound. If for example there were two people in a bar and one of them said that if the other rowed his canoe around the world the speaker would eat his hat, a court would probably not consider that to be a contract because there was no serious intention to eat the hat. It was a figure of speech, meaning that 'If you canoe around the world I'll be very surprised'.

5   The offer and the acceptance do not actually have to be in writing in most cases. They can be oral or written or a combination. And they can be in a course of correspondence rather than one document.

But some contracts do have to be in writing, such as agreements that relate to land or the legal assignment of copyright. You can agree to assign copyright verbally but the actual assignment must be done in writing.

Ancilliary rights

This describes all the rights that are 'ancilliary' to the minimum rights required to make and exploit a film or programme. Video, cable, cinema and TV are not considered to be ancilliary rights; publishing, radio, stage or merchandising rights, which don't actually involve exploiting the film itself, are usually considered as ancilliary rights.

Assignment/Partial Assignment

Making a film involves a bundle of rights; that is, there are a number of different material forms, including writing, music, pictures - still and moving - which can be protected by the law of copyright. These rights, as a whole or in part, can be sold or assigned for the purposes of making and exploiting a film or programme(s).

As the rights necessary to make and exploit a movie do not need to include all the copyrightable elements in a work, so writers sometimes need to sell only partial copyright, while reserving certain copyrightable elements.

Assignment to Third Party/Direct Covenant

A chain of rights can be involved in assigning to third parties. You can increase your chances of being paid by taking the following steps.

1   When two parties enter into a contract with each other, only the parties who sign the contract are bound by it, not 3rd parties.

2   If you have sold the rights to your script to a 2nd party and they have promised to pay you money for the script, if they sell the script on to a 3rd party (which is quite common), your claim to the money you are owed is not against the 3rd party, but only against the party with whom you made the deal (ie the 2nd party).

3   In all probability the party to whom you sold the rights, when they made their deal with the 3rd party, will have secured from that 3rd party a promise of payment in their (the 2nd party's) favour. But you won't normally be a beneficiary of that payment because you don't have a contract with the 3rd party.

4   So, it is sensible to only permit an assignment to 3rd parties of the rights you sell or license to a second party, on condition that the 2nd party procures a direct promise to you by the 3rd party that the 3rd party will pay you what you are entitled to under your deal with the 2nd party.

Furthermore, only if and to the extent that the 3rd party actually does pay you, should you be prepared to relieve the 2nd party of their obligations to pay you. In this way you will be getting a promise to pay you from two parties instead of only one, which must be better! There is no reason at all why either the 2nd or 3rd party should refuse to agree to this provision in the agreements, which is sometimes called 'a direct covenant'.

Best of Knowledge and Belief

Every contract under which you sell or licence rights will probably include warranties that what you are writing is original, true (if you claim it is a fact), doesn't invade anyone's privacy, is not defamatory or obscene, and so on. Since it is not always possible to know that something is true, or is not defamatory, it is advisable to qualify such warranties with the words 'to the best of my knowledge and belief'. This still imposes a fairly onerous obligation on you to be sure of what you are writing, but it is not as sweeping as the warranty without these words.

Buy-out

Many deals involve paying the writer 'residual payments' according to sales of the film or programme. These are sometimes also called 'repeat' or 're-use' payments. For instance, the sale of a TV movie by a UK broadcaster to a German broadcaster will, if the original contract for the writer included residuals, oblige the person who hired the writer to make an additional payment (a proportion of the original, basic fee). Similarly if the sale is to Australia. Each territory has a fee agreed in the contract.

However, instead of residual payments, some producers prefer to pay a lump sum in advance of sales. This is called a buy-out, as it, in effect, 'buys-out' the residuals. It is usually paid on the first day of principal photography. Buy-outs are commonly between 100% and 150% of the original fee and the rule of thumb is that sales in many territories will produce a larger sum than the buy-out, but a) there is a risk that those sales will never be made, and b) the buy-out is usually paid on the first day of principal photography and is guaranteed as long as the film or programme is made.

Collecting Agencies

There are various collecting agencies, such as ALCS in the UK and others in Europe like the SACD. They collect monies for writers, composers and directors that is due usually as a result of agreements within the industries in different countries of the world. This money is intended to go to the writers and other creative roles, not to the producers. But if writers are not registered with the WG or SOA in the UK or with ALCS, the monies from the UK or abroad may end up going to the distributor or producer. The WG/PACT agreement notes that a producer cannot claim any monies payable to the writer via foreign and/or domestic collecting societies. (See also reference to ALCS in the chapter on research.)

Completion Guarantee

A completion guarantee is necessary to obtain most forms of industry film finance. This is a form of insurance guarantee given by completion guarantors to the financiers of a film that the film will be completed and delivered.

Often the financiers will pay their contribution towards the budget of a film on the basis that payment will only be made if and when the film is delivered. The producer of the film will take the financiers' promise to pay on delivery (which may take the form of bankable letters of credit) to his or her own bank, who will lend the producer the money to make the film against these promises of payment. But the producer's bank will be at risk if the film was not delivered. Hence the requirement of a completion guarantee (also known as a completion 'bond').

However, the completion guarantee or bond will not guarantee the shortfall in a film's budget if one or more of the financiers fails to put up the money promised. The completion guarantor will only put up the amount of money by which the production costs exceed the agreed budget. It works as follows: if the budget is agreed, and subject to their satisfaction that the budget is realistic and that the producer is likely to raise the necessary finance, the guarantor will provide 'insurance' against certain uninsurable events.

If a camera breaks, that is insurable. But if the weather is appalling or the director is too slow, with the result that the film goes over budget, then subject to the financiers who agreed to put up the budget having done so, the guarantor will put up the money necessary to complete and deliver the film.

The guarantee is given not to the producer but to those who finance the film and therefore provides considerable reassurance to the primary investors, who may not commit their money unless there is a completion guarantee. The guarantor, if required to put up additional monies because the film has gone over budget, can, under certain circumstances, take control of the film away from the producer. If the guarantor believes that the film can never be financially viable, it can abandon the project and return the monies invested so far to the investors.

Confidentiality (or Protecting your Work)

Breach of confidentiality is dealt with in Chapter 17. The other sort of 'confidentiality' that occurs in writers' contracts can refer to the writer being obliged not to divulge any information relating to the production. The clause in the current WG/PACT Agreement reads: 'The Writer will not divulge any information of any nature or kind relating to the production or furnish any statement or announcement relating to any other work or other matter connected with the production.'

This is too sweeping and you should establish that you may state on your CV that you are writing this project for the particular producer. It is important to be able to use this information to promote your career. It is also reasonable that you should not be able to reveal details about the production which the producer may not want revealed.

Copyright – see Chapter 17.

Copyright Line – see Chapter 17.

Credits

All agreements should spell out exactly what the credit provisions are. In the UK the WG/PACT agreement deals with screen credits according to the Screen Credits Agreement that was made between 'the Writers' Guild in 1974 and the then British Film and Television Producers Association or as subsequently amended.'

There's a useful clause in the current WG/PACT Agreement dealing with the fact that if a producer or director tries to claim any screenwriting credit, it's automatically referred to the credit arbitration procedure of the Writers' Guild. This does not apply of course if the producer or director is the sole writer.

The American Writers' Guild (WGA) also has strict credit provisions with tightly controlled arbitration procedures. The WGA, not the producer, decides on the credits which are appropriate.

Writers rarely get both front and back-end credits, and they usually come after the director and the stars. It is indicative of the relative lack of power of writers in the industry that major directors tend to be remembered for the films they direct. Few people remember that *Thelma & Louise* was an original script by Callie Khouri; it is usually thought of as a film 'by Ridley Scott'. Without wishing to detract from his superb directing on the film, it seems to me that Ms Khouri has as much right to it being called 'a film by Callie Khouri'.

Cut Off

Most contracts provide for the producer to replace the writer if the script is not acceptable to the producer. This can happen even if it is the writer's original idea or script. Writers must generally accept the principle of cut-off, except that they should insist on being given the right to do at least one rewrite (which is usually not paid for, unless the contract agrees that it should be).

If your first draft is not very good (and few first drafts are), you should have the right to expect the producer or script editor to provide you with detailed notes. These should make clear exactly what changes they require. If the notes are given verbally, make detailed written notes, send a summary of them to the producer for confirmation, and then start the rewrite.

If your rewrite still is unacceptable, then the producer should have the right to make a cut-off decision: you may not, in the producer's view, be able to fix the script, or get it up to the standard required. The difficulty arises when there is a 'difference of opinion' about the plot, character motivation, the ending or some other aspect of the script.

There is not, usually, only one way that a script will work. Who is to say whether you or the producer are right. However, it is ultimately up to the producer, who is paying you, and is also responsible to the financiers, to make decisions like this. If the decision goes against you, be professional and bow out. However many other writers are brought in, the sum of money payable on principal photography and the share of profits agreed in the contract is often divided pro rata between all the writers, according to how much of their work is in the shooting script. Hence the need for objective arbitration.

A useful negotiating point for a writer to make, when asked to accept a reduction in profit or other participation if some form of cut-off takes place, is that the writer will agree to to a reduction in their participation (eg from 5% profits to 3%) but only if the 2% which is deducted goes to the other writer. This stops the producer bringing in another writer and benefitting, in terms of the profit participations, from the cut-off.

Deal Memos

When negotiating on your own behalf, it can be risky to take short cuts unless you know what you are doing. If you use a short letter of agreement or deal memo bear in mind that, should there be a dispute and should you end up in court, you only have the short letter agreement to defend yourself with. Short agreements may omit important points which can only be covered in a longer document.

It's true that the other side have also only got the short letter agreement to defend themselves with. And if you feel fairly confident in your ability to handle a situation like that you may decide that it's worthwhile.

If your deal goes beyond the treatment stage, then the parties tend to enter into a much fuller contract. An increasing number of producers and agents prefer to keep it simple to start with. This avoids lengthy and costly negotiations at an early stage, since it is statistically improbable that the film will actually be made.

Defamation

Defamation is either libel or slander. Libel takes place when someone is defamed in writing (ie in permanent form), slander when it is spoken (ie in a transitory form).

For defamation to take place, several things can have happened. If only one of these occurs and is established in court, then the defamation allegation could be upheld:
a) Does the alleged defamation lower the plaintiff in the estimation of society (meaning 'right-thinking' members of society)?
b) Does it bring the plaintiff into hatred, ridicule, contempt or dislike by society?
c) Does it tend to make the plaintiff shunned or avoided or cut off from society?

There are other refinements and qualifications but the point should be clear.

Writers should be particularly aware of the dangers of defamation. Most contracts that writers sign relating to their work include a 'warranty clause'. In a typical one the writer (or Owner) warrants that '...the screenplay and all products of the Writer's services shall except insofar as the same may be based on material supplied to the Writer by the Production Company be original with the Writer and shall not be obscene or to the Writer's best knowledge and belief be defamatory or infringe the copyright or any other right of any person firm corporation or company.'

A warranty is a contractual matter. The writer makes certain promises about the treatment or script. It is usual to link these promises to an indemnity, so if the writer is in breach of any of the warranties, such as the warranty that the work is not defamatory, he or she may be obliged to pay all the loss and damage including legal and other costs occasioned by the breach. The sums of money involved can be substantial.

The agreement between writer and producer, in which both parties may cross-indemnify each other for the 'material supplied' by the other, or alternatively restrict the damages either may have to pay the other, will not, however, protect either from an action by a 3rd party who is defamed. This is because the 3rd party is not a party to the agreement. And the action can be against both writer and producer, irrespective of who may have been responsible for the alleged defamation.

It is possible, if you were employed by a company to write or research a script, or if you were a journalist on a newspaper or current affairs programme, to put into your contract of employment a one-way reverse indemnity. This would state that it is up to the employer to check the script/research and if they get sued they can't ask you to indemnify them, and if you are sued personally (which is very likely in a defamation action), then your employer will protect you. This clause imposes a duty on the employer to take precautions against publishing or broadcasting something defamatory.

You would be wise to provide all source material to your employers, whose lawyers might advise you to make changes. If you did not follow their advice the indemnity might not apply. Similarly it is advisable for people writing books and scripts which they think might be contentious, to request that the publisher or producer gets the script read for any libel problems. It shifts the onus slightly onto the other party, though you would still be open to a defamation action.

With fiction there are similar warranties, for example, concerning originality, defamation and so on. If you are unaware that something is defamatory, even if it's fictional, you can still be sued for defamation. It is possible to libel someone by accident or unintentional innuendo. The most likely occurrence of this would be if you chose a name for a character in a screenplay or novel, which turned out to be the same as someone real, and you, in effect, portrayed that person in a seriously demeaning way.

There are several defences against defamation:

1 Justification: in other words, that the matter is true. If you repeat a defamatatory remark you may be guilty of defamation.
2 Fair comment: if you wrote something that was a matter of public interest, and you wrote it in good faith, you might have a defence against a libel action. However, if you were shown to have acted maliciously towards the plaintiff the defence would fail.
3 Privilege: certain statements are considered 'privileged'; something said in Parliament, or an accurate contemporaneous report of a public judicial proceeding in England.

4 If you can prove that what you wrote was not defamatory, you will have a defence.

5 Apology: this is not a defence, although if speedy and appropriate it can lessen the damages.

The remedies if found guilty are usually a combination of paying compensation and an apology. Sometimes a fulsome apology can be enough, although in Britain libel damages can be very high under certain circumstances.

Delivery Schedule

A contract for a writer should clearly identify the schedule for delivery of the different drafts of the work. This applies to the treatment as well as to the script. The delivery schedule should also state how long the producer will take to read the material and respond. It is essential to obtain this information from your producer, otherwise you may be left waiting, not wanting to take on other work, in case it conflicted with your obligations to do a rewrite. Put in a clause to the effect that if the producer is X weeks late in paying for the previously delivered work then you are entitled to add the same additional period onto your agreed delivery date for the current stage of the work.

Writers should always build in sufficient time to do first and subsequent drafts, then add extra time as a contingency. Some writers sensibly work out how long the first draft will take, then allow several days or more to put it aside before doing a rewrite of their own which is what they submit, calling that the first draft.

Beware of the phrase 'time shall be of the essence' here. It makes the delivery time specified an important material clause. Try to negotiate the phrase out of your contract. If you succeed, or if it is not in, you should nevertheless attempt to be 100% professional as a writer and deliver on or before your agreed date.

It is important that writers understand the problems of producers, who have to juggle with numerous financial, creative and administrative demands in pulling the film together. It is rare for writers to be sued or fired for being a little bit late, because most producers (even not very good ones) know that to get the best creative work writers cannot be bullied by threats and litigation.

Disputes

The Writers' Guild/PACT agreement has a disputes procedure. They have set up a Standing Joint Committee which consists of up to three members of the Writers' Guild and three members of PACT who have no direct involvement or cannot gain directly from the project and they will arbitrate in a dispute.

If they can't resolve the dispute it may be taken to ACAS, the Advisory, Conciliation and Arbitration Service.

But it's important to note that pending completion of the disputes procedure you can't stop work. And it's also the case that the disputes procedure doesn't stop either party going to a court of law.

In many other countries there are similar arbitration procedures. Should you get into a dispute check your contract and take advice early on in the dispute, before it becomes set. That way you can assess your chances and make a calculated decision on what course of action to take.

Escalators

An escalator is a method for increasing an agreed fee or royalty, due to an event or performance subsequent to the signing of a contract. You can have escalators for all sorts of things including increases in the budget, the box office take of the film, whether the book on which the film is based gets into the best-seller lists and so on.

If you agree a fee for someone to buy the rights to your script, it can be useful to put in an escalator. This is particularly relevant where the buyer negotiates a relatively low price. One way of doing this is to make the purchase price a percentage of the budget. If the producer agreed to pay you a fee equivalent to 2% of the final approved budget, and the budget is £1 million, you will get £20,000 for the rights. If the budget turns out to be £2 million, you will get £40,000.

There will probably be a ceiling (also known as a 'cap') put on what you can get, but producers have been known to go into the initial negotiation claiming a low budget when in fact they know it's going to be higher. That's a reasonable business trick - but so is an escalator clause. You may also agree that there should be a minimum fee (known as a 'floor') so that if the budget was less than £1 million and 2% was less than £20,000, you would still get the 'floor' of £20,000.

Producers will often insist that the budget on which the writer's percentage is based should be the below-the-line budget. But if quality above-the-line elements are drawn to the film, and the budget goes up, it will probably be because of your script. The fee you get should therefore be higher, which it will if your contract stated the fee for example in the following way (assuming the budget is £1m): '...the writer will receive a fee of £20,000 or 2% of the budget whichever is the greater with a ceiling of £50,000...'

The final approved budget of the film is that which the financiers authorize being spent. The cost of production is what the film actually costs, which may be more or less than the budget. This production cost is 'certified' by a production auditor or accountant specified by the financiers. There are certain acceptable exclusions from the budget (in calculating your percentage): these include the contingency fee, financing changes, insurance and monies paid to you.

Escalators established in the sale of a novel to film or TV, and negotiated into the contract with a producer who buys the audiovisual rights in the novel, usually relate to whether the book gets into one of the bestseller lists, how high it gets in the list, and for how long it stays there. Often a lump sum is payable when the book has been in a list for a certain period of time, which can be as little as one week. When selling a book to a publisher, escalators can be built in, based on appearances in best-seller lists or on TV broadcast or release as a movie.

Exercise of Option

An option is the right to acquire certain rights in a creative work. The actual acquisition of those rights results from 'the exercise of the option'. The option is usually exercised by giving notice, and possibly paying the monies agreed in the option agreement. The acquisition document (which has been pre-agreed as part of the option agreement and is usually annexed to it), which is called the 'assignment' or 'licence', is then signed.

The rights granted are usually exclusive, though exclusivity is not a necessary feature. The issue as to whether actual payment should be a condition of effecting the exercise of an option is something that can be the subject of negotiation.

Formats

In the UK there is currently no copyright protection for formats as such (ie the idea for a film or programme). One of the reasons that people are willing to pay format fees is because they would rather pay these than face claims against them by the originators or owners of the format for 'passing-off'. By entering into an agreement with the originators or owners they are also able to acquire goodwill and know-how associated with a series or show. It is usual for broadcasters and/or producers to control format rights. Writers can attempt to reserve these rights but are likely to be less able to exploit them than producers.

The writer should try to negotiate at least 50% of revenue (after any commissions are deducted) from a sale of so-called 'changed-format' rights. A changed-format is usually the adaptation of a series: *All in the Family* is the American changed-format version of the British series *Till Death Us Do Part*, with Alf Garnett becoming Archie Bunker.

Grant of Rights

In the assignment there are various rights which may be transferred to the purchaser. These usually include the right to write scripts, the sole and exclusive right to make or produce film(s) or television programmes based on the work (book or script), the right to perform or exhibit or transmit the work to the public by any means and in any media.

Also included can be the right to print and publish synopses of the work, the merchandising rights, the right to make remakes, prequels and sequels, the right to register the copyright in the purchaser's name, and the right to assign or authorize others to use the rights listed above. (This list is not exhaustive but should give you a general idea what the phrase 'grant of rights' refers to.) Some of these rights can be reserved by the writer.

Ideas, Protection of – see Chapter 17.

Libel – see Defamation

Material

In contracts the word 'material' is an adjective meaning 'important' or 'essential'. It is a form of emphasis. It can be a useful qualifying word. You should attempt to insert it wherever you are asked to sign something which seems to you to be too sweeping. If you have to warrant, for example, that everything you've written is true, you could put in the words 'materially true' - it qualifies it in your favour. If there is a provision penalising you in some way in a contract for breach of a warranty, try to change the wording to 'material breach'.

Merchandising

Merchandising is the manufacturing and exploitation of goods based on or connected with characters or stories which occur in copyright works. Because merchandising involves using the promotional spin-off or goodwill associated with one 'property', such as name recognition, to promote the sale of other goods, it usually involves a payment of some sort to the owners of the copyright in the original property.

In the WG/PACT Agreement there is an important clause about formats and merchandising, which states that: 'When the layout or format of a production is contributed by a writer, such writer may have an interest in merchandising.' It goes on to say that the extent of that interest or any financial participation shall be the subject of mutual agreement.

This is often tacked on at the end, or indeed sometimes left off. Generally speaking, if you're getting a share of the profits and the merchandising revenue of the film goes in towards the film's profits, then you are potentially but indirectly getting a share of the merchandising. This is the most common arrangement. But as very few films ever show a profit, the money that comes in from exploitation like merchandising goes towards the apparent running loss on the film, and therefore you may not actually receive anything from the merchandising.

So it is preferable to get merchandising rights separately accounted and your share paid separately, not set against the film's cost as a whole. This is particularly important if your film has real merchandising potential. The writer's share could be, say, 30% of merchandising revenue. Most films, however, have little or no merchandising potential. What creates real merchandising potential is constant exposure. TV series with many episodes are very valuable to merchandising, whereas a single TV movie is not.

Merchandising is usually handled by specialized agencies and their commission usually comes off before there is any split in revenues between the writer and the producer. So the writer's share would be 30% of what is left after the agent's cut. (See the *Writers' and Artists' Yearbook* for more details on merchandising.)

Minimum Terms

As with many union-negotiated agreements the WG/PACT agreement is a minimum terms agreement. Some writers get significantly more than the minimum terms, and some get less. In Europe we don't have the American situation, where production companies have to sign the minimum terms agreement and risk being blacklisted if they try to pay below the minimum rate. PACT members should however subscribe to the minimum terms.

The Writers' Guild provides a 'model form of engagement', that is, a model contract. The members of PACT are supposed to inform the Guild when they have engaged a writer under this agreement and PACT recognises the Guild as the exclusive representative for the purpose of collective bargaining. Even if you are not a WG member you can try to base your negotiations on WG agreements.

The important point about 'minimum terms' is that while you should not be expected to write for less, you are also reasonably entitled to expect more if you have a track record, or if you have a script or idea that more than one purchaser wants to buy.

The BBC and ITV consider the agreed minimum rate to be appropriate unless you have had between two and four hours of your scripts broadcast. But what one writer gets as opposed to another may depend on negotiation. If you don't ask, you are unlikely to get.

The WG/PACT Agreement also has a 'Schedule of Minimum Fees and Use Payments'. These are important and there is a copy of the figures in Appendix 4.

There are four separate sets of figures for deals between writers and independent producers: the first is for feature films budgeted at £2 million and over, the second for feature films between £750,000 and £2 million or television films at £750,000 and above, the third is for films budgeted at below £750,000, and the fourth deals with TV series.

For films there are usually seven points at which payment is made, two for the treatment, two for the first draft, two for the second draft, and one on principal photography. As a rough guide the proportion of the total payable for each of these stages is as follows:

Treatment

Commencement payment	10%
Acceptance payment	10%

First Draft

Commencement payment	20%
Delivery payment	20%

Second Draft

Commencement payment	10%
Delivery payment	10%

Principal photography   **20%**

Total   **100%**

There is usually an additional fee as an advance against repeats, and other residual payments, on top of the 100% basic fee, might be paid. For television there are four equal payments, for the treatment, the first-draft script on commission, first draft on delivery and the second draft on acceptance.

Residual payments are payments to the writer for uses (sales) of a film or programme outside the country of origin or repeated over and above domestic repeat(s) included in the basic payment. They are in addition to the basic fee. If there is a buy-out then residuals are not paid. The buy-out is a lump sum paid in lieu of residuals, usually equivalent to 100-150% of the basic fee.

The significance of 'acceptance' and 'delivery' payments is that if a payment is to be made only on acceptance, then if the treatment is considered not acceptable, the writer does not get paid the second part of the payment. This may mean that the writer has to rewrite the treatment again and again, until it is acceptable.

If the writer has failed to deliver a treatment according to the brief, this is fair. However, if the producer has 'moved the goalposts' and is asking for something different from what was agreed originally, then it is not fair to withhold the payment, and the writer should not be penalized under those circumstances. A compromise may be for the producer to add in an extra payment to take into account the new instructions and additional work that the writer has been asked to do.

'Delivery payment' should mean what it says: payment on delivery of the treatment or script whether or not it is actually accepted. Unfortunately some writers abuse this and deliver scripts that are patently not acceptable, so producers sometimes ask for additional stages to be put into contracts, entitling them to ask for one or two rewrites at each stage without any further payment.

Producers can also argue that the delivery of 120 pages does not constitute delivery of what was commissioned. The producer therefore does not accept that delivery has taken place. This is a subject capable of considerable argument. Producers sometimes attempt to put in a clause to the effect that '...delivery shall mean full and complete delivery in accordance with the requirements of the producer communicated to the writer from time to time...' This turns delivery, in effect, into acceptance.

It is an anomaly that the treatment attracts about 20% of the total basic fee for a script, and the first draft about 40%. In practice the treatment should take longer to develop and write than the first draft. It is difficult to persuade producers to change this, because the money they lay out on the treatment is the highest risk. Many treatments don't proceed to a script at all. The reason for this is that frequently the time the writer can afford to spend on the treatment - because they are being paid so little - is simply not enough to turn it into a bankable document.

Writers working speculatively on their own treatments can short-change themselves by being too superficial. A fully-developed treatment, or a bible for a long-running series, should be the single most intensive item in the schedule, and should be paid accordingly. If you are doing it in your own time, give yourself time. Get as much feedback from writers and other people in the industry. Then write it again. And again. And again.

Moral Rights (*Droit Moral*)

As part of the general law of copyright, there are some personal rights called MORAL RIGHTS. The most important of these are known as the right of 'paternity' and the right of 'integrity'. Paternity involves the right to be identified as the author of a work; integrity is the right not to have your work mutilated or altered so as to bring you into disrepute.

These rights of authors' are recognised as inalienable in some countries (such as France) and cannot be waived or transferred to third parties. In the UK, under the most recent Copyright Act, authors can waive both of these rights under certain circumstances.

The right of paternity needs to be asserted with a statement on the title-verso, such as: 'The author asserts the moral right to be identified as the author of the Work.'

The right of integrity does not prohibit a producer or director from altering a script. The right of integrity protects authors from alterations that damage the work and the author's reputation in such a way as to bring the author into disrepute. The complainant has to show that whatever use is being made of the work really does mutilate or transgress the work in detrimental way.

In the UK it is usual in the film and television world for purchasers of copyright to want the right of integrity to be given up when the property is sold. It is important to purchasers for the future, because they don't want to be in a position where, having invested in order to exploit the property, they could find that they're subject to the threat of an injunction from an author who now says the work has been treated in a way he or she doesn't like.

In the UK the law tends to treat copyright as an ordinary property right that can be bought and sold like a car or plank of wood, whereas in other jurisdictions (that tend to have stronger author's rights), works tend to be viewed as cultural/artistic products and the commercial treatment of the works tends to be slightly different.

Non-Delivery

There can be various penalties for non-delivery. The simplest actions the producer has against the writer are to withhold the payments that would have been due if the writer had delivered and to fire the writer. This money due on delivery may have to be used to contract a new writer.

Some agreements stipulate that if the writer fails to deliver because of illness or injury then the writer has a certain number of days in which to deliver, but after that the producer isn't bound to accept the work or pay the fees due on delivery. The producer may be able to insist on an independent medical examination, and if the writer is pulling a fast one the contract might be terminated.

Options

An option is an agreement in which the owner of the audiovisual rights in a Work, in return for a 'consideration' (which is usually money), grants to the purchaser the exclusive opportunity to acquire some or all of those rights. The exclusive opportunity is for a fixed period - usually one year - and the purchase price is agreed at the time of the negotiation of the option deal. In the event that the purchaser 'exercises' the option, there is no further negotiating about the purchase price or other terms on which the acquisition takes place, such matters having been agreed as part of the option deal.

The option agreement is attached to the 'assignment agreement', which comes into force when the option is exercised. When the assignment is signed and the exercise monies paid, the rights assigned pass over to the purchaser.

Always try to link this to the payment to you of the money due on exercise, to avoid the disappointing experience of signing exercise documents but finding that the cheque from the producer takes ages to arrive.

A suitable wording here might be (from the point of view of the writer to producer): 'You may execute your option by giving me notice that it is exercised and by paying the exercise price.'

In such circumstances, if there is no payment then it would not be a valid exercise.

If a producer wants to 'option' a treatment, script or novel without making any payment, what the producer wants is for you to agree to take the property off the market for an agreed period of time while they attempt to raise some finance (perhaps to pay you a normal option). Producers sometimes simply have no money and they are prepared to put time and effort into raising finance. It may be worth while having a good producer dedicate energy to set up a film based on your work.

But be careful. Your promise not to sell the property or the relevant rights in it to anyone else during this period should be qualified. If a producer cannot pay you anything at all - and £250 or £500 is often satisfactory for a short option (which protects them as well) - you should not lose a *bona fide* offer for that property from another party.

I would recommend that if you are asked for a 'free option', and you are inclined to let the producer 'run' with the project, insist that should you receive a *bona fide* offer you will communicate it to the producer and he or she will have 14 or 28 days to make a better offer, or you will be free to accept the offer.

If the producer will not agree to that, pointing out that the time, effort and - in effect - money that they are investing in your project must be protected, then I think that you should negotiate the whole deal in the normal way, with two exceptions;
1   you agree to defer the option payment usually due on signature;
2   the producer agrees to add £1000/ £5000/£10,000 - or whatever you can negotiate - on to the back-end of the deal.

Passing Off

Passing-off may take place when a person or company passes off their own goods or services as those of another so as to wrongfully benefit from the goodwill established by the other in their own goods and services. Similarities of name, packaging or title may be used to confuse a purchaser in this way. While there may not be copyright in titles, if it appears that the choice of a same title is confusing, and misleads people, then an action for passing-off may be successful.

Payment Schedule

Payment is often tied to delivery, but there may be other key dates, such as, for example, the first day of principal photography, or first release, or first exploitation of a particular kind, or the date of a repeat, etc.

Writers should preferably be paid at least something in advance, ie on commission of the work that they are contracted to do. Should a writer be asked to do work without payment at the point of commencement, then a sum, additional to what has already been agreed should, in my opinion, be added on to one of the later payments.

Agreeing to take payment at a later date (or possibly only on the occurrence of an uncertain future event that might never happen) of money that one would normally expect to be paid at an earlier date is called 'deferring'. Deferred payments sometimes attract a bonus. It depends on the negotiation. A writer writing without payment should, in my opinion, be treated as an investor in the project. And I believe that copyright should not pass to the producer until a significant sum, equal to at least all the payments due up to and including delivery of the first draft script (or even the first day of principal photography) have been received.

Privacy Laws/Secrecy

There are stringent privacy laws in America, and some in France and other countries, but none (yet) in Britain, although there has been an increasing amount of talk about their introduction. Privacy laws normally protect a person's private life against unjustified intrusion and disclosure. However, if a person is in the public eye, eg a politician, there may be good public interest reasons which would justify breaching their right to privacy. Other laws may protect certain other kinds of secrets. Most countries, for instance, have laws to protect military and state secrets.

Profits

Distinguish between:

1 the 'net profits' of a film (an expression which is usually defined in the production, financing and distribution agreements for that film), and
2 'the producer's share of the net profits', which is that share retainable by the production company after first paying out all the shares of net profits payable to the other net profit participants in the film.

Beware of the expression 'producer's net profits', which is, I believe, ambiguous and might mean either of 1. or 2. above.

Writers usually receive between 2.5% and 5% of the film's net profits. It is not uncommon for there to be approximately 5% in aggregate of the net profits available for the creators of the script and underlying rights together (eg to the scriptwriter and novel author if the script was based on a novel).

Profits can be worth a great deal. But few films actually make profits, so if a writer is offered profits in addition to an acceptable fee, then there is little to lose in accepting. But if the profits are offered as an alternative to guaranteed fees, the writer must consider the deal something of a gamble.

The reason for pessimism when it comes to profits is partly explained by the William Goldman dictum about the film business: 'Nobody knows anything'. In other words, there are NO guarantees. But it is partly because of the financial structure of the cinema distribution and exhibition business. The exhibitor, the cinema, will usually keep at least 50% of the box-office takings. If the film is a re-issue it can be as high as 75%. If the local distributor has a 40% commission deal with the studio or the producer and is also entitled to recoup the costs of releasing the film, then the distributor will keep 40% of what the exhibitor returns. The distributor will then deduct the costs of prints and ads, which could be 20% of what they get from the exhibitor, leaving only 40% of what the exhibitor sends to the distributor (called the 'film rentals') to go back to the producer.

So from every pound or dollar taken in by the cinema, the producer might only get 20%. They have to recoup the cost of the actual production, plus all the financing costs (interest, insurance, completion guarantee costs, etc.), from that 20%, which is why a film usually has to gross more than five to six times its cost before it goes into profit.

Protection of Ideas – see Chapter 17

Reality-based Drama

During the early 1990s broadcasters discovered that by following up real disasters or police stories, they could offer viewers a hybrid between true stories and highly melodramatic drama, at a significantly lower cost than conventional drama. Audience figures for reality-drama programmes peaked by 1994, although there are still shows like this where the cost-per-audience ratio is good from the broadcaster's point of view.

There have also been shows about the supernatural, in which hosts like Sir David Frost take us into a world where truth is supposed to be literally stranger than fiction. These shows sometimes 'dramatize' real events. On a larger scale the drama departments of TV companies, and some film directors (Oliver Stone in *JFK*) present as drama stories loosely based on real stories. But the production values are usually those of high-budget drama, and the scripts pay attention to the needs of fictional storytelling. In other words, in the interests of better drama, there is no absolute fidelity to the truth.

There are some pitfalls and problems in this genre which writers ought to be aware of. Truth may be a justification against charges of defamation, but the assertion of truth needs to stand up in court. Writers are usually advised to avoid the possibility of going to court. There are a number of things that writers (and of course producers) can do to protect themselves.

It does not necessarily help you avoid a potential action for defamation or invasion of privacy, if you simply change an idea or characters or elements in the events that took place. Nor do you stop something being defamatory just by changing characters' names. If an idea was given to you in circumstances in which it was protected by the law of confidence, and you 'adapt' it, you will not necessarily avoid legal action if you use a protected idea as the 'springboard' for your own idea. Writers and producers sometimes think that they can get away by disguising elements in a story or documentary, but that's not necessarily the case.

If you add certain facts in an attempt to disguise the basis of your programme or film, and if what you have added may be prove to be defamatory, you could worsen the situation. The best defence may be to stick to the facts. If this means that you cannot use the material, perhaps you should not write the script or make the film.

There are other ways of protecting yourself, if you're going to do a story about real people. If you are able to obtain from the real people involved a release form (see below), this will give you some protection.

But that may not be sufficient protection, because there may be other people, minor characters from whom you do not get a release, who you think are unimportant, who could be, directly or by implication, defamed by you. Although you can't defame the dead themselves, you may directly or by implication libel close associates of the dead person, eg a husband or wife or professional advisor.

Registering Scripts – see pp 144 and 149

Release Forms – see Chapter 17

Release forms sent to writers are short contracts in which companies demand that writers release them from certain obligations in return for the company reading a script or novel. For example, you could be asked to waive any legal actions should the company make a film based on an idea the same as or very similar to that proposed in your script.

Bona fide companies are concerned at the increase in litigation and accusations of plagiarism; they want to protect themselves from being sued. This does not mean that they intend to steal your idea. The costs of an idea or script are relatively small, and the risks too great, for genuine companies to try and use other people's work without paying.

But it does leave a bad taste in the mouth when you are asked to sign. My advice though is that unless you expose you work to the industry you are unlikely to sell it, so where there is a small risk you should sign and submit. Often scripts submitted through a lawyer or agent do not require a release form to be signed.

What lies behind the insistence of many larger companies for writers to sign release forms? There is a mix of reasons, though the central idea is protection against legal actions from writers. The companies' arguments tend to be along the lines that there are hundreds of ideas around; they may or may not have had similar ideas to those submitted by the writer. So if you wish to submit your idea to them then you must accept that no confidentiality attaches to your submission and the company is not bound to treat it as confidential.

This is naturally worrying to a writer who believes that they have a really good idea. But the reality is not very comforting. If you don't submit the idea or script, how can you sell it?

The second part of some release forms specifies that should the company be accused of lifting material (which is protected by copyright laws), then you must agree that you will not injunct them, you agree to specified arbitration, and should they be found 'guilty' by the arbitration, the damages will be limited to what they might have paid you if they had purchased the material in the first place.

The most cautious action for a writer is to try to avoid signing the release form. Usually this can be done by making the submission through a lawyer or agent known in the industry. The alternative is not to submit it to that company but to find others.

'Real' people can also 'release' a writer or producer who wishes to use facts about themselves, or interviewees can sign release forms, quit-claims or waivers, giving permission for the interview in which they participated to be used without further permission being required. Having signed the release form you cannot object to the use of the interview, unless it distorts what you said or is used in a way that you did not authorise. You may be able to take action if defamation or misrepresentation has taken place.

Remakes and Sequels

Producers prefer to acquire the rights to make as many films as they like based on the material from one book or script. If you are a novelist or a scriptwriter you should attempt to restrict them. You can do this by ensuring that what they acquire is a single-film licence. This permits them to make one and only one film based on the work. They do not acquire remake rights or spin-off sequel rights. It is a limitation, however, that can make it more difficult for producers to raise the money for the film.

If the producer insists on the right to make remakes and sequels, and most major companies will insist, then fight for proper payment. Sequels also include so-called 'prequels'. A sequel, defined from the writer's point of view, is a substantially new or different story containing one or more of the characters in the original. *Friday the Thirteenth, Part 2* is one example. A prequel is like a prologue or introduction coming before the story of an existing film. *Young Sherlock Holmes* could be seen as a prequel to *Sherlock Holmes*.

For a sequel or remake producers normally expect to pay only 50% of what they paid for the original script. But why should they pay only half as much? After all, they are not going to make a sequel or a remake unless the first film has been successful. Time will have passed, and inflation will have reduced the value of your original fee.

There's also less risk involved in making a sequel than in making an original, though a remake may be safer than a sequel It may therefore be possible to persuade producers that there is more justification for paying 100% for a remake, as in a sequel there does need to be more creative work, new characters and situations, which may be devised by people other than yourself.

I believe that the payment for sequels and remakes should nevertheless be at least the same as or, in the case of a remake, in excess of the payment for the original.

The other terms of the contract for the original should apply, or be better, in the new contract for the remake, prequel or sequel. This also includes any profit share. Make sure you not only continue to get your profit participation, but that it increases with the growing success of your original work. Put in escalators too if you can. Unfortunately producers won't agree to all of this. But it is a battle that I believe writers need to fight, because the argument is reasonable. Sometimes you will win, or at least achieve a compromise.

In some contracts the producer will acquire the right to make a producer-originated sequel (which should be distinguished from an author-originated sequel). A producer with this right can make a film or series of films using the characters from the original novel or script, with new stories that the producer, or hired writers, come up with. There should be an appropriate payment negotiated in the original contract - for any sequel, whether producer- or author-originated. The rights to an author-originated sequel should cost a producer more than one created by the producer.

The original novelist should not be precluded from writing more books with the same characters. It is likely however, that the producer will get the novelist to agree in the original contract that should there be any new novels with the same characters, then the producer must have the first right to make an offer for the audiovisual rights. The details of the new deal should be subject to a new negotiation and should not be the same as the previous deal. You can argue that the new deal must be a better one than the original. Similarly it is worth arguing that the deal for a sequel to an original script should be an improvement on the original deal.

If the first film has been a big success, the producer might argue that he/she should not be penalized by being made to pay a much higher price for the next novel. This argument rests on the assumption that the added value to the next novel comes from the producer's film. While there is some truth in this, the producer will have received his/her reward from the success of the film (including now being able to raise money more easily), and the novelist or script writer on whose work the film was based, should also be entitled to receive the (increased) market price for their next work.

Reserved Rights – see p 134

Residuals – see pp 140, 181 and 190

Reversion and Turnaround

If you write a script or novel, and licence or assign movie or TV rights in it, there should always be an agreed period of time for the purchaser to make the film or programme. If they have not made it within that time, or have not negotiated and paid for an extension, then the rights should come back to you. Whether you get them back automatically, without having to pay any money to the producer, or whether you do have to pay to re-acquire the rights, reversion (in appropriate circumstances) is something writers should insist upon.

In the current WG/PACT Agreement there is an interesting buy-back clause. This says: 'The Writer shall have the right to buy back an original script on payment of 50% of sums received if principal photography has not begun within two years of delivery of the last material for which the Writer has been commissioned.'

This buy-back clause is better than the situation that existed a few years ago. Then it was not uncommon for scriptwriters (or novelists) to have to pay at least 100% of what they were paid if they wanted their rights back.

There are still some contracts in which, if the film is not made rights will only revert to the writer if the writer pays back the fee that was paid to them, plus interest and even a contribution towards the other development monies that were spent on their project. Since the writer had no control over the development expenditure, and since the producer is supposed to have 'purchased' the rights for a period of time, not lent the writer that money, and since the producer has in effect failed to produce the film, it seems harsh to penalize the original writer for what could be said to be the producer's failure.

Faced with having to repay, say, the full fee paid in order to re-acquire rights to the script or book, the writer sometimes has the frustration of not being able to raise the money. There are ways of improving this situation by negotiation. For instance, it is possible to argue that the money to be paid back to the producer, whether 50%, 100% or whatever, should be paid back at the rate of, say, 51% (or less) of any new money received by the writer for the rights should he/she resell the property. This leaves the writer (and their agent) some income to cover the costs of selling it again.

So, instead of paying the producer a fixed sum as agreed in the contracts, before being able to sell the rights elsewhere, the writer pays say 51% of any monies that come in from such a sale, until the total owing to the producer (such as the 50% mentioned in the WG/PACT agreement) is repaid.

If the writer sells the work a second time for a very small sum, the producer will only get 51% (or whatever is agreed) of what the writer receives. This enable the writer to sell the property, and hopefully see it realized as a film. This way it does return some money to the producer. If the producer had originally paid a large sum, and the writer was required to pay this back, unless the writer could find an equivalent large sum to make the repayment, which on an old property is not very likely, the script or novel would perhaps never be made. For a writer's career this is a serious situation, which is why it is so important to keep open possibilities of selling the rights.

Ideally, from the point of view of the writer, the rights should revert automatically at the due date without any monies having to be repaid. But 'free reversion', as it is sometimes called, is relatively rare. Producers will argue that their purchase of the copyright should be for its duration, and many contracts are for that period, with no time limit imposed on the producer. But this is a matter of negotiation, and the shorter the period of assignment or licence, the smaller the sum of money is likely to be. Writers, like producers, have to gamble at times.

Turnaround is a form of reversion. The rights have been acquired by another party who fails to exploit them (go into production is usually the defining criterion) by a certain date. The original owner of the rights gets a window of time in which they can buy back the rights. That is a 'turnaround period'.

A 'revolving turnaround' means that should the original owner not purchase the rights back, the other party gets a window in which to exploit the rights before it 'turns around' again to the first party.

There are many permutations and provisions, including when turnaround may take place, for how long one party may have the right to buy back the rights, on what terms, what happens if they don't buy the rights back in the agreed time, and so on. In American contracts these are called 'turnaround provisions'.

Sequels – see Remakes

Suspension/Termination – see Index, 'writer, firing of'

Television

In a contract for the purchase of audiovisual rights in a book or script, fees are negotiated. The producer may intend to make a feature film, but he or she will also require 'television rights', in case the end product is a TV movie or a mini-series. In the latter case the contract will state how much the original rights holder receives per TV episode or if it is to be a TV movie.

Termination – see Chapter 16

Time shall be of the Essence

This means that if you have agreed to do or deliver something by a particular date and time is 'of the essence', failure to deliver is considered to be a serious breach of the contract. Which means that the contract could be repudiated.

Every time you are asked to sign a contract in which there is a clause with the phrase 'time shall be of the essence', try to modify it. You might be able to argue that you've already undertaken in the contract to use your best endeavours (or reasonable endeavours) to deliver everything on time and that should be good enough. You're not a writing machine and you can't just churn words out to order. When you negotiate the time periods for delivery, you should build in safe margins for yourself. Not to do so is risky both to the producer and to your reputation.

There are a couple of useful things to bear in mind here:
a) Unless it is explicitly stated that time is of the essence, then it's not.
b) Time can be made of the essence after a contract has been signed. This can also be done by only one party to an agreement. So, for example, if you are consistently paid late, one remedy is to write to the person owing you the money stating that you are now making time of the essence in respect of the outstanding payments.

A court would probably back you up if for example you give a reasonable period of notice to pay. If, say, you send a letter stating that they have to pay by tomorrow morning, that would probably not be seen as reasonable. But if you propose several weeks after the deadline, that might be acceptable to a court. If the producer still fails to pay, then they may have repudiated the contract. If so, what rights they may retain will depend on the wording of the contract.

Titles, Copyright in

Writers often worry about the duplication of titles. If you look through reference works like *Books in Print* you will discover literally dozens of occasions where the same title is used two, three or even more times for different books.

The danger to be aware of is in being accused of 'passing off'. If you use the same title as someone else in a way that could mislead the public to think that your book is, say, by a much better known author, you might attract a charge of passing-off. Certain names like Coca Cola are registered trademarks, so you could not call a film or book Coca Cola without permission.

Titles are usually not 'substantial' enough to be accorded copyright protection. Unless the title were, say, several lines long, in which case it might have such protection. The Society of Authors has a Quick Guide on the protection of titles, which is worth looking at if you are faced with a problem of this sort.

Turnaround – see Reversion

Warranties

The writer of a script will probably have to warrant, for example, that the script is original, that it does not infringe anyone else's copyright or other rights, and that it will not (perhaps to the best of the writer's knowledge and belief) be defamatory. Without such warranties producers will not sign agreements, and will not be able to raise the finance. Writers usually agree to indemnify the producer against loss and damage caused by a breach of these warranties.

Beware of agreements which include the phrase 'breach or alleged breach'. A nuisance claim, that you stole someone else's story, could be proved totally unfounded.

But if your contract included the words 'alleged breach' you could end up indemnifying the producer. So attempt to get the word 'alleged' out of the contract.

Another formulation to be aware of is the proposal that you will pay if the matter is settled on the advice of Counsel approved by both parties or if no agreement is reached on Counsel then he or she can be appointed by a third party, such as the President of the Law Society. This is not unreasonable. But be careful of wording that says you indemnify the producer if the producer's advisers decide to settle.

Writers' Guild/PACT Agreement – see Appendix 4

Appendix 4.

Writers' Guild Minimum Terms

Writers' Guild/Producers' Alliance for Film and Television (PACT) Minimum Terms

These were the figures agreed by the two representative organisations effective from 3 February 1992. Add at least 30% to the figures to ascertain what would be appropriate in the year 2000 (or until the WG and PACT agree uptodate figures, which will probably be in the first half of 2000. Check the WG website at www.writers.org.uk/guild for the latest situation).

There are four separate schedules of minimum payments: the first deals with feature films budgeted at £2 million and over, the second with feature films between £750,000 and £2 million or television films at £750,000 and above, and the third deals with films budgeted at below £750,000. The fourth one deals with TV series.

Writers' Guild/PACT Minimum

Section 1:

Feature Films Budgeted at £2 Million and Over

Treatment:	Commencement payment	2,500
	Acceptance payment	1,500
First Draft:	Commencement payment	4,800
	Delivery payment	4,800
Second Draft:	Commencement payment	2,400
	Delivery payment	2,400
Principal photography payment		4,800
Total minimum payment		23,200
Additional use pre-payment		8,000
Total guaranteed payment		31,200

The Total Minimum Payment buys all rights except those listed below. The Additional Use Pre-payment is an advance against the payments listed below.

Payment for Uses

UK TV* (per transmission)	2,000

Limited to 7 years and subject to
    a minimum payment of   6,000
US Network TV Primetime   13,000
US Network TV Non-Primetime   2,000
PBS   1,500
US other TV   1,500
Rest of the World Free TV   6,000
US Major Pay TV   5,500
Other US and Rest of the World Pay TV   2,000
Video   3,000
* UK TV rights shall include the right to simultaneous European Cable television transmission.

Section 2

A: **Feature films budgeted at £750,000 up to £2 million**

B: **TV Films budgeted at £750,000 and above and not subject to any budget ceiling**

Note: the figures set out below refer to television productions of 90 minutes duration. For television productions or more or less than 90 minutes the script fee shall be pro-rated.

Treatment:	Commencement Payment	1,000
	Acceptance Payment	1,000
First Draft:	Commencement Payment	3,500
	Delivery Payment	3,500
Second Draft:	Commencement Payment	1,200
	Delivery Payment	1,200
Principal Photography Payment		2,600
Total Minimum Payment 14,000		
Additional Use Pre-Payment		5,000
Total Guaranteed Payment		19,000

Payment for Uses

The producer opts before the first day of principal photography to take within the total minimum payment Either
a) Worldwide theatrical rights, or
b) Two UK network TV transmissions and a limited theatrical release in the UK over a period of three months in not more than ten cinemas which shall not be all in the same circuit. This limited theatrical release may take place within a period commencing nine months before the first television transmission in the UK and terminating three months after.

Subject to the option as above, the total minimum payment buys all rights except those listed below. The Additional Use Pre-Payment is an advance against the payments listed below.

a) If the theatrical rights are taken:
  UK TV 1,250 per transmission, limited to seven years and a minimum payment of 3,750
b) If two UK television transmissions are taken: additional UK Television transmission within 7 years, per transmission: 2,000.
  UK (Full) theatrical: subject to negotiation
  US theatrical: subject to negotiation
  Rest of the world theatrical: 1,200.
Whatever the option taken up either a) or b) the following residuals will apply thereafter:
  US Network TV Primetime 9,750
  US Network TV Non-Primetime 1,800
  PBS 1,000
  US Other TV 1,000
  Rest of World Free TV 2,500
  US Major Pay TV 2,750
  US and Rest of World Pay TV 1,250
  Videogram Use 1,200.
* UK TV rights shall include the right to simultaneous European Cable transmission.

Section 3:

Films budgeted below £750,000
The terms for films in this category to be exactly the same as for films budgeted at £750,000 and up to £2 million except that the Producer is not required to make the £5,000 advance payment against additional uses. The Total Guarantee Fee is therefore the same as the Total Minimum Payment of £14,000, for the fee the Producer opts, before the first day of principal photography, to take either worldwide theatrical rights or two UK network television transmissions*.

Treatment:	Commencement Payment	1,000
	Acceptance Payment	1,000
First Draft:	Commencement Payment	3,500
	Delivery Payment	3,500
Second Draft:	Commencement Payment	1,200
	Delivery Payment	1,200
Principal Photography Payment		2,600
Total Minimum Payment		14,000
Total Guaranteed Payment		14,000

Payment for Uses
The producer opts before the first day of principal photography to take within the total minimum payment either worldwide theatrical rights or two UK network TV transmissions. Subject to that option the total minimum payment buys all rights except those listed below.
  If the theatrical rights are taken: UK TV 1,250 per transmission, limited to seven years

and a minimum payment of 3,750. If two UK Television transmissions are taken:
Additional UK television transmissions within 7 years per transmission 2,000

UK theatrical: subject to negotiation
US theatrical: subject to negotiation
Rest of the world theatrical: 1,200
Whatever the option taken up the following residuals will apply thereafter:

US Network TV Primetime	9,750
US Network TV Non-Primetime	1,800
PBS	1,000
US Other TV	1,000
Rest of World Free TV	2,500
US Major Pay TV	2,750
US and Rest of World Pay TV	1,250
Videogram Use	1,200

* UK TV rights shall include the right to simultaneous European Cable transmission.

Section 4:

Television Series and Serials With Format Provided By the Producer

Note: The figures set out below refer to productions of 60 minutes slot length. For productions of more or less than one hour the script fee shall be pro-rated.

Treatment	1,375	25%
First draft on commission	1,375	25%
First draft on delivery	1,375	25%
Second draft on acceptance	1,375	25%
Total minimum payment	5,500	

The total minimum payment buys one UK Network Television* transmission and all other rights except those listed below.
* UK TV rights shall include the right to simultaneous European Cable transmission.

Principal Photography Payment
On the first day of principal photography the Associate shall pay a further sum equal to 100% of the script fee therefor paid for which he acquires worldwide television rights except those listed below.

Provided always that if on said day the Associate confirms in writing that the series is intended solely for UK domestic transmission said payment shall be a sum equal to 75% of said script fee for which it acquires a first UK repeat transmission only.

The Total Guaranteed Payment is thus, at the minimum level, either £11,000 or £9,625.

Provided further that if only the first UK repeat is paid for pursuant to the foregoing and subsequently the programme is offered for sale abroad, the 100% worldwide buy-out will additionally become due on the earlier of the dates on which the programme is first licensed to a foreign buyer (other than a foreign buyer in the list below) or transmission by such a buyer.

Payment for Uses
    UK Network Television second repeat 50%
    UK Network Television third and subsequent repeats (limit 7 years) each
        transmission 25%
    US Network Television Prime Time 100%
    Non-Prime Time 50%
    PBS 15%
    US Other Television 15%
    US Major Pay Television 20%
    Other US and Rest of World Pay TV 10%
    Video 7.5%.
* UK TV rights shall include the right to simultaneous European Cable transmission.

The total minimum payment buys all rights except the payments relating to uses which are mentioned separately.

> **Note** What the producer has to do as a result of this particular contract is to pay you an advance against those uses. This is called 'the additional use pre-payment'. So for a film budgeted at over £2 million a writer in the UK should not get less than a guaranteed payment of £31,200. It is very rare these days for producers to leave the use payments open as they are on the sheet. Some producers prefer what's called a buy-out. A buy-out means the producer pays the writer a lump sum and the writer gives up his or her right to claim money under the use payments. The rule of thumb is to try and establish a buy-out at over 100% of the total guaranteed payment. Some producers will argue that the buy-out should be paid on the total minimum payment because the additional £8,000 that the writer would have got is a use payment. That's not unreasonable although you can sometimes get round it.

The Guild and PACT have agreed a number of points relating to these payments in Section 1. It's important that you are aware of them.
1   The fees are minimums.
2   Treatments and draft scripts must be delivered within the time agreed and the producer has thirty days in which to accept and request revisions. The writer has fourteen days in which to complete the revisions and the producer then has fourteen days to signify acceptance or rejection.
3   If the producer accepts the treatment, it means just that: that you've done what you have been required to do. So the acceptance money is due. However, if the treatment is rejected then there are two possibilities:
a) If the writer supplied the original treatment and the producer rejects it, the writer remains the owner of all the rights. The producer is not obliged to pay an acceptance fee. Try and get all those references to 'acceptance' payment changed to 'delivery'. That means you get paid when you deliver even if they don't like what you have delivered.

b) If the writer writes a treatment based on an idea or a format provided by the producer and the producer rejects the treatment then all rights remain with the producer. The contract says that in this case the payment must be made for both commencement and acceptance. It's bad wording because how can they pay for acceptance when they are rejecting it? What it actually means is that the acceptance payment is due even if the producer rejects your treatment if the original idea or format was provided by the producer.

4   There are occasions where no treatment is required. Sometimes the producer will commission the first draft script without requiring a treatment. In that case the treatment money still has to be paid and they pay the commencement payment with the first draft script commencement payment, and the treatment acceptance payment is added to the first draft delivery payment.

5   The Agreement says that all the payments are negotiable above the minimum. In other words, you must always remember that these are minimums and you may be able to get more. Copyright only passes to the producer at each stage of the payment as and when these occur.

6   The Agreement says rather blandly and quietly 'cut-offs apply at each stage from treatment to completion'. What this actually means is that you can be fired. It means that the producer is entitled to bring in another writer. Much as I don't like this, it is another one of those clauses where I think on balance the producer has got to have the right to cut off as long as the writer is paid what he or she is due and has also been given at least one chance to rewrite.

The writer who gets the credit should be entitled to a proportionate share of the end payments even though that writer may have been cut off earlier. This is important as the writer may lose out on the share of principal photography money that is properly due to him or her. If the writer has delivered everything, including the second draft, and the only payment due is the principal photography payment, then he or she can't be cut off. At that point, when principal photography starts, the principal photography payment is due.

7   The additional use pre-payment is an advance against all the use payments and it does not form part of the minimum payment.

8   It also says that once UK television uses, purchased over a period of seven years from the date of first transmission, have elapsed, each further transmission on UK television may be purchased by payment of 20% of the current scale fee for that use. Note the word 'current'. It does not mean the fee that existed at the time you signed the agreement, but the fee which is current at the point at which the new transmission is taking place.

In Section 2, which is the medium range of feature films or TV films at over £750,000, you'll see that there are still two payments for the treatment, two for the first draft and two for the second draft.

Where this section differs is that if it's a television production it relates to a 90-minute duration production and if it's more or less than 90 minutes the fee will be pro-rated more or less. Because we are now taking about television there are an increasing number of slightly different points. The producer has to decide before the first day of principal photography to include within the total minimum payment either worldwide theatrical rights or two UK network TV transmissions and a limited theatrical release in the UK.

The additional use pre-payments vary depending on whether theatrical rights were taken or the two UK television rights were taken. If theatrical rights are taken then you get £1,250 per UK TV transmission limited for seven years for a minimum payment of £3,750. If, on the other hand, the two UK television transmissions were taken then you get £2,000 for each additional UK TV transmission within seven years. Theatrical rights in the UK and US are subject to negotiation but there's a one-off payment of £1,200 for the rest of the world theatrical rights.

However, whichever of the above options were taken, there are additional residuals covering US television, pay television, the rest of the world pay television and video use.

You should note that UK TV rights now include the right to simultaneous European cable transmissions. For example, countries like Holland and Belgium receive BBC transmissions 24 hours a day. Whenever there's something on here it's on there.

Section 3 deals with low-budget movies. There's one notable difference from the higher-budgeted films, in that there is no advance payment for additional use. So the guaranteed fee is the same as the total minimum payment. The figures are proportionately less than before although the payments for uses are more or less the same as for section 2.

Section 4 deals with television series and serials where the format has been provided by the producer. The figures relate to 60-minute slots and if you are being asked to write for a 90-minute slot then it's one and a half times as much or if it's only 30 minutes it's half as much. There are four equal payments, one for treatment, one for commission of first draft, one for delivery of first draft and the final one which is acceptance of the second draft.

This fee buys one UK network transmission on television but does not include other payments such as a principal photography payment, which is a further sum of 100% of the script fund for which the producer acquires worldwide television rights.

In practice, these minima are often used for original series too, but in theory original series should be more expensive.

You get 75% of the script fee for a first UK repeat. This effectively means that if your minimum payment is £5,500 then if the producer pays you 100% of the fee to acquire worldwide TV rights you effectively get a total guaranteed payment of £11,000. However, if the producer only wants to pay for one UK repeat then your guaranteed minimum is £9,625.

If the producer only buys the rights to show the repeat in the UK and subsequently the programme is bought abroad, then the 100% buy-out will additionally become due. There are some qualifications to this but you are also entitled to certain residuals for American television news, video, pay TV, and second or third UK repeats. These are the most likely. You get 50% for a second UK network television repeat and 25% for a third.

Conclusion

The Writers' Guild uses a model form of engagement. This refers to all the clauses that we've covered dealing with commission and fees, writers' undertakings and copyright, and then gives particulars of the work such as the title, the length of production, delivery and reading periods and revision periods, the amount of time the producer has in which to commission the various drafts once they've been delivered.

It then lists all the payment stages and deals with the pension contributions which get deleted if they are not applicable. There are two model agreements. The first deals with single productions and the second with television series and serials.

This is not a perfect contract, but it is not a bad one. However, no two contracts are ever exactly the same, no two situations are ever exactly the same, therefore don't assume that any contract will be suitable in all respects for your purposes. Copies of the various contracts negotiated by the Guild and PACT, the BBC and ITV can be obtained from the organizations in question. PACT and the Guild may prefer you to be a member.

BBC TV and the Writers' Guild Minimum

If you are offered a contract with the BBC, the form and the terms will be somewhat different from the PACT agreement. In general, BBC contract terms are reasonable, although the money may be less than from ITV or PACT. The basic rates that have been agreed by the Writers Guild and the BBC fall into two categories: rates for published material and television rates. Check Writer's Guild website, www.writers.org.uk/guild for latest figures.

BBC Television Drama Rates

Column A shows the going rate for established writers, Column B the minimum rate for beginners.

	A	B
Original Drama		
60 minutes	£7410	£4703
per minute	£124	£78
Series/Serial		
50 minutes	£5605	£3880
per minute	£112	£78
Dramatisation		
50 minutes	£3989	£2707
per minute	£80	£54
Adaptations		
50 minutes	£2390	£1632
per minute	£48	£33
Light Entertainment		
sketch material per min	£68.36	£34.18

ITV and the writers' guild minimums

Off-peak repeats

The Guild has agreed new rates with the ITV companies for repeats. When a repeat is made in peak hours (between 16.00 and 22.29 on Monday to Friday and 22.59 on Saturday and Sunday), the payment will be 100% of the initial fee, as now. Where a broadcast is made in the day-time off-peak hours (between 10.25 and 15.59, and from the end of peak hours to 23.29), the payment will be 50% of the initial fee, and where a broadcast is made in the night-time off-peak hours (any times outside the specified hours), the payment will be 15%. A similar arrangment has been reached with Equity. These new rates were agreed to facilitate repeats of home-produced drama in the daytime.

Duration of rights in Teleplays

ITV may now broadcast a drama contracted under the Teleplays agreement for the duration of copyright, on payment of the usual fees.

Credits

ITV have agreed a new credits clause, which obliges them to include a credit to the writer in all publicity or programme material provided to third parties where the Director is also credited, in addition to the screen credit obligations.

Rewrites

The ITV companies are now obliged to negotiate an additional fee in good faith in the event that they require 'substantial additional writing service' as a result of 'material change' in their original requirements. In return the Guild agreed that the companies should have 70 days from delivery rather than the current 48 to ask for minor rewrites. This takes account of the additional delays caused by the role of Network Centre in the consideration of scripts.

Comment from the Writers' Guild

Agreement has been reached on the two new fee rates (part-network commissioning and off-peak repeats) on the basis that they will help to bring about, respectively, additional regional drama commissioning, and additional repeats of ITV produced drama. With respect to part-networking, the Guild has been given two assurances by ITV representatives: firstly, that the rates will only be used for genuinely regional drama commissions which will be in addition to rather than in substitution for the companies' current normal commissioning; and secondly, that they will be used primarily when commissioning new and inexperienced writers and that they will be unlikely to form the basis of offers to established or senior writers. The Guild has made it clear that if the companies do not abide by these restrictions the Guild will not hesitate to revise the position.

Rates

	Established	New to TV*	New to TV
Teleplays			
not less than 30 mins	£5553	£3940	£3775
not less than 60 mins	£9245	£6568	£6296
not less than 75 mins	£11112	£7891	£7562
not less than 90 mins	£13833	£9855	£9437
Dramatisations			
not less than 60 mins	£5793	£4173	£4000
Adaptations			
not less than 60 mins	£3647	£2627	£2517
Series & Serials *(where episodes are written by more than one writer)*			
up to 20 mins	£2789	£2010	£1921
21 to 30 mins	£3647	£2627	£2517
31 to 45 mins	£5482	£4515	£3779
46 to 60 mins	£7300	£5254	£5038
Serials *(where writer provides script only)*			
up to 20 mins	£1810	£1300	£1250
21 to 30 mins	£2425	£1750	£1674
Series & Serials *(of a finite length where writer writes all the episodes)*			
30 minutes	£5553	£3940	£3775
60 minutes	£9245	£6568	£6296
75 minutes	£11112	£7891	£7562
90 minutes	£13883	£9855	£9437

Children's drama for Series or Serial
£85.70 (per minute)

* (reputation in another field)

Bibliography

Reading scripts, whether from films you have seen or not, or TV shows, is as valuable as reading about writing. Suggesting a shortlist of books on writing is difficult and necessarily subjective. If I could only recommend one book, it would be the *Complete Works of Shakespeare*.

There are literally hundreds of books on screenwriting and novel writing. Most deal with the craft of writing, and provide advice on how to create well-structured scripts and manuscripts. I am restricting myself to only twenty, a fraction of the good books available. These have all, in some way or other, been important to me and to my clients.

1   ANSORGE, Peter. *From Liverpool to Los Angeles: On writing for Theatre, Film and Television* (Faber & Faber 1997). A thought-provoking book about the context in which much of the best (and worst) British scriptwriting took place up to the late 1990s, by ex BBC and Channel 4 drama specialist.

2   BLAKE, Carole. *From Pitch to Publication: Everything you need to know to get your novel published* (Macmillan 1999). The most detailed guide available to the inner-workings of the publishing industry, an invaluable insider's guide for anyone wanting to be published or already being published.

3   BOORSTIN, Jon. *The Hollywood Eye* (HarperCollins, 1990). Boorstin's eye-opening book is subtitled 'What makes movies work'. He examines the basic principles behind the film-maker's attempts to grab and hold and move an audience.

4   DALE, Martin. *The Movie Game: The Film Business in Britain, Europe and America* (Cassell 1997). If you thought you understood the more arcane parts of the film business, check again. The best single volume on the subject.

5   DIBELL, SCOTT CARD & TURCO. *How to Write a Mi££ion* (Robinson, London 1995). This is a collection of three previously-published books in one volume: PLOT by Ansen Dibell, CHARACTER & VIEWPOINT by Orson Scott Card, and DIALOGUE by Lewis Turco. Although these books are really aimed at novelists they provide a formidable amount of information for any fiction or drama writer.

6   ELGIN, Suzette Haden. *More on the Gentle Art of Self-Defence* (Prentice Hall, USA 1983). A sequel to her previous book, The Gentle Art of Self-Defence, this also has great insights into the use of dialogue. Intended as self-help books, these should be invaluable to script writers. The books show how language is used to attack, and how you can defend yourself with words. Useful for ideas on subtext in dialogue.

7   FRIEDMANN, Julian. *Writing Long-Running Television Series Vols 1 & 2*. These books contain the edited lectures from the first two years of PILOTS workshops. The most comprehensive collection of lectures on long-running series. Available from University of Luton Press. More are to be published by Intellect Books.

8   GOLDMAN, William. *Adventures in the Screen Trade* (Abacus, London 1985). No bibliography should be without the most entertaining book on the business of screen writing. Filled with humour and insight it is as likely to put prospective writers off (if they think carefully about what Goldman is saying) as to turn them on. Hollywood is the villain of the piece, and like all well-written villains you can't help liking it.

9   HAUGE, Michael. *Writing Screenplays That Sell* (Elm Tree Books, London 1989). One of the clearest statements of what makes good scripts different from bad ones. A classic.

10 HILTUNEN, Ari. *Aristotle in Hollywood: The Anatomy of Successful Storytelling*. At the time of going to press this book was not signed up to a publisher, but it will be published in 2000. It is an inspiring account of

Aristotle's theories of drama applied to blockbuster movies, top-rating television and best-selling novels. One of the most important books about writing, because it both explains Aristotle's theories so clearly and provides an accessible and exciting explanation of how readers and audiences are affected by the way something is written.

11 HOWARD, David & MABLEY, Edward. *The Tools of Screenwriting: A writer's guide to the craft and the elements of a screenplay.* (St Martin's Press 1993). With an introduction by Frank Daniel. The book identifies the tools for writers to use to tell their stories in more cinematic ways. Analyses of sixteen major films helps focus the theory in a practical way.

12 HUNTER, Lew. *Screenwriting* (Hale, London 1994). Published in the USA as the book is based on one of the most famous courses in America (UCLA). Starting with getting the idea, building characters, Hunter guides you through the differences between the three acts and has a long and important chapter on rewrites.

13 KENNEDY, Gavin. *Pocket Negotiator* (Economist Books/Hamish Hamilton,London 1993). It is difficult to conceive of being any good at negotiating without either experience or study (or both). This little book is accessible and relevant to those working in the film and television industry, and that includes writers. Also valuable for insights into the behaviour of fictional characters whose motivation is too thin.

14 McKEE, Robert. *STORY: Substance, Structure, Style and the Principles of Screenwriting* (Methuen, 1998). The famous three-day lecture in book form. Will be a classic!

15 SEGER, Linda. *Making a Good Script Great: A guide for writing and rewriting* (Samuel French, USA 1987). Another classic, Linda Seger's book is the key to great rewriting, the activity that makes or breaks most scripts.

16 STANISLAVSKI, Constantin. *Building a Character* (Methuen, London 1968). Together with his other books *An Actor Prepares* and *Creating a Role* this is a stimulating guide to creating better characters. Stanislavski describes the physical realisation of the character on the stage, including expressions, movement and speech. Invaluable for getting the writer deep into the characters being written about.

17 STORR, Anthony. *The Dynamics of Creation* (Penguin, 1991). A provocative examination of creativity: '...psychologists...have not made much distinction between art and neurosis; and since the former is one of the blessings of mankind, whereas the latter is one of the curses, it is seems a pity that they should not be better differentiated.' This book explains why people choose the subjects of their creativity. A fascinating journey for all writers and producers into the choices we make. Also invaluable for scriptwriters is his *Music and the Mind* (HarperCollins, London 1993). By examining music and its effects on the listener, we begin to see both the significance of music from the pov of the scriptwriter, and the importance of non-dialogue scenes in the process of engaging the audience's emotions. This book convinced me that music in the movies is often more important than dialogue.

18 SWAIN, Dwight & SWAIN, Joyce. *Film Scriptwriting: a practical manual* (Focal Press, London 1988). Emphasis on the practical: looks at the differences between proposal, outlines, treatments, step outlines, shooting scripts, master-scene scripts, as well as other aspects of the scritpwriting such as storyboarding and judging screen time.

19 VOGLER, Christopher. *The Writer's Journey: mythic structures for storytellers & screenwriters* (Macmillan, revised edition 1999). No one disputes the importance of Joseph Campbell's analysis of myth in storytelling. But Campbell is difficult to read and Vogler makes it so accessible and relevant to scriptwriters today. Campbell has influenced film-makers like Lucas and Spielberg. Vogler was advisor to Disney on films like *Aladdin* and *The Lion King*. Great pedigree.

20 WOLFF, Jürgen & COX, Kerry. *Successful Scriptwriting* (Writer's Digest Books, USA 1988). A clear and concise guide to writing feature films, sitcoms, soaps, serials and variety shows. Using great insight into the psychology of the writer, the book charts a course through all forms of dramatic scriptwriting.

Trade papers

Out of the many available, read one or two closest to your areas of interest. Unless you read them regularly you will not benefit from the mass of information and opinion to be found between their pages. Don't think that a subscription of £70 a year is a lot of money. It will repay itself many times over in the first year, and perhaps prove to be the best investment you can make.

Broadcast: the UK's main television weekly. Good on international as well as domestic news and analysis.

Screen International: the UK's main weekly film trade paper. Also good on international news and analysis (in fact all the trades are these days).

Television Business International (TBI): strong on business, very international. Good in-depth coverage of selected subjects and geographical areas.

TV World and *C21*: monthly with good in-depth programme analysis; also particularly good on audience analysis. The most readable trade papers, partly because they are monthly and do not try to be an instant provider of transient news.

Variety: the weekly international edition. Best American coverage but also perceptive views on Europe. Essential for feature film writers.

Amongst the more specialised are *The Rights Report*, an interesting magazine dealing with the interface of publishing, film and television - who is buying what, who the players are. Not cheap but worth checking out (published by Whittakers, London). Check the Screenwriter's Store for details of the latest scriptwriting magazine *Scriptwriter* (www.screenwriterstore.co.uk).

Index